Rhetorical Secrets

RHETORIC, CULTURE, AND SOCIAL CRITIQUE

SERIES EDITOR
John Louis Lucaites

Rhetorical Secrets

Mapping Gay Identity and Queer Resistance
in Contemporary America

DAVIN ALLEN GRINDSTAFF

THE UNIVERSITY OF ALABAMA PRESS
Tuscaloosa

Typeface: Bembo

∞
The paper on which this book is printed meets the minimum requirements of American National Standard for Information Science—Permanence of Paper for Printed Library Materials, ANSI Z39.48–1984.

Library of Congress Cataloging-in-Publication Data

Grindstaff, Davin Allen, 1970–
    Rhetorical secrets : mapping gay identity and queer resistance in contemporary America / Davin Allen Grindstaff.
        p. cm. — (Rhetoric, culture, and social critique)
    Includes bibliographical references and index.
    ISBN-13: 978-0-8173-1506-1 (cloth : alk. paper)
    ISBN-10: 0-8173-1506-3
    1. Gay men—United States—Identity. 2. Homosexuality, Male—United States.
3. Rhetoric—Social aspects—United States. I. Title. II. Series.
    HQ76.2.U5G75 2006
    306.76′ 620973—dc22
                                                                    2005028937

Contents

Acknowledgments

Portions of this book have been previously published elsewhere. Some paragraphs on performativity and ideographs from Chapter 1 and the analysis of same-sex marriage debates from Chapter 2 appeared in "Queering Marriage: An Ideographic Interrogation of Heteronormative Subjectivity," *Journal of Homosexuality,* 2003, vol. 45, no. 2/3/4, pp. 257–76.

The analysis of *Lawrence v. Texas* from Chapter 2 were presented at the 13th NCA Alta Conference on Argumentation, held on July 31–August 3, 2003. The conference proceedings are published in *Critical Problems in Argumentation: Selected Papers from the 13th Biennial Conference on Argumentation.* Ed. Charles Arthur Willard. Washington DC: National Communication Association, 2005, pp. 187–93.

Over the past eight years, many have contributed to the development of *Rhetorical Secrets.* First and foremost, I thank Kevin Michael DeLuca for encouraging me to find my own voice. You remain an invaluable mentor and a great friend. Stephen Browne, Thomas Benson, Richard Doyle, and Vincent Lankewish also deserve much gratitude for their sage advisement and unwavering faith in the early development of this project at the Pennsylvania State University. I also thank my colleagues in the Department of Communication at Georgia State University for their continuing support. David Cheshire and Mary Stuckey, in particular, provided vital comments on parts of this manuscript and furthered my intellectual development in countless ways. Finally, I recognize the contribution of those at The University of Alabama Press. I had always been told how frustrating it was to publish an academic book. I now believe this presumed truism to be a myth. The reviewers' comments and John L. Lucaites's guidance have infinitely improved the writing and scholarship herein. Charles E. Morris's piercing and exhaustive insights, in particular, have challenged and sharpened my own thoughts on queer theory and rhetoric. The value of your brilliance and friendship cannot be overstated. Debbie Posner is worthy of great praise for her editorial diligence. I thank them for making this process enjoyable at every turn.

Rhetorical Secrets

Introduction

Identity as a Rhetorical Resource

Non-heterosexual citizens' experiences, both personal and political, are influenced greatly by various and conflicting concepts of sexual identity. Such concepts of identity do not appear fully formed in public consciousness, but, rather, as Smith and Windes have observed, "Identity is forged in combat" ("Identity" 29). Sexual identity, in other words, is created through rhetorical contests over its meaning in public discourse. "Identity" has served as a rhetorical resource for non-heterosexual citizens in everyday life and public policy decision making for over fifty years. Elizabeth Armstrong, in her sociological analysis of the lesbian and gay movement in San Francisco, reminds us: "Homophile organizing in the 1950's and 1960's began the process of transforming homosexual identity from a private group consciousness into a public collective identity. It established the legitimacy of creating public organizations of homosexuals and the notion that homosexuals were a group deserving rights that could be won by engaging in interest group politics" (3). Collective consciousness of a distinctive homosexual "identity" was born from the emergence of gay bars in postwar urban America as well as publications such as Donald Webster Cory's *The Homosexual in America* (1951) and Alfred Kinsey's *Sexual Behavior in the Human Male* (1948) (D'Emilio). Homosexuality became viable as a social identity through public modes of association and rhetorically charged discourse.

The term "identity" remains a significant rhetorical resource for non-heterosexual citizens today. In the following pages, I explore gay male identity as it is formulated in American public discourse at the turn of the twenty-first century. The study of gay male identity, as a product of public discourse, is important because it directly engages contemporary questions regarding social power and resistance in American society. The interrelatedness between identity, power, and resistance is more complicated than it first appears. In the first instance, being gay in America means different things to different people. Recognizing one's sexuality, making that sexual identity publicly known, creating relational-sexual bonds, becoming a member of a minority community, and confronting the social forces of homophobia are common events in the lives of non-heterosexual persons; yet each individual experiences these moments differently. Additionally, a conceptual incoherence lies at the core of modern homosexuality. As David Halperin has recently noted: "'Homosexuality' is at once a psychological condition, an erotic desire, and a sexual practice (and those are three quite different things)" ("How to Do" 110). Such a fundamental incoherence thwarts defining "homosexuality" or "gay male identity." Finally, any study of gay male identity must recognize that political activism based on sexual identity has become more and more problematic in the past two decades. Although critiques of identity politics rightly observe its many shortcomings, the category of "sexual identity" remains an important one for activists and scholars alike.[1] For philosophical and political reasons, then, this project confronts pivotal issues in contemporary American life.

Focusing exclusively on gay male identity, thus neglecting other queer subject positions constituted within the discourse on sexuality, must be understood as a necessarily strategic limit on the scope of rhetorical inquiry. In other words, the isolation of gay male identity as this book's subject matter should not be read as a statement about its significance relative to other queer experiences of heteronormative power. This decision, on the contrary, reflects the utmost sensitivity toward differences within what might tentatively be called the "queer community," for historical and contemporary discourse commonly conflates male homosexuality with other queer subject positions. From its nascence at the turn of the century, for example, the term "homosexual" has often carried a specifically male connotation (Sedgwick, *Epistemology*). More recently, male homosexuality has unfortunately served as the paradigm in both queer activist and academic venues, effectively homogenizing non-heterosexual citizens' experiences and struggles. Politically speaking, this equation of homosexuality with *male* homosexuality has repeatedly proven to be troublesome, if not dangerous, as it often renders political interests specific to women and people of color invisible. Despite political alliances between lesbians, transsexuals, transgender persons, bisexuals, and gay men, sexual identity construction and experiences of heteronormative power remain unique to each group (Edelman, *Homographesis;* Seidman, "Identity and Politics"; Smith and Windes, *Progay/Antigay*). In fact, tensions that derive from different, gendered experiences of heteronormative power continue to disrupt a fully coherent lesbian *and* gay identity politics today (M. McIntosh, "Queer Theory"; Vaid, *Virtual Equality*). Shane Phelan clarifies, "We are united not by sexuality but by oppression based on categories of sexuality. We may thus share a legal and political interest, but this is not a cultural or familial link" (*Getting Specific* 3). Male biases also taint lesbian and gay scholarship such that male homosexuality becomes a paradigm for understanding all queer experiences of power.[2] These observations rightly question the legitimacy and validity of scholarship that does not overtly recognize the different experiences of different non-heterosexual subjects in a heteronormative society. I aim, in focusing selectively on gay male identity, to avoid such a fate.

The Queer Turn: Notes on Sexual Identity and Social Power

Simply put, I investigate gay male identity as a rhetorical resource in contemporary American public discourse. Yet rhetorical studies in the field of speech communication currently stands ill equipped to address the influential connections between sexual identity and social power. Engaging questions that surround "identity" construction will build upon the growing scholarship on lesbian and gay movements in communication studies[3] while simultaneously traversing relatively unexplored terrain in rhetorical studies. Rhetorical studies of lesbian and gay discourse frequently (but not always) rely on traditional argumentation methodologies rather than drawing from the abundance of research on sexuality in literary studies, philosophy, and sociology.[4] This trend often limits questions of power and resistance to social institutions and public policies.[5] Yet social-political relations also exist outside the scope of institutions and formal policies and deserve the attention of rhetorical scholarship. When rhetorical scholarship does address cultural forms of representation, their available means of persuasion is often characterized as false stereotypes rather than ideological constructs worthy of philosophical inquiry. I argue, in contrast to most previous studies of lesbian and gay discourse, that public discourse plays a constitutive role in forming sexual identities.[6] Gay male identity, we must understand, is essentially public, essentially a product of rhetorical invention, and essentially the residue of social-political contests. This conceptual foundation makes truly unique research questions available to the rhetorical scholar without dismissing the importance of previous research.

To this end, I bring together the rhetorical tradition and queer theory in ways that expand both fields of study. R. Anthony Slagle's essay on Queer Nation's construction of collective identity was one of the first attempts to introduce queer theory to rhetorical studies. Although Slagle's analysis provides insight into Queer Nation's "politics of difference," its ties to social movement theory prevent it from fully engaging the intersection of queer theory and rhetorical theory. Robert Brookey later identifies this shortcoming and the essay's general inattentiveness to Foucault's critique of the repression hypothesis ("A Community"). Thus, Slagle problematizes sexual identity as a foundation for social movements without examining queer theory's contribution to our understandings of social power. Yet Brookey's essay errs in the other direction, leaving queer theory's insights into the rhetorical construction of sexual identity alone. The potential bridge between rhetorical scholarship and queer theory thus remains relatively absent. Only in 2003, with the publication of a special issue in the *Journal of Homosexuality* entitled "Queer Theory and Communication: From Disciplining Queers to Queering the Discipline(s)," has a series of essays that promises to fill this gap in our scholarship finally emerged.

The relationship between rhetorical studies and queer theory, however, remains tenuous. Ralph Smith's contribution to the special issue, while hopeful about the consequences that might derive from bringing queer theory to communication studies, displays common anxieties that surround this interdisciplinary relationship, anxieties that merit our attention. Queer theory, at its worst, privileges discursive texts over the material world, expresses an historical relativity to the point where lesbian and gay persons are deprived of universality, ignores political action in favor of cultural analysis, and obscures its ideas with jargon ("Queer Theory" 346–347). Of course, Smith is not alone with these concerns, nor can we ignore the warning signs he illuminates. Examining gay male identity's role in American public discourse, I implicitly address these concerns and provide correctives that prevent rhetorical analysis from falling into these interdisciplinary pitfalls while substantively and critically importing queer theory into rhetorical studies. Clarifying the relationship between sexual identity and social power is an important step in this process.

The academic invention of queer theory often begins with struggles over sexual identity's nature and its role within political activism. In

1993, Michael Warner's observation that the essentialist vs. construction-ist debate seemed "exhausted" encouraged queer theory to move be-yond merely proving the social construction thesis, and instead, to be-gin specifying the ways in which homosexual identity is constructed politically, historically, and in this instance, rhetorically ("Introduction" x). Cindy Patton, in an analysis of recent public discourse on homosexu-ality, acutely argues, "The crucial battle now for 'minorities' and resistant subalterns is not achieving democratic representation but wresting con-trol over the discourses concerning identity construction" ("Tremble" 173). Identity's contested terrain thus remains politically vital. Rather than something very private, I contend that sexual identity is essentially a public matter, for it resides in discourse. Moreover, the public discourse on sexuality is never merely descriptive; it remains forever normatively and thus rhetorically charged. Finally, and most important, the public discourse on sexuality is more than a mere source of social-political power; it is equally the residue from social-political contests. In the chapters that follow, I map these rhetorically charged spaces of identity.

Queer theory is equally demarcated by competing theories of social power, which are intricately connected to our understandings of sexu-ality and identity. In 1978, Michel Foucault drafted the haunting words that reverberate throughout queer theory today: "Homosexuality ap-peared as one of the forms of sexuality when it was transposed from the practice of sodomy onto a kind of interior androgyny, a hermaphrodism of the soul. The sodomite had been a temporary aberration; *the homo-sexual was now a species*" (*History* 43). Foucault's claims about modern homosexuality's constructed nature cannot be isolated from his larger discussion of social power, nor can they be disassociated from his cri-tique of the repression hypothesis in the *History of Sexuality.*

Although recent legal battles over sodomy laws and same-sex mar-riage might suggest that we examine heteronormativity from a juridi-cal conceptualization of power, Berlant and Warner define "hetero-normativity" as "the institutions, *structures of understanding, and practical orientations* that make heterosexuality seem not only coherent—that is, organized as a sexuality—but also privileged" (548). In other words, heteronormative power extends beyond the law into cultural concepts of "sexuality" itself. This definition abandons the ubiquitous equation of power with repression, and encourages scholars to examine power's productive side.[7] Foucault contends, "[P]ower is strong . . . because, as we are beginning to realize, it produces effects at the level of desire—and also at the level of knowledge" (*Power/Knowledge* 59). In short, the effects of power experienced by queer or non-heterosexual subjects in America are productive and normative as well as repressive. Limiting questions of power to matters of law and repression often forecloses on an understanding of, and potential resistance to what Foucault has called "the regime of sexuality" and the disciplinary production of sexual subjects. Although heteronormative power clearly influences the equality afforded by social institutions and revisions of public policy, public discourse equally reinforces heteronormative power relations through its rhetorical constitution of gay male subjects. Gay life in America is not simply a matter of public policy; it is forever a matter of our very existence.

Even though the discourse on sexuality and identity is familiar territory for those engaged in LGBT studies and queer theory alike, I render such territory strange, creating new maps of social power and investigating new paths of resistance. The necessary fiction called "queer theory" slides along multiple axes, between sexual identity and social power, raising new questions about contemporary sexual politics and offering different opportunities for resistive action. For instance, how do cultural narratives about sexuality and identity work? Through what rhetorical operations do they emerge? How do the heteronormative power relations that suffuse their texture sustain themselves? How might these relations of power be disrupted? Reworked through rhetorical inquiry? How might we thematize resistance within such networks of power?

Rhetorical inquiry has much to offer lesbian and gay studies or what has recently become "queer theory." Mostly taking place in English and Sociology departments, queer theory frequently relies on literary and sociological methodologies in order to advance its understanding of modern sexuality.[8] Yet there exists an important intersection between the study and practice of rhetoric and the study and politics of sexuality. Introducing rhetorical theory to the study of lesbian and gay discourse contributes a unique analytic style, extending beyond formal literary devices to include the available means of persuasion that animate public discourse on sexual identity. The study of rhetoric equally advances social theory. Textual analysis, using rhetorical theory as a guide, makes studying public discourse central (rather than peripheral) to our understandings of how sexual identity is constructed. This methodological shift does not leave literary studies and sociology behind, but, rather, it imbricates diverse academic lenses in order to see more clearly the ways in which public discourse constructs gay male identity in twenty-first-century America.

Extending the Critical Rhetoric Project

The critical rhetoric project crystallizes what has been called the "ideological turn" in rhetorical studies (Deetz; Crowley; Wander, "Ideological Turn"; Wander, "Third Persona"). In his inaugural essay, McKerrow advances the claim that ideology is built through "rhetorical creations" ("Theory and Praxis" 92). The study of ideology thus examines public discourses that mobilize and sustain power relations. The critical rhetoric project more systematically imports Foucault's social theory into rhetorical studies, although it is not the first attempt to do so (Biesecker; Blair; Blair and Cooper; Foss and Gill).

Yet, critical rhetoric is not without its own critics, who launch two main concerns: first, what is the status of "knowledge" in critical rhetoric? and second, how might critical rhetoric advance "judgment" through its ideological critique of domination and freedom? Both questions are symptomatic of Foucault's centrality to critical rhetoric, echoing criticisms toward Foucault's genealogical project, the knowledge/power dyad in particular. These concerns justify extending the critical rhetoric project by way of Butler's thematization of performativity (*Gender; Bodies; Excitable*).

In critical rhetoric's third principle, as McKerrow articulates it in "Theory and Practice," doxa [opinion] supplants epistemic knowledge as rhetoric's true province. Knowledge production has long been of concern to rhetoricians, as privileging philosophy over rhetoric derived from opposing epistemic and doxastic knowledge. Knowledge has somewhat more recently been recognized as an effect of rhetorical invention (R. Scott) and social interaction (T. Farrell), and as such, has been described as a means of establishing "status" or power relations within a society (Hariman, "Status"). These power relations, McKerrow ("Theory and Praxis") observes, are grounded in an epistemic rhetoric founded upon universal standards of judgment. Yet McKerrow's simple inversion of the episteme-doxa hierarchy, as a corrective to this problem, maintains its binary form and thus remains reductionist (Hariman, "Critical"). The relationship between doxa and episteme, Hariman argues, is "linear, not oppositional . . . There is not more opinion, or more reliance upon status in the center, only more benefit from a particular but pervasive pattern of authorization" (69–70). Some distinction between epistemic and doxastic knowledge, however, remains significant to the critical rhetoric project, for, as McKerrow maintains, "[critical rhetorics] respond to the demands of a critique of domination and of freedom . . . A rhetoric encased in principles of universalism, and bound to seek certitude, fails that task" ("Postmodern" 77). Like criticisms of Foucault's genealogical project, concerns regarding knowledge's thematization lead to questions of judgment and intervention. How might the critique of social knowledge avoid being charged with either "transcendentalism" [universal standards of judgment] or "relativism" [lacking standards of judgment]? What grounds for critique exist in the critical rhetoric project? More important, what is the character of such grounds?

In avoiding universal principles as the ground of critique, McKerrow recommends instead that critical rhetoric engage in "permanent criticism" ("Theory and Praxis" 96), a cleavage that leaves critical rhetoric open to accusations of relativism, a raft afloat without direction in the ideological sea (Charland, "Finding"; Gunn and Beard; Kuypers; Ono and Sloop, "Commitment"). McKerrow's response to these skepticisms returns to Foucault's ethics, in which he finds "the possibility of holding to the theoretical stance of non-privilege with respect to any one set of power relations, while at the same time participating in the politics of one's era" ("Postmodern" 76; see also, McKerrow, "Propaganda Studies").[9] Critical agency, however, remains a central question in rhetorical scholarship, a discipline that accounts for social change and political engagement. Judith Butler's thematization of performativity enables the critical rhetoric project to better conceptualize rhetorical agency within the postmodern condition.

Judith Butler, addressing universal standards of judgment as the foundation for democratic activity, reconciles structural (formalistic) and historical (strategic) accounts of universality. After revisiting the paths mapped by Hegel (in which the particular always contaminates the universal) and Laclau (in which the particular is elevated to the status of the universal), Butler imagines universality as a claim, as a matter of rhetorical invention within a specific historical context. As a potential corrective to the problems facing critical rhetoric, her account deserves to be cited at length:

The claim to universality always takes place in a given syntax, through a certain set of cultural conventions in a recognizable venue. Indeed, the claim cannot be made without the claim being recognized as a claim. But what orchestrates what will and will not become recognizable as a claim? Clearly, there is an establishing rhetoric for the assertion of universality and a set of norms that are invoked in the recognition of such claims . . . Thus, for the claim to work, for it to compel consensus, and for the claim, performatively, to enact the very universality it enunciates, it must undergo a set of translations into the various rhetorical and cultural contexts in which the meaning and force of universal claims are made. ("Restaging" 35)

If, as Butler suggests, the universal, as a foundation for knowledge production, is "staged" or performatively called into being through utterance, then how does the dominant discourse invent its own universality? Butler later writes, "The established discourse remains established only by being perpetually re-established, so it risks itself in the very repetition it requires" ("Restaging" 41). This repetition, this performativity, then, is the site of entry into universal standards of judgment that ground knowledge production, and becomes a means of challenging and rearticulating those universalities.

Additionally, Butler's critical objectives parallel those outlined in McKerrow's critical rhetoric, specifically: "The aim is to understand the integration of power/knowledge in society—what possibilities for change the integration invites or inhibits and what intervention strategies might be considered appropriate to effect social change" ("Theory and Praxis" 91). Adopting a performative rhetoric provides the "intervention strategies" toward which McKerrow gestures. Critical rhetoric's fourth principle—"*Naming* is the central symbolic act of a *nominalist* rhetoric" (105)—is in need of methodological elaboration. Although this principle implicates the production of subjectivity, and, we might add, its necessary incompletion, these rhetorical processes' theoretical and political details remain largely unexamined. Ronald Wendt's essay on the genealogical poaching of texts also suggests that nominalist rhetorics might operate in resistive ways, but, like McKerrow's inauguration of critical rhetoric, fails to specify *how* the "poaching of texts" (266–67) exerts rhetorical force or initiates rhetorical appeals. Likewise, John Murphy's "novelization" (10–12) and Ono and Sloop's "pastiche" ("Vernacular" 23–25) appear overly optimistic about the possibility of rhetorical agency within a discourse of power. Appropriating a performative rhetoric will enable us to construct a potentially resistive critical methodology without reinventing a humanist agency that seems implausible (at best) and dangerously naive (at worst) in the postmodern condition. A performative rhetoric enables possibility at the moment of historical emergence. As Butler concludes, "The reiterative speech act thus offers the possibility—though not the necessity—of depriving the past of the established discourse of its exclusive control over defining the parameters of the universal within politics" ("Restaging" 41).

Performative Ideographs

"Identity," as a category of contemporary political thought, limits (even disables or thwarts) our resistance to heteronormativity's everyday, non-institutional forms. The discourse on sexual identity thus functions as an apparatus of power, establishing heterosexuality as the universal condition for knowledge production. Public discourse equally stands as material evidence of heteronormative ideology or mass consciousness, for as rhetorician Michael Calvin McGee observes, "If a mass consciousness exists at all, it must be empirically 'present' . . . ideology in practice is a political language, preserved in rhetorical documents" ("Ideograph" 4–5). Bridging the gap between material and symbolic conceptions of social power, McGee defines ideographs as "one-term sums of an orientation" within a society (7). Additionally, any analysis of ideographic terms examines their rhetorical appeal "in their concrete history as usages, not in their alleged idea-content" (10). In other words, how ideographs function to produce material effects of social power significantly outweighs their supposed meaning. In 1950, for example, "homosexuality" was characterized as a specific type of "sex perversion," which ultimately prevented homosexuals from being employed by the government. Borrowing from the psychiatric discourse of the time, the U.S. Senate reported, "In the opinion of this subcommittee, homosexuals and other sex perverts are not proper persons to be employed in Government for two reasons; first, they are generally unsuitable, and second, they constitute security risks" ("Employment" 243). The subcommittee's association between homosexuality and sex perversion does not merely produce meanings; it materializes heteronormative ideology through public discourse and the rhetorical means of enacting that ideology.

Discourse is thus material in two senses: first, discourse renders mass consciousness as observable in rhetorical documents, and second, discourse engenders material power relations through its public circulation. Discourse's materiality, however, poses two problems for the practice of critical rhetoric. First, might not the materiality of discourse hypothesis take on an "idealist" stance, one that ultimately "detaches texts from their material (rather than intertextual) contexts" (Cloud, "Materiality" 152)? And second, doesn't discourse's materiality presuppose a relativist stance such that "there is no distinction between the real or material and the discursive," a position that prevents judgment and social action (Cloud 153)?[10] The controversy that whirls around both McGee's and McKerrow's materiality of discourse hypothesis probes our very definitions of discursive "texts" and physical "objects," one that questions the very notions of representation that undergird contemporary understandings of language. Returning to Foucault's formulation of discourse as "incorporeal materiality," rhetorical scholar Martha Cooper observes, "The paradox arises because materiality implies existence of some physical object, while incorporeality implies a non-physical phenomenon, lacking in substance" (4). Yet, as an event, Foucault contends, discourse itself takes material form. As empirical documents, McGee argues, discourse renders ideology an observable phenomenon. These characterizations of discourse take us far from conventional theories of language and representation. Cooper notes, "For if discourse functions incorporeally, takes on a life of its own, it is presentative as surely as it is representative . . . [prompting] an examination of how [objects] are given form by the statement" (6).

Ideographs and their usages in public discourse, it must remain clear, are neither transcendental nor corporeal, neither pure consciousness nor adequate substitutes for physical objects themselves. Ideographs, as material discourse, both make ideology visible and enact ideology in a society. Ideological productions of "identity," for example, inform and guide gay [male] politics and activism. "Identity" becomes an effect of power; it mobilizes ideology in and through public discourse, for it creates the very objects to which it refers. Yet "identity" must not be taken as a physical object itself, but, rather, as a concrete social category with rhetorical force.

"Identity," as an ideological force within contemporary discourse on sexuality, must also remain open to resignification.[11] As an ideograph, "identity" is salient in what Lucaites and Condit call our "public vocabulary" or ideology (8). Ideographs, such as "identity," thus become powerful rhetorical resources for those who participate in public deliberation about sexuality and power in contemporary American society. These usages, of course, can take on "culturetypal" and "countercultural" forms (Lucaites and Condit). "Homosexual identity," for instance, took on countercultural usages with the emergence of the gay liberation movement in 1969.[12] Rather than the in-group consciousness raising of the Mattachine Society in the 1950s and the Homophile movement's focus on legal and institutional changes during the 1960s, gay liberation created a collective identity based on lesbian and gay persons' increasing public visibility, the formation of a distinctly gay identity, and the nascent concept of "gay pride" (Armstrong; Bronski; Jagose). Gay and lesbian identity, in its countercultural form, thus became a public identity rather than merely a private experience. The rhetorical association of gay identity and pride was equally countercultural. Carl Wittman, in "A Gay Manifesto" (1969), wrote, "Homosexuality is *not* a lot of things. It is not a makeshift in the absence of the opposite sex; it is not hatred or rejection of the opposite sex; it is not genetic; it is not the result of broken homes except inasmuch as we could see the sham of American marriage. *Homosexuality is the capacity to love someone of the same sex*" (381). These radical shifts in the use of "identity," an ideograph in gay liberation discourse, were neither instant nor commonly accepted. Linking homosexual identity to "pride" and advocating "coming out" as a form of public visibility remained controversial acts within the lesbian and gay population as well as in heterosexual society (Blasius and Phelan 380). How might rhetoricians account for these divergent usages of "identity" in public discourse? How might the audience reception of such usages be understood?

Performativity, specifically its attention to discursive limits and constraints, enables further thematization of ideographs as rhetorical resources in public discourse. Rhetorical action, in other words, is grounded in specific and historically situated discursive conditions. Such conditions both enable and restrict rhetorical action and thus must be attended to in order to develop a worthwhile rhetorical theory. Without locating the discursive conditions of contemporary society, critical rhetoric risks becoming idealistic or relativistic to the degree of explaining nothing at all. Conceptualizing ideographs as performative prevents critical rhetoric from taking on a purely relativist stance in which ideographs can take on either culturetypal or countercultural forms on account of a speaker's will, his or her unfettered rhetorical agency.

Establishing ideographs' performative dimension as well as their rhetorical circulation within a discourse clarifies and supplements McGee's notion ("The 'Ideograph'"; "Text") of the ideograph in three ways: 1) when we conceptualize ideographs as performative entities, we necessarily conceptualize social power as contingent rather than as deterministic force, 2) performative ideographs rely on cultural conventions for their rhetorical efficacy, and 3) the repetition or citation of performative ideographs potentially resists their normative power relations.[13]

To begin, the power relations produced through the deployment or circulation of ideographs are necessarily contingent rather than deterministic. McGee writes:

> [Mass] consciousness, I believe, is always false, not because we are programmed automatons and not because we have a propensity to structure political perceptions in poetically false 'dramas' or 'scenarios,' but because 'truth' in politics, no matter how firmly we believe, is always an illusion. The falsity of an ideology is specifically rhetorical, for the illusion of truth and falsity with regard to normative commitments is the product of persuasion. ("The 'Ideograph'" 4)

Rejecting ideology as false consciousness (citizens as "programmed automatons" and perceptions as "false dramas"), McGee conceptualizes political and cultural claims of truth and falsity as "illusions" that are "the product of persuasion." Judith Butler claims similarly in her discussion of the "sex"-ed body: "[I]f 'sex' is a fiction, it is one within whose necessities we live, without which life itself would be unthinkable" (*Bodies* 6). In Butler's terms, an ideological "illusion" is not necessarily "false"; in fact, Butler challenges "fiction/truth" and "fantasy/reality" as symmetrical binaries (6). Rather, these characterizations of social reality are the effects of rhetorical invention. Both McGee's discussion of ideographs and Butler's theorization of performativity cast power relations as contingent and open to contest.

Butler's discussion of performativity transforms what she terms the discursive law [ideology] from a deterministic origin of power into a rhetorical space or *a site of invention*. This transformation begins by establishing the performative utterance as a *nominalist* practice—a rhetoric of naming—which follows J. L. Austin's distinction between perlocutionary [traditional persuasion] and illocutionary [performative] utterances, between doing something "*by* saying something" and doing something "*in* saying something" (94–103). Although we are considering performative utterances as a substantive part of rhetorical discourse, we must be wary of "the tendency to characterize (or rather reduce) this relationship to a relation between an 'inner' cause and an 'outer' consequence" (Gould 26) such that we might foreclose "a place of possible utterance"

(41). In other words, we must retain rhetorical discourse's inherent contingency, leaving its ideological operations open to future interrogation.

To begin conceptualizing a performative rhetoric, I turn to Butler's *Bodies That Matter:* "In the first instance, performativity must be understood not as a singular or deliberate 'act,' but, rather, as the reiterative and citational practice *[in] which discourse produces the effects that it names*" (my italics, 2). Butler's elaboration of performative utterances or citations locates the rhetorical text (a text that "produces effects") in an interval space, a space between. The performative utterance is brought into existence by a discursive practice rather than by the speaking or "deliberate" subject; it repeats a particular constitutive statement based upon a discursive law [ideology] that *appears to precede* the utterance. This textual repetition or citation acquires its rhetorical authority, or capacity to influence, from this seemingly a priori discursive law because the law appears to come before and thereby verify the citation itself. The power mobilized by discourse [ideology] not only results in the emergence of the performative citation, but also enables that utterance to have rhetorical force or influence. Thus, the citation appears to be located between the discursive law [ideology] and the citation's rhetorical effects; it is mobilized by the former and produces the latter.

The rhetorical relationship between the discursive law [ideology] and the performative citation is contingent, rather than deterministic, in Butler's account. For if we follow the linear causality presented thus far (the discursive law constitutes its effects through the performative citation), a discourse's normative, disciplinary, or ideological effects remain unquestionable.[14] This conceptualization merely reiterates a deterministic notion of discursive power [ideology], thereby foreclosing resistive critical acts.

Butler's transformation of the discursive law from a stable origin of power into a rhetorical space begins by critiquing a particular (mis)reading of Foucault, which conceptualizes power as a quasi-humanist subject that has an unquestioned agency or ability to produce effects (*Bodies* 9). Butler rehearses this depiction of power-as-agent. For instance, citations are "compelled" by the law (13, 15); they possess a "binding" force (225). Also, "the symbolic ought to be rethought as a series of normativizing injunctions that secure the borders of sex through the threat of psychosis, abjection, and psychic unlivability" (14–15). Finally, the citation's performative repetition of the discursive law is characterized as "forcible" (15). Ideology, materialized in discourse, appears here as a solely imposing figure: it compels, binds, secures through injunction, threatens, and forces the subject to comply.

These passages simultaneously challenge power's absolute agency, however. In terms of the sexed body, Butler explains, "the norm of sex takes hold to the extent that it is 'cited' as such a norm, but it also derives its power through the citations that it compels" (*Bodies* 13). And later: "[the discursive law] is produced through citation" (14). Here, the discursive law's strategic agency is significantly limited by its reliance on the citation, yet its force is not completely eliminated. The law has a rhetorical capacity, a certain authority, but it simultaneously relies upon the performative citation for its efficacy. Butler's text, itself a performative citation, re-cites the discursive law of heteronormativity in order to "produce it differently." A critical rhetorician, moving similarly, might locate the discursive law that appears to govern a particular set of power relations. More important, Butler's conception of performativity allows for resistive citations to occur and potentially affect change within those power relations—it enables a resistive act. This mode of resistance does not, and cannot, completely subvert the power relations that are produced by the discursive law, for any performative citation functions partially within the law rather than wholly outside of it. The resistive citation, therefore, creates a capacity for difference within the law without guaranteeing a revolution or totalizing liberation.

Before examining how Butler enables these resistive citations, however, it remains necessary to understand *how* performative ideographs become repeated. In other words, what secures their ability to govern any particular scene of social power? How do discursive laws [ideologies] appear to precede their citations?

Performative ideographs rely upon cultural conventions for their rhetorical efficacy; their usages must be "accepted" by the society in which they circulate and influence relations of power (Austin; McGee, "Ideograph"). The rhetorical character of ideographic terms, their conventionality, exists both diachronically and synchronically. A diachronic analysis indicates how ideographic terms maintain their influence over time (McGee 10). Homosexual identity, for example, must continually confront its ubiquitous association with mental illness and sinfulness. These usages of "homosexual identity" in public discourse clearly rely upon conventionality and widespread cultural acceptance for their repetition. If one is tempted to believe that equating homosexuality with disease and sinfulness are merely old worn-out stereotypes, one only has to remember the 1998 Center for Reclaiming America ads in Fort Lauderdale, Florida, that promised to "cure" homosexuality through religious teachings and that only recently in 2003 did the Supreme Court finally overturn the *Bowers v. Hardwick* decision upholding sodomy laws in Georgia.

A synchronic analysis, in contrast, indicates how different ideographs come into conflict with each other. DeLuca argues that synchronic analysis "enables us to understand how ideographs . . . function presently as rhetorical forces" (36–37). The conventional usage of "homosexual identity" as a source for unified political activism and the achievement of civil rights legislation, for instance, have often conflicted with differences that permeate the queer community. These rhetorical contests over "identity" and its nature are most salient when the political interests of non-heterosexual citizens diverge along lines of gender, race, and class.

A performative rhetoric expands McGee's methodology to explore why conventional usages are accepted in the first place and why certain ideographs win out over others in a particular ideological contest. In short: what cultural appeals influence these ideographic consequences? Supplementing McGee's concept of the ideograph with Butler's discussion of performativity enables critical rhetoricians to identify these rhetorical elements and potentially transgress contemporary relations of power. This observation brings us directly to our third question: how might we deploy ideographic terms in order to articulate resistive modes of social identity and relation?

Repeating or citing performative ideographs potentially enables resistance to their normative power relations. Butler raises this question explicitly: "What would it mean to 'cite' the [discursive] law to produce it differently, to 'cite' the law in order to reiterate and coopt its power, to expose the heterosexual matrix and to displace the effect of its necessity?" (*Bodies* 15). Resistive citations, what Butler terms "resignifications," involve conditional agency in order to reinvent an ideographic terms. Although performative citations do not rely on a willful, intentional subject to maintain their efficacy (2, 227),[15] the agency of the subject is not eliminated (7); rather, agency is qualified or "constrained" in specific ways (12, 228). For instance: "Where there is an 'I' who utters or speaks and thereby produces an effect in discourse, there is first a discourse which precedes and enables that 'I' and forms in language the constraining trajectory of its will" (225).[16] Here, the discursive law's power, its force, enables the subject to perform resistive citations and simultaneously limits their potential outcomes. The rhetor's intended effects are thus constrained by the discursive law [ideology] due to the ideograph's historicity and its conventional usages. We must be careful not to associate the resistive citation's limitations with a disabling of political and cultural change. The performative citation of ideographic terms has the potential to effect change via "reiteration" or citing the law differently. This potential is the social agent's resistive capacity, an observation that leads us to rethink identity politics, for identity becomes both foundational *and contingent* (Butler, "Contingent"; Elliot).

A Genealogy of Gay Male Identity

Adopting and adapting Michel Foucault's genealogical method provides the analytic tools required to present a series of textual analyses that examine the public discourse on gay male identity in order to uncover the rhetorical means by which social power and resistance take hold in American society today. The term "genealogy" generally invokes a sense of history, a sense of the past. Foucault's genealogies, however, work to "isolate different scenes" of power and knowledge in the present (Foucault, *Language* 140). Yet these scenes of knowledge-power are not "the final term of an historical development"; rather, they constitute "merely the current episodes" (148). A genealogy of gay male identity in contemporary America thus isolates rhetorical scenes of power and resistance in the public discourse on sexuality. Following Foucault and extending his social theory, I map these rhetorical forces in places other than the state, social institutions, and public policy.[17] This book's most important contribution to rhetoricians and activists alike is its thematization of the available means of persuasion for queer resistance in America. To this end, I have structured my argument about the rhetorical secret and its various modes of inventing male homosexuality in American discourse according to three dimensions of genealogical inquiry: descent [*herkunft*], emergence [*enstehung*], and critique. Although these methodological choices have significant implications for rhetorical scholarship more generally, such implications derive from the extended case study of gay male identity as a rhetorical resource in contemporary America. I note several of these consequences at the end of each chapter, attending primarily to the historically situated analytics of knowledge-power in gay male culture.

To begin, Chapter One returns to the so-called birth of modern (male) homosexuality in Western culture—its historical descent. The invention of modern homosexuality at the turn of the twentieth century is marked by historical, conceptual, and discursive struggles. Although the modern term "homosexuality" first appeared in scientific discourse, literature is the most ideal setting in which to observe and analyze its public modes of representation, for to represent homosexuality in public required literary devices such as metaphor. Returning to Herman Melville's *Billy Budd* as well as Eve Kosofsky Sedgwick's reading of its literary texture illuminates the discursive conditions necessary for speaking about homosexuality in the modern era. These conditions of speaking, the discursive ground upon which rhetorical action takes place, employ and deploy the rhetorical secret, itself composed out of multiple, intersecting performative contradictions. Inventing homosexuality, for instance, requires (among other things) the performance of private sexuality in public discourse. Thus, it is here, in this discursive realm, where we can begin to map the rhetorical means of creating knowledge and enacting power.

Moving forward one century, Chapters Two and Three investigate productions of male homosexuality today—its contemporary emergence. These chapters bear witness to the discursive regimes that discipline gay male bodies in American culture. I examine, to use Foucault's terminology, the struggle of discursive forces and the corporeal exercise of power that engender gay male identity in law and medicine. In Chapter Two, more specifically, I turn to the legal discourse on homosexuality in contemporary America, mapping ideographic uses of "identity" and "secrecy" as rhetorical resources for both enacting and resisting heteronormative power relations. *Lawrence v. Texas* [eventually overturning sodomy laws] and *Baehr v. Lewin* [provoking public debates over same-sex marriage] exemplify how the rhetorical secret enters into and ultimately directs the legal discourse on homosexuality. In this context, the rhetorical secret enacts its performative contradictions thus inventing essentialist and ethnic forms of gay male identity. Although such rhetorical resources advance social justice in many ways, they also elide the collective and normative dimensions of sexuality and identity. Chapter Three moves the analysis of male homosexuality's historical emergence to medical discourse. Dominant scientific narratives on HIV transmission, those found in epidemiology, immunology, and virology, employ a notion of "identity" governed by the rhetorical secret and its performative contradictions, thus inventing gay male communities in ideologically charged ways. Ultimately, an ethics of monogamy damages these collective forms of identity and sexuality.

The final two chapters perform a critical intervention into heteronormative modes of knowledge and social power, uncovering rhetorical resources for queer resistance. In so doing, they demonstrate genealogy's capability for critique. To engage a critique of the rhetorical secret, Chapter Four illuminates the rhetorical force of hypermasculine body images and their various modes of reception.

Hypermasculine images, a key instance of homoeroticism in both mainstream society and gay subcultures, operate as a public code for private homosexuality, circulating homoeroticism in public spaces. Both mainstream and gay viewers, however, inscribe heteronormative knowledge upon hypermasculine bodies, thus disciplining gay erotic culture in specific ways. Mastering the rhetorical secret and its performative contradictions, gay male culture is driven by the desire to be private and the desire to be normal. Recuperating homoerotic elements of gay male subculture provide an alternative ethical model, one resistant to the forces of heteronormative power. Gay life thus becomes public life, a (re)invention of collective identity.

The fifth and final chapter illuminates coming out as a rhetorical practice, reworking the rhetorical secret and its performative contradictions through genealogical critique. Novelist Allan Gurganus's autobiographical story is an ideal text for rearticulating the rhetorical practice of coming out for several reasons: although coming out itself is directed at diverse audiences, coming out narratives are most often consumed by gay audiences in search of identification; authored by a writer, Gurganus's story possesses a literary quality akin to the public language of modern homosexuality; and finally, Gurganus writes of a time in which coming out was not reduced to its function in visibility politics. Bringing together the social theories of Foucault and Deleuze and Guattari, I return to the actual conditions of speaking about homosexuality: its public character, its inventiveness, and its enslavement to discourse. These discursive conditions enable a critical resistance to heteronormative power and the ethics of gay life in American culture.

It has been slightly more than one hundred years since the invention of modern male homosexuality in Western culture, and the rhetorical secret continues to influence and reproduce relations of heteronormative power in American societies. Mysteriousness haunts these performances of male homosexual identity and thus creates opportunities for living differently. Within the modern discourse on sexuality, this book creates new maps of social power and investigates new paths of resistance.

The Rhetorical Secret

> [F]ar from being a category of resemblance . . . The search for de-
> scent is not the erecting of foundations: on the contrary, it disturbs
> what was previously considered immobile; it fragments what was
> thought unified; it shows the heterogeneity of what was imagined
> consistent with itself.
>
> —Michel Foucault

In *The History of Sexuality,* Foucault writes, "We must not forget that
the psychological, psychiatric, medical category of homosexuality was
constituted from the moment it was characterized—Westphal's famous
article of 1870 on 'contrary sexual sensations' can stand as its date of
birth" (43). Herman Melville's *Billy Budd* and Oscar Wilde's *The Picture
of Dorian Gray,* Eve Sedgwick contends, represent "a particular historical
moment, culminating in 1891, a moment from the very midst of the
process from which a modern homosexual identity and a modern problematic of sexual orientation could be said to date" (*Epistemology* 91).
The so-called birth of homosexual identity, however, is marked by historical, conceptual, and discursive struggle, not by resemblance and coherence. This historical moment bears witness to a struggle between different, coexisting models of erotic life rather than one conceptual model
usurping another; as queer scholars have recognized, this period does
not observe a "Great Paradigm Shift" (Halperin, "How to Do"; Halperin, "Forgetting"; Sedgwick, *Epistemology* 44–47).[1]

This historical period also constitutes the moment when, as Sedgwick notes, "secrecy itself becomes manifest as *this* [the homosexual]
secret . . . In such texts as *Billy Budd* and *Dorian Gray* and through their
influence, the subject—the thematics—of knowledge and ignorance
themselves, of innocence and initiation, of secrecy and disclosure, became not contingently but integrally infused with one particular object
of cognition: no longer sexuality as a whole but even more specifically,
now, the homosexual topic" (Sedgwick, *Epistemology* 74). The rhetorical
equation of secrecy and homosexuality is the subject of this chapter, yet
in ways that are distinct from both Foucault's analysis of the psychoanalytic confession and Sedgwick's treatment of the closet in literary docu-

ments. If Foucault displays how "sexuality" emerged historically, and if Sedgwick demonstrates the damaging effects of power that result from the predominance of sexual object choice and its structuring of the closet, then this chapter returns to the discursive exclusions, constitutive excesses, and conceptual struggles that are manifest in this historical moment.

The Rhetorical Secret

Reading and Knowing: Modern Performances of Homosexual Identity

Mapping the struggles inherent to male homosexuality's descent in the modern era, I follow Sedgwick's observation that Herman Melville's *Billy Budd* provides access to the "texture" of "a particular historical moment" (*Epistemology* 91). Melville's final novel, *Billy Budd* was drafted in 1891, yet it wasn't published until 1924. Although the story is set aboard a British naval vessel in 1790, its historical accuracy and portrayal of naval law have been criticized (Sealts 417–419). The representational significance of *Billy Budd* thus appears to lie within its ideological context and its possible connection to Melville's personal feelings of loneliness toward the end of his life (Martin 95–102). With regard to the novel's historical context, literary critic F. O. Matthiessen concluded, "By turning to such [historical] material Melville made clear that his thought was not bounded by a narrow nationalism, that the important thing was the inherent tragic quality, no matter where or when it was found. As he said in one of the prefaces to his verse: 'It is not the purpose of literature to purvey news. For news consult the *Almanac de Gotha*'" (501).

The story itself, once stripped of its bypaths and mysteriousness, is quite simple. Transferred to the *Bellipotent* from another warship, Billy Budd—described as a paragon of beauty and strength—is introduced to a world of power and discipline, represented in the figures of Captain Vere and master-at-arms John Claggart. Witnessing scenes of punishment and the exercise of authority, Billy is quickly instructed into obedience and docility. One night, Billy is roused from his sleep by a stranger who bids him to meet him at a secluded part of the ship. Once there, the stranger invites Billy to join a gang of mutinous sailors, a proposition that Billy vehemently rejects. Sometime later, however, John Claggart reports the potential mutiny to Captain Vere and names Billy Budd as one of the key conspirators. To resolve the issue, Vere calls upon Billy to defend himself against such charges. Later that day, within the confines of Vere's cabin, Claggart accuses Billy directly. Vere commands Billy to defend himself. Unable to speak, due to his uncontrollable stutter, Billy strikes Claggart, murdering him. Following the strict martial code, against his personal feelings about the matter, Vere orders Billy Budd's execution.

Melville's tale of mutiny, however, has evoked diverse and conflicting interpretations, from symbolizing the religious conflict between good and evil to providing social-political commentary on capital punishment (Sealts 421–424). It was F. O. Matthiessen's *American Renaissance* that, in 1941, introduced Melville's work into the canon of American literature and the study of American culture more generally (Bergson; Pease). Moreover, Matthiessen's seminal study of American literature presented what David Bergman has called "a covert celebration of the homosexual artist" (94). "Matthiessen," Bergman argues, "erected in *American Renaissance* virtually a gay canon of American literature" (96). Matthiessen's criticism thus renders *Billy Budd,* among other literary works, a significant part of American culture and a representation of queer American culture. Georges-Michel Sarotte, for example, contends that Melville's *oeuvre* is "essential to any discussion of the homosexual in the American novel before the 1940's" (12). Sedgwick's reading of *Billy Budd* in *Epistemology of the Closet* thus provides entry into the discursive world in which modern homosexuality was conceived.

Universalizing and Minoritizing Homosexuality

The birth of modern male homosexuality, Sedgwick argues, is wrought with competing accounts of identity, namely, universalizing and minoritizing, which produce particular effects of paranoid homophobic power.[2] Sedgwick locates modern male homosexuality within a regime of power that is at once repressive and productive, at once "murderous" and "generative" (*Epistemology* 90). Engaging the texture of modern male homosexuality, Sedgwick's reading of Melville's *Billy Budd* exposes the repressive effects of the closet and its epistemology, the struggle between universalizing and minoritizing accounts of homosexuality. More specifically, she argues, masculinist-homosocial regimes of power must repress their own homoerotic dimension in order to come into being. In one account, homoerotic desire is universal aboard the *Bellipotent,* for as Sedgwick notes, "*[E]very* impulse of *every* person in this book that could at all be called desire could be called homosexual desire, being directed by men exclusively toward men" (92). In the minoritizing account, on the other hand, the same-sex desire that appears to be everywhere is cast as "mutiny," as a threat aboard the ship *Homosociality* [with its presumed heterosexuality]. Sedgwick's primary line of questioning reveals the tension between these accounts of male homosexual desire: "Is men's desire for other men the great preservative of the masculinist hierarchies of Western culture, or is it among the most potent of the threats against them" (93)? Sedgwick later suggests: "A better way of asking the question might then be, What are the operations necessary to deploy male-male desire as the glue rather than as the solvent of a hierarchical male disciplinary order" (94)? These operations, it becomes clear, are repressive enactments of power.

Consider the title of Sedgwick's chapter on *Billy Budd,* "After the Homosexual" (*Epistemology* 91), which claims to identify "the most murderous plots of our culture" (90). Power is thus set against desire in a repressive relation. Robert Martin's discussion of the homoerotic in *Billy Budd* comes to the identical conclusion: "[This is] a tale that could bear witness to the power of eros and its conflict with authority . . . Power depends, in *Billy Budd,* on the suppression of eros" (124). *Billy Budd* renders theatrical, in Sedgwick's terms, "the fantasy trajectory toward a life *after the homosexual*" (127) or the contemporary "genocidal fantasy" of Western culture (129). This repressive relation between power and *eros* is central to Sedgwick's thesis on universalizing and minoritizing accounts of male homosexual identity. The "murderous plot" of *Billy Budd* performs two different, yet compatible operations or modes of repression: 1) phobia and 2) display (*Epistemology* 104). The first of these is the repression of the self by the self. This internalized homophobia, embodied in John Claggart, is initially enacted when he accuses Billy of mutinous engagement (a metaphor for homosexuality). Claggart's homosexual desire is ultimately repressed through his murder. The second type of repression, performed by Captain Vere, is the repression of the homosexual self by others. This display of power is performed thrice: Billy witnessing a formal gangway-punishment, Billy striking and killing Claggart, and Billy's own execution at the end of the story.

Whether it is read as a tale about capital punishment or as a tale about homophobic violence, *Billy Budd* is often received as a story about power, repressive power at that. And at some level, Melville's story is indeed such a tale. Barbara Johnson, in her analysis of *Billy Budd,* argues, "[I]t is reading, as much as killing, that is at the heart of Melville's story" (238). Johnson's comment suggests that the narrative also displays specific modes of reading and knowing. *Billy Budd* is as much about the production of knowledge as it is about the display of power. Sedgwick's analysis probes further, disclosing the homosexual-homophobic implications of the closet, as a way of reading and knowing the world, such that the production of knowledge about homosexuality is necessarily linked to the display of homophobic power. But how does this relationship between knowledge and power become invisible, normalized beyond reproach? How does the epistemology of the closet appear to be other than what it is? How does the rhetorical secret persuade us of its innocence rather than revealing its undeniable guilt? Returning to Sedgwick's commentary on the closet, I explore these questions as a matter of rhetoric.

The Temporality of Ignorance

The temporal structure of secrecy/disclosure is evident in Sedgwick's discussion of the relationship between "ignorance" and "knowledge." Ignorance is characterized in two conflicting ways, one that treats it as a simple lack of knowledge [a matter of repression] and one that conceptualizes it as a claim [a matter of invention]. Ignorance, as a lack of knowledge, is illustrated through the instance of U.S. President Ronald Reagan lacking linguistic skills in his interactions with Mitterrand (*Epistemology* 4). Because Reagan is merely "ignorant," his hypothetical learning of the French language in the future (presuming he learned it well) would not alter the language itself. The French language, previously unknown by Reagan, would not in itself change upon being learned. This instance of not knowing a foreign tongue stands in marked contrast to the examples that follow. Sedgwick notes, "The epistemological asymmetry of the laws that govern rape, for instance, privileges at the same time men and ignorance, inasmuch as it matters not at all what the raped woman perceives or wants just so long as the man raping her can claim not to have noticed (ignorance in which male sexuality receives careful education)" (5). This second type of ignorance is also demonstrated in cases of workplace discrimination against persons with AIDS in which firing them is justified by a claim to ignorance of that medical fact (5). Ignorance, in such situations, is a rhetorical invention rather than the simple lack of some incontestable information, such as a foreign language. Ignorance can thus function as if it were a "stubborn fact" even though it might be, on the contrary, "a pretense," its invention in discourse (6). Through these inventions of ignorance, misogyny, AIDS-phobia and homophobia are effectively displaced—in the closet—on the other side of secrecy and disclosure. Relations of power clearly operate in these instances yet advance the claim of "not guilty."

How do we arrive at this verdict? How do we turn a blind eye to the effects of power?

The temporal structure of the rhetorical secret enables both forms of ignorance to function in the conventional discourse of lesbian and gay politics. It allows us to believe that the contents of the secret remain unaffected by their disclosure, and that simply acknowledging the facts of homosexuality and homophobia will remedy the social effects of heteronormative power. It assumes that the revelatory act of coming out will secure the rights of citizenship and that the documentation of homophobia will provide legal recourse against it. The opening pages of *Epistemology of the Closet* seem to reference the popular fantasy of lesbian and gay politics that endows the public act of coming out with the capacity to liberate: "Inarguably, there is a satisfaction in dwelling on the degree to which the power of our enemies over us is implicated, not in their command of knowledge, but precisely in their ignorance. The effect is a real one, but it carries dangers with it as well . . . [the] privileging of ignorance as an originary [productive], passive innocence" (7). Sedgwick thus disavows ignorance's status as a stubborn fact or mere lack of knowledge, disavows accounts in which ignorance is seen as "a single Manichaean, aboriginal maw of darkness" or "pieces of the originary dark" (8). The rationale derives from Foucault's repression hypothesis: "[A] writer who appeals too directly to the redemptive potential of simply upping the cognitive wattage on any question of power seems, now, naïve" (7). The rhetorical secret, therefore, functions retroactively. Its temporal structure, the belief that secretive contents *precede* their disclosure, attributes a certain "truth" status to the contents themselves. In other words, disclosure does not alter or change the secret contents, for in actuality they existed *prior to* the act of disclosure. Under this discursive regime, we remain unable to question the relations of power that are at work in the production of knowledge and the invention of ignorance. Rather than rely upon the rhetorical secret's temporality, we must examine the ways in which the secret contents of the closet change upon disclosure—their modes of invention.

The Spatiality of Privacy

In addition to its temporality, the rhetorical secret relies upon the spatial relationship between public and private. Emerging as "the love that dares not speak its name," forever under the threat of repression, modern male homosexuality could only make public appearances under a rubric of codes (Beaver 104; Creech 77–78; Chauncey 288). Although what

Charles E. Morris III has called "homosexual double-consciousness" might be considered a mechanism that simply reinforces the repressive nature of the closet (262), his analysis of literary critic F. O. Matthiessen encourages us to recognize the resistive potential in the "homosexual palimpsest." Passing, Morris optimistically argues, "affords obscured agency, and immersion in the mainstream, precisely so that one might swim against the tide, undermining the homophobic order of things" (263). Such agency, especially in oppressive contexts, requires the performance of the private in public, in a word—the closet.

The epistemology of the closet thus operates through the practice of reading metaphorically, translating public codes into private meanings. As Sedgwick's reading of *Billy Budd* demonstrates, the literary site became a confessional of sorts, a means of making the private fact of homosexuality public. We have already witnessed how "mutiny" becomes a metaphor or code for the universalizing account of the male homosexual subject (*Epistemology* 100–101). John Claggart, on the other hand, embodies the minoritizing account. The language describing Claggart— "mysterious," "exceptional," "peculiar," "exceptional" again, "obscure," "phenomenal," "notable," "phenomenal" again, "exceptional" again, "secretive" (94)—announces his homosexuality because within the discourse on sexuality in 1891 these terms were taken up as effective euphemisms. Claggart's nature is put to the reader as a mystery to solve, yet as Sedgwick proves, "the answer to the riddle" comes not from substantive explanations, but, rather, it emerges from "a series of intensifications of [the mysteriousness]" surrounding Claggart (94). Put otherwise, these answers derive from "representationally vacant, epistemologically arousing place-markers" (95). The answer appears because it does not appear; it is present, ironically, by virtue of its very absence. The riddle of Claggart, which answers itself by repeatedly refusing to answer, is instead answered within the medical and legal taxonomies of homosexuality. Sedgwick admits, "Arguably, however, there can be no full or substantive answer at all to the question . . . Claggart represents a pure *epistemological essence*" (96). The paradox herein is that the male homosexual [fundamental essence] is known by and as his unknowability [epistemological contingency]. His stubborn mysteriousness, in Sedgwick's words, "is not, however, enough to drive doctor, lawyer, clergyman, once summoned, from their place of consultation at the door of the text" (96). In sum, the diagnostic taxonomies that compose the metaphoric relation between unspeakable depravity and homosexuality are rhetorical inventions rather than full answers to the riddle. Yet they eschew their status as inventions, and instead, present themselves as deterministic, unequivocal codes.

The formal logic of the closet appears to be one in which acts of secrecy and disclosure oppose each other, for to keep a secret refuses to reveal it. Yet, upon closer examination of the discourse that equates "homosexuality" and "secrecy," we learn that this is not at all the case. Rather, secrecy and disclosure are fully compatible, even necessarily so. D. A. Miller, for one, has illuminated the theatrical force of the open secret: "in theatrically continuing to keep my secret, I have already rather *given it away*" (*Novel* 194). Gay men today know this double bind all too well. Upon coming out to a friend or relative (or heck, even a total stranger), we are often jolted by the comment, "Oh, *that?* I figured *that* out a long time ago. I was just waiting for you to feel comfortable telling me." It appears we wear our homosexual secret on our sleeve, so to speak. Our insistent attempts at passing for heterosexual only seem to announce our homosexual desire even further. Miller later writes, "Sometimes, certainly, this open secret is actively *opened* . . . [but] dramatic revelation even of this order is superfluous" (205). The closet, formally speaking, is thus no closet at all. The closet, its trope of secrecy/disclosure, cannot be understood as pure knowledge, but, rather, must be implicated in historically situated power relations. How does the rhetorical secret disguise these insidious functions? How does it convince us that disclosure is simply a matter of exchanging information about oneself? How does it appear so innocently? These are the questions that require a rhetorical analysis, an examination of "identity" and "secrecy" as ideographs in public discourse.

The Mastery of Discourse

The temporal and spatial structuring of the rhetorical secret is further conditioned by a leap of faith, by desire itself. In depicting how the male homosexual riddle is solved, Sedgwick begins, "If there is a full answer to this question at all then there are two full answers . . . that Claggart is depraved because homosexual, or alternatively depraved because homophobic" (*Epistemology* 96). In other words, the answer, any answer, requires us to act "as if" there is an answer to be had, "as if" one is possible. The diagnostic taxonomies of Melville's historical-cultural texture are thus fundamentally mobilized by a desire for secrets, by what Foucault has called "pleasure in the truth of pleasure" (*History* 71). The rhetorical secret, its ability to provide an answer, is compelling due to the promise of textual mastery that is held out to the reader. The reader, in other

words, becomes endowed with a capacity for reading unequivocally, co-
herently, and assuredly—the reader becomes a master of knowledge,
an agent. The appeal to mastery, however, is no agency at all—it is an
empty promise. Sedgwick observes: "The inexplicit compact by which
novel-readers voluntarily plunge into worlds that strip them, however
temporarily, of the painfully acquired cognitive maps of their ordinary
lives (awfulness of going to a party without knowing anyone) on condition of an invisibility that promises cognitive exemption and eventual privilege, creates, especially at the beginning of books, a space
of high anxiety and dependence" (97). Within the appeal to textual
mastery, the reader oscillates between "vulnerability" and "promise,"
"threat" and "flattery," "disorientation" and "tentative empowerment,"
"terrorism" and "rescue" (*Epistemology* 97–99). The anxiety produced in
these reader-relations produces a desire for mastery, for agency. To read
otherwise would be to subject oneself to a constant state of anxiety,
vulnerability, threats, disorientation, and terror. Textual vulnerability
and textual mastery, in this schema, appear to be contradictory forms of
readership that compel us to choose between subservience and master-
ful agency. These two relations between reader and text are, in fact, one
and the same—to become a master of the text requires one to become
subservient to it. Sedgwick explains: "The reader, thus, is invented as a
subject in relation to the 'world' of the novel by an act of interpellation
that is efficacious to the degree that it is contradictory, appealing to the
reader on the basis of an assumed sharing of cognitive authority whose
ground is hollowed out in the very act of the appeal" (99). To become
an agent in this literary world thus requires the reader to enter into a
relationship with the text while providing the very ruse that allows him
to imagine himself outside the text. Isn't this relationship between
reader and text identical to the homosexual-homophobic epistemology
of the closet? "It takes one to know one."

Historical Forgetting

If ignorance is performed as invention, if the private is performed in
public, and if slavery is performed as mastery, then what rhetorical operation enables these contradictions to disappear into the textual fabric
of modern homosexuality? In other words, what differences must be
excluded in order to produce identity as a coherent sameness? What
must we leave behind, what must we forget in the process of leaping? As
David Halperin suggests, the history of male homosexuality must explore the "historical process of accumulation, accretion, and overlay . . .

the play of identities and differences" ("How to Do" 89–90). This dynamic interaction between sameness and difference, which results in the production of a coherent modern male homosexuality, requires rhetorically charged exclusions. Knowledge thus requires forgetting, an absence of knowledge.

Modern definitions of male homosexual identity effectively reduce themselves to the gender of one's sexual object choice such that "the word is now almost universally heard as referring to relations of *sexuality* between persons who are, because of their sex, more flatly and globally categorized as *the same*" (Sedgwick, *Epistemology* 158–59). This production of homosexual "identity," however, requires rhetorical work. "Identity" cannot be taken as an historical given, but, rather, must be shown to have emerged from the exclusion of erotic difference. "The plot of [Oscar Wilde's *Dorian Gray*]," Sedgwick illustrates, "seems to replicate the discursive eclipse in this period of the Classically based, *pederastic* assumption that male-male bonds of any duration must be structured around some diacritical difference—old/young, for example, or active/passive—whose binarizing cultural power would be at least comparable to that of gender" (160). Perhaps the greatest historical irony is that Wilde's conviction of "gross indecency" required the presence of such differences rather than their absence. Differences within social/erotic relations became, in this instance, the mechanism by which the "homosexual" person [someone prone to relations of sameness] was diagnosed, revealed. More important, however, such processes of diagnosis/conviction were then elided. Ed Cohen, analyzing the newspaper accounts of the Wilde trials, argues that because the specific sexual acts [sodomy] of which Wilde was accused were deemed as "unrepresentable" in public discourse, other signs of sexuality were used to diagnose him as a "homosexual" person. It was suggested that "his 'friendships' with [several younger, usually unemployed, working-class men] could not be 'proper' because they were marked by gross disparities in class, age, position, and social and educational background" (166). Cohen later concludes that this diagnostic process, which took place in the courtroom as well as in the press, was founded upon "a topology of difference" (190). The Wilde trials teach us, perhaps most dramatically, that erotic relations are never fully manifest as relations of sameness or relations of difference, but, rather, continually slide along the axis between the two.[3] The treatment of these loose strands in the fabric of modern male homosexuality evidences how the rhetorical secret governs this scene of disciplinary power, and produces the coherence of the subject it promises. My aim then is to detail the rhetorical operations that enable such attachments, forces, compulsions, and seductions.

The Pleasures of Reading

The epistemological relationship between text and sexuality lies in the former's failed attempts to fully know and represent the latter. We know, from our critical engagement with Sedgwick's *Epistemology of the Closet,* that sexual knowledge carries with it a series of performative contradictions, statements in which "the propositional content of what the speaker says contradicts the conditions of the asserted proposition itself" (M. Morris, "On the Logic" 740): ignorance requires invention, the private must be performed in public, to promise epistemological mastery is to seduce one into slavery, to know is to forget. These performative contradictions, I contend, produce pleasure, enabling the rhetorical secret to seduce us. Reading the rhetorical secret is thus an erotic act.

To claim that reading has an erotic dimension is to evoke a double valence such that engagement with literary texts results in two different modes of knowledge: the sexual and the erotic. The former, as we have witnessed in the modern discourse on male homosexuality, promises subjective coherence at the same moment that the latter thwarts it. The erotic, writes Alphonso Lingis, is an event in which "the individual is carried through the experience of psychic shattering, a threat to the stability and integrity of the self, by the pleasure of erotic excitement, a pleasure inherently masochist" (*Foreign* 120). Elsewhere, Lingis elaborates, "Eroticism is the inner experience of being violated in sexual contact, and of violating another. The erotic craving is a craving to be violated" (*Imperative* 148). Already we can see the immense difficulty in wrenching apart the erotic and the sexual. Thank goodness, then, that this is not the task we have set for ourselves here. What I do want to suggest, rather, is that the oscillation between the erotic and the sexual performs two modes of knowing, constituting different relations between the self and the other. In these erotic moments, we are often left without our disciplinary maps.

When pleasure and literary texts collide, language ultimately fails to represent, to cohere to its object. In fact, the more expressive texts become, the less they express. Roland Barthes sets us straight, so to speak: "The text of pleasure is not necessarily the text that recounts pleasures; the text of bliss is never the text that recounts the kinds of bliss afforded literally by an ejaculation. The pleasure of representation is not attached to its object" (*Pleasure* 55). Later: "*Writing aloud* is not expressive" (66). Borrowing from Barthes, Corey and Nakayama's literary persona, Mark Stark comes to the stark realization: "Desire seemed so fleeting at that moment, as if no text, despite pornography's claim otherwise, could capture and hold desire. Desire was always already beyond the text, beyond the ability of any system, including capitalism, to contain and control it" (64). Stark eventually concludes, "Language fails me" (67). Is Stark lamenting this fact? Expressing his ultimate disappointment in his inability to come to any sort of epistemological conclusion? Or is perhaps the representative failure of language a reason for celebration? For Barthes, it appears this failure to express pleasure is no reason for dismay: "I enjoy a text bursting with legibility *for the reason that it does not speak*" (*Pleasure* 123). The text's inability to "express," "recount," "speak," "capture," "hold," "contain," or "control" taunts us.

A text's eroticism, however, does not require readers to participate in an economy of secret codes waiting to be deciphered. Roland Barthes reminds us, "The pleasure of the text is not the pleasure of the corporeal striptease or of narrative suspense. In these cases, there is no tear, no edges: a gradual unveiling: the entire excitation takes refuge in the *hope* of seeing the sexual organ (schoolboy's dream) or in knowing the end of the story (novelistic satisfaction)" (*Pleasure* 10). The pleasure of the text does not strip the text of its secrets, the reader does not eventually see what s/he hopes to see, know what s/he hopes to know. The texture never fully reveals that which it promises to disclose; it remains mysterious, reorienting the relation between self and other, as well as our knowledge of that relationship, and, finally, the pleasure that accompanies such modes of knowing. Barthes realizes, "I am often struck by the obvious fact that the other is impenetrable, intractable, not to be found; I cannot open up the other, trace back the other's origins, solve the riddle. Where does the other come from? Who is the other? I wear myself out, I shall never know . . . [T]he other is not to be known; his opacity is not the screen around a secret, but, instead, a kind of evidence in which the game of reality and appearance is done away with" (*Discourse* 134–35). The epistemological relation between self and other, however, is not done in. The murder of knowledge ["I shall *never* know"] is a ruse. The other becomes "a kind of evidence" rather than a "riddle" or a "secret," and thus engenders competing claims rather than final discoveries. We have not witnessed a murder here. We have, instead, witnessed the usurping of the secret by its mysterious underside.

Eroticism, the collision of pleasure and texture, is, above all else, performative, for it ultimately confuses being and doing, identity and conduct. In the translator's preface to *Pleasure of the Text,* Richard Howard attempts to distinguish between "pleasure" and "bliss": "Pleasure is a state, of course, bliss (*jouissance*) an action" (vi). The presumptive "of course," betrays, of course, the simplicity of this separation. It is as if to say that states and actions can be easily distinguished, that we can know the difference between them—a task that Barthes has much difficulty with throughout this text on text. In fact, perhaps, does he not find it impossible to separate them fully? Doesn't bliss continually fold back onto pleasure? The blissful text is an impossible performance (*Pleasure* 7, 22), for its essential condition is its utter foreignness. The blissful text is "asocial" (39), "darkness" (39), the "limit of speech" (45), the "undoing of nomination" (45), and the "non-cultural" (62). The blissful text is the limit of text, a performance of otherness par excellence. Yet, Barthes writes, "every language becomes old once it is repeated" (40). The oxymoron is evident: to be blissful, the text must be new; to be a text, it must be old. In its repetition, the blissful text folds back onto the pleasurable text, the possible text, a text that is forever "disappointing" (58). Pleasure is produced by the "embarrassed figuration" of representation, for representation announces the coming of that which it represents and simultaneously bears witness to the emergence of "nothing" (56–57). The erotic subject, inhabiting this texture, becomes a "split subject," for "he enjoys the consistency of his selfhood (that is his pleasure) and seeks its loss (that is his bliss)" (14). Put another way, he "simultaneously enjoys, through the text, the consistency of his selfhood and its collapse, its fall" (21). Erotic texts thus set the sexual subject "adrift" (63).

The Masochistic Economy of *Billy Budd*

Narrative as Rhetorical Form

Billy Budd performs modern male homosexuality, its texture, its modes of invention, its public discursiveness, in narrative form. Melville's story, in so doing, so explicitly displays the troublesome nature of narratives that we would be remiss to ignore the rhetorical ways in which the narrative disrupts and prevents the story from ever reaching its end; it remains "unfinished" (Hutchinson 397).[4] Mizruchi, in fact, goes as far as to suggest that "Billy, in striking Claggart dead, disables the story . . . a draining of the very possibility for story" (300). Rather than accept Claggart's death as the *telos* of this narrative, as its ending, this analysis explores the ways in which Claggart's death sets off a series of events that undermine narrative coherence. The narrative's *mysterious* quality extends from both a generic tension in the narrative as well as its formal imperfections (J. McIntosh, "Billy Budd").

Following a depiction of Billy Budd's physical beauty and corporeal perfection, the narrative focuses our attention to his "vocal defect," his stutter. From this revelation, questions surrounding the story's genre emerge: "The avowal of such an imperfection in the Handsome Sailor should be evidence not alone that he is not presented as a conventional hero, but also that the story in which he is the main figure is no romance" (Melville, *BB* 302)[5]. This refusal of the romantic genre is supported by a defect in the central character—an imperfection at the core of the narrative. This imperfection sweeps across the text, producing ambivalence throughout the story. The negation of "romance" in this passage and the presence of particular romantic elements in the novella allow its generic classification to remain contingent (Hendershot; Martin). Literary critics have understood the story's contingency differently. While McElroy contends that *Billy Budd* presents "deliberate violations of historical realism" (47), James McIntosh maintains that Melville "broadens the common conception of 'romance'" (225). The problem of literary genre is exacerbated by the way in which the narrative casts its potential hero. Rather than a "conventional hero," Billy is "the main figure." Once again, literary scholars do not concur as to the effect of this passage. Martin, for example, refers to the narrative texture as "a heroless world" (118). Refusing to cast Billy Budd and John Claggart as "heroes," Hocks recommends Captain Vere as the potentially tragic hero (61), a reading that Martin explicitly and vehemently rejects (114). *Billy Budd* thus displays the "larger historical problem of subjectivity and agency in the late nineteenth century," which was tied significantly to the generic problematics of American literary realism (Mizruchi 272).

The formal discontinuities of *Billy Budd* also invite a high-resolution reading of Melville's novella. For instance: "The symmetry of form attainable in pure fiction cannot so readily be achieved in a narration essentially having less to do with fable than with fact. Truth uncompromisingly told will always have its ragged edges; hence the conclusion of such a narration is apt to be less finished than an architectural finial" (*BB* 380–81). The narrative experiences a broader tension between form and chaos, which is not resolved within its borders (Hocks; Ruttenburg). The narrative's formal imperfections are achieved both spatially and temporally.

Staging the events upon a ship creates what Casarino calls "heterotopia": "To represent, to contest, to invert: one can think of Foucault's heterotopia as a mode of representation, as a particular kind of space from and through which one can see and make new and different sense of all other spaces" (2). Readers of *Billy Budd* are thus located within a heterotopic space, a space of invention. As we open the pages of Melville's novella, Casarino maintains, as we board the spatial architecture of the ship, we position ourselves in the historical texture of "the crisis of modernity" (12), "the dramatization of paradigm shifts in conceptions and definitions of sexuality" (13) and the troublesome site of narrative itself (5). The ship-as-heterotopia thus displays the problematics that swarm around modern inventions of sexuality, its incoherences. Casarino concludes, "It is precisely such a paradoxical symbiosis of fragment and monad, of homogeneity and heterogeneity, of sameness and difference in respect to social totality that generates the space of the ship" (4).

Billy Budd equally troubles the temporality of teleological narrative, thus problematizing the production of knowledge itself. Melville's "inside narrative" displays its "ragged edges," its "bypaths" in plain view such that narrator and reader are situated as "mediator[s] among various systems of knowledge" (Mizruchi 303). Considering the disavowal of "romance" in the text, which for many scholars constitutes the story under the genre of late-nineteenth-century realism, *Billy Budd* might be said to "invent a truth," serve as "an instrument of knowledge," and "create a new reality" (G. Levine, 5, 13, 20). If "the mysterious [is] a key subject of the text" (J. McIntosh 227), then *Billy Budd* surely "call[s] attention to the uncertain status of what one can know in fiction" (234). These epistemological "bypaths," however, are not predetermined secrets waiting to be discovered by readers. *Billy Budd,* in its mysteriousness, demands that we read with greater and greater precision. Yoder, for instance, argues, "Melville's tale will never be finished, of course, because its life exists in the minds of readers" (97). Yoder's commentary also suggests, "[T]he novel transcends simplicity through the varying responses of readers, with the emergence of the contention that all responses can be but partial truths about protagonists who represent the complexity of human experience" (100). It is not difficult to notice the double valence in Yoder's evocation of "partial truths," for truth is both incomplete and contingent. The question of truth, which circulates within the narrative economy of *Billy Budd,* is indicated further by the name "Starry Vere." Hendershot explains, "[Vere is] an allegorical name (Vere=Truth)" (100). Yet his nickname "Starry Vere" derives from the observation that "Captain Vere though practical enough upon occasion would at times betray a certain dreaminess of mood" (*BB* 310). Can we not conclude, then, that the narrative figure of "Starry Vere" lives on the very border between truth and fiction, between fact and fantasy?

These questions of social knowledge ultimately become questions of power. Most critics insist upon the repressive character of power in *Billy Budd,* for Billy's death is unanimously read as the patriarchal and/or homophobic repression of the feminine and/or homoerotic (Hendershot; Koffler; McGowan; West). Robert Martin's analysis is most instructive on this point: "The sexuality of *Billy Budd* is a sexuality divested of its subversive power: it is the sexual attraction between power and powerlessness" (108). The power that mobilizes the erotic events of the text is thus absolutely repressive. This becomes clear as Martin concludes that Melville's story is "a tale that could bear witness to the power of eros and its conflict with authority . . . Power depends, in *Billy Budd,* on the suppression of eros" (124). But what disallows viewing the forces of power and eros differently? Martin claims, "*Billy Budd* is above all a study of repression . . . since there is no one in the story to respond to the events" (107). What would this response need to look like in order to stage a resistance against patriarchy and homophobia? Martin's answer: "[*Billy Budd*] also makes it clear that beauty alone is not redemptive; indeed because it lacks speech it must always be condemned to misunderstanding and failure" (123). Beauty and speech are, of course, mutually exclusive, for we are speaking of "beauty alone" and "lacking speech." The hierarchy of speech over image and its gendered character are even more explicit in West's articulation of feminism and its relationship to *Billy Budd.* Resistance is said to be absent in the narrative because Billy is "impotent" or "because Billy is so annoyingly and maddeningly *silent*" (19). Casting silence as a form of impotence reinforces a conventional association between dominant male sexuality and speech. If this is not clear enough, the next statement in the passage certainly is: "The bottom line for women [and homosexuals?] is just this. Women must break this silence. If we wish to avoid Billy's fate, then we must articulate a defense when we aggress against those who would victimize us" (19). What these guidelines for resistance fail to recognize is their dependence on the very productive forms of power that they reinforce: speech = power; silence = repression. In contrast, I contend with the following analysis that the erotic character of this text does not witness the repression of eros by authority, but, rather, it constitutes an erotic *suffused with* authority.

On Masochism and Sexuality

Billy Budd, while representative of the discursive texture of late-nineteenth-century modernism, cannot be reduced to the emergence of "sexuality" as a discrete, coherent object of knowledge. Its composition also derives from interwoven elements, threads and particles that undermine our reliance on what Foucault has termed "the agency of sex." These loose threads are staged within and through a masochistic erotic economy, "an invention of the late nineteenth century . . . [that arose out of] crises in liberal concepts of agency" (Noyes 6–8). The modern problematics of agency, subjective coherence, sexuality, and gender make themselves conspicuous in the works of Krafft-Ebing and others. Scholars, considering masochism's historical situatedness, observe its connection to anxieties surrounding both middle-class ideology (Cosgrove) and nationhood (Noyes).

The late-nineteenth-century taxonomy of "sadomasochism" finds its most elaborate articulation in the work of Krafft-Ebing. *Psychopathia Sexualis* constructs the "sadomasochistic entity" out of the literary texts of Marquis deSade and Sacher-Masoch, yet converts their distinctive erotic economies into a symmetrical psychic entity (Deleuze, *Masochism* 12–14). The binary taxonomy of sadomasochism begins by establishing sadism and masochism as distinctive, yet complimentary sexual activities. Krafft-Ebing observes rather simply, "Masochism is the opposite of sadism. While the latter is the desire to cause pain and use force, the former is the wish to suffer pain and be subjected to force" (127). The symmetry between sadistic and masochistic activities is echoed several times throughout the text (148–49, 181–82, 187), until Krafft-Ebing finally concludes that they are "perfect counterparts" (190). Such symmetry is founded upon the premise that sexual activity organizes itself around distinctively active and passive roles. For instance, "The parallelism [between sadism/masochism] is perfect. All the acts and situations used by the sadist in the active role become the object of the desire of the masochist in the passive role. In both perversions these acts advance from purely symbolic acts to severe maltreatment" (191). The second part of this passage also reiterates the ways in which the sadomasochistic entity, as conceived by modern sexology, fixates on the element of pain and suffering, whether symbolic or physical in nature (87, 116, 181–94).

The perverse character of sadomasochism is strictly tied to modernist notions of gender and sexual activity. In other words, masochism on the part of men appears to be perverse due to the inversion of active and passive roles in the sexual encounter. This implication first appears in Krafft-Ebing's dismissal of "masochism in women." "In women," he writes, "voluntary subjection to the opposite sex is a physiological phenomenon. Owing to her passive role in procreation and long-existent social conditions, ideas of subjection are, in women, normally connected with the idea of sexual relations" (177). This positioning of women in the passive role leads to the conclusion that masochism in women is "to a certain extent a normal manifestation" (178). Masochism in men, on the contrary, is characterized as "a partial *effemination*," for "the masochist considers himself in a passive, feminine role toward his mistress and that his sexual gratification is governed by the success his illusion experiences in the complete subjection to the will of the consort" (189). Kaja Silverman, in her essay on masochism, explicates that the patriarchal regime depends upon the binary form of gender and its understanding of men and women in complimentary active and passive roles (33). Tyler concurs and argues effectively that viewing masochism as a mere inversion of sex roles [the adoption of passivity on the part of men] is such that "the meaning of the phallus and its 'privileged' signifiers [the penis] could remain unanalyzed" (51). I extend this critique of Krafft-Ebing's conceptualization of "sadomasochism" to include its heteronormative implications. Krafft-Ebing, for the most part, reduces the sadomasochistic entity to heterosexual encounters. This taxonomy readily dismisses same-sex sadomasochistic relations. For instance, a male committing a sadistic act toward a member of the same sex is considered to be merely an act of substitution: "the impulse is really directed toward women, and that only as a makeshift the nearest attainable objects (pupils) are abused" (119). Masochism, on the other hand, is "frequently found in homosexual men," but is cast as merely an extension of the gender inversion that already defines their "homosexuality" (189–90). In this sense, we can immediately detect the taxonomic trouble that might be caused by a serious consideration of masochism and male homoeroticism.

The erotic economy of masochism, however, already haunts the taxonomy laid out by Krafft-Ebing, for his study borrows directly from the literary texts of Sacher-Masoch (see *Psychopathia Sexualis,* pages 127–28, 138, 142). The literary quality of masochism is vital to our study, for it is the literary, performative, and narrative character of this erotic economy that enables us to stage resistances to heteronormativity within *Billy Budd.* In fact, descriptions of the masochistic narrative parallel those used to depict the narrative style of Melville's novella. Silverman, for

instance, defines the perversion of masochism as "the temptation to engage in a different kind of erotic narrative, one whose organization is
aleatory and paratactic rather than direct and hypotactic, preferring
forepleasures to endpleasures, and browsing to discharge" (33). Likewise,
Cosgrove writes, "The masochistic narrative is void of cause and effect,
and a series of arbitrary *decoupages* unlinks continuity in the quest for
mise en scenes whose goal is the moment of stimulus" (432). The anti-
teleological aspects of the masochistic narrative make it an ideal tool for
mapping *Billy Budd*'s mysterious character, for it enables the reader to
improvise, browsing the forepleasures, moments of stimulus, and bypaths
that are laid out before us, rather than simply translating these mysteries
into secrets to be uncovered by the reader. Sacher-Masoch's own philosophical viewpoint presents his writing as "the revolutionary element in
literature" (qtd. in Noyes 54). The masochist, Noyes explains, "masters
nature by staging his loss of mastery" (76), a staging that occurs in
"writing itself" (79). These conceptualizations of masochism as a literary
staging of the "loss of mastery" lead us to inquire as to the precise narrative techniques that produce such an effect.

The masochistic economy, as theorized by Deleuze, is characterized by four operations that garner our attention here: the contract,
disavowal, expiation, and rebirth. Deleuze's work on the masochistic
economy transgresses the binary form of active/passive [male/female]
relations, which dominates the sadomasochistic entity found in modern
sexology. The masochistic economy, for instance, finds its founding gesture in a contract that establishes a mutually active relationship between
the subject and the torturer. Deleuze contends, "The masochist appears
to be held by real chains, but in fact he is bound by his word alone. The
masochistic contract implies not only the necessity of the victim's con-
sent, but his ability to persuade, and his pedagogical and judicial efforts
to train his torturer" (*Masochism* 75; see also, Abel, "Fargo"). In this depiction of the masochistic contract, we observe not only the relational
qualities of erotic agency, its ability to undermine the notion of distinctly "active" and "passive" participants in the erotic, but we also witness the rhetorical processes by which these relations take place. Namely,
masochism (unlike sadism's demonstrative enactments of power and
status) operates through persuasion and pedagogy. "We are dealing,"
Deleuze reminds us, " . . . with a victim in search of a torturer and who
needs to educate, persuade, and conclude an alliance with the torturer in
order to realize the strangest of schemes" (*Masochism* 20). But what style

of erotics does this contract aim to realize? And how does it go about realizing it?

Masochism's contractual relations are performed through disavowal or suspense; they are recognizable by their ability to slow or delay gratification. I wish to argue, whereas Deleuze appears to imply, that the masochistic staging of disavowal occurs at the level of performativity [citational] as well as at the level of performance [theatrical]. Disavowal, in other words, is performed in the act of reading as much as it is performed in the act of writing; it is a matter of historical-cultural texture in addition to being an element of literary text. Rather than the narrative acceleration that occurs in sadistic relations (Abel 318–19), masochism affects a "frozen quality" (Deleuze, *Masochism* 34). Borrowing from the work of Theodor, as Deleuze does, Silverman explicates that masochistic narrative is one of "endless postponement" through the enactment of ritual (46). It is the very staging of rituals, then, that performs a disavowal of conventional power structures, for it denies them a teleological resolution to the story. Masochism's tactical, ritual performance thus "works against anything approximating psychic coherence" (Silverman 48). The processes of disavowal are characterized by their attention to the aesthetic, formal, and dramatic dimensions of erotic pleasure such that "[the masochist is] able to deny the reality of pleasure at the very point of experiencing it" (33). The impact of disavowal, Deleuze is quick to point out, is the creation of a space in which "a new horizon opens up beyond the given and in place of it" (*Masochism* 31). The masochistic contract, therefore, effects a transformation in the erotic relations it constitutes.

Such transformations take place through the processes of expiation and rebirth. The masochistic contract differs significantly from the sadomasochistic entity, which relies upon the repression hypothesis in order to imagine its resistances (Deleuze, *Masochism* 57). The effect of confusing and/or conflating elements of sadism and masochism is made clear: "Modes of equivalence and translation are mistaken for systems of transition and transformation" (58). Is this outcome at all surprising considering what we now know about the rhetorical economy of secrecy and disclosure? In collapsing the distinctions between sadism and masochism, do we not consequently replace the mysteriousness of erotic relations with secrecy? And, finally, might the masochistic operations of expiation and rebirth become ways of resisting the secret's rhetorical potency? The process of expiation that structures the masochistic contract enacts a resistance to the patriarchal themes of sadism and "conventional heterosexuality" (Silverman 35).

In order for masochism to expiate the patriarchal Father, Deleuze explains, he must first appear on the scene. The character of the Greek in Masoch's *Venus in Furs* serves as a key example of how the Father appears in the masochistic fantasy of expiation and rebirth. The Greek's presence in the masochistic scene does not confirm the sadomasochistic entity; on the contrary, he functions as a threat to the masochistic contract, a threat that must be overcome in order to fulfill the ideals of expiation and rebirth (Deleuze, *Masochism* 65; see also, Whang). In the masochistic scenario, then, the Father, or the Greek, or the sadist becomes the beaten rather than the beater (60–61). The beating of the Father sets in motion the masochistic contract and performs its ideals of expiation and rebirth, the creation of a "new horizon," the inhabiting of possibilities. The beating of the Father performs a "shattering" of phallic coherence (Silverman 38; Tyler 47), "a sardonic mockery of authority" (Cosgrove 421), and a "disruption of paternal authority" (Gearhart 393).

Rather than finding avenues of resistance outside of the law, or within the juridical model of power and resistance, the masochistic formulation inhabits a transgressive space that cuts across the law. Deleuze concludes, "[the masochist] simply attacks the law on another flank . . . irony" (*Masochism* 88). In order to affect such a transgression, however, it must first stage the law and display its absurdity by submitting to it (84–88). Noyes explains, "Law only functions if it is not taken too literally. Sacher-Masoch's violation of the law lies in its all too literal fulfillment" (78–79). For Noyes, this transgression is a wholly historical one that contests the late-nineteenth-century ideals of liberalism and reason by demonstrating how these ideals are ultimately tied to systems of violence (79). Masochistic parodies of the law occur through performance, narrative and display. We must remember that display is both highly formalized and ritualized within the masochistic economy (Deleuze, *Masochism* 109). It is wholly without content (83–85). In contrast to the sadistic economy, then, display and theatricality—in a word, spectacle—is not a means of achieving sovereign power, but, rather, it becomes a tactic for undermining such ideals. It is expiation. It is a transgression that plays out along the gendered, binary axes of activity/passivity (Noyes; Silverman).

The problem with the sadomasochistic entity, Deleuze argues, is that it maintains the categories of active/passive in binary form. The masochistic contract and its ideals of expiation and rebirth should not be understood as "passive" (*Masochism* 110), but, I would suggest, as a relational form of agency in which the terms "active" and "passive" no longer make sense. "Masochism is a story that relates how the superego was destroyed and by whom, and what was the sequel to this destruction" (Deleuze, *Masochism* 130). Within this story, "death can only be imagined as a second birth" (131). If sadism or "conventional heterosexuality" is thwarted in the masochistic narrative, then what role do male homoerotic images play in this transgression? Kaja Silverman's psychoanalytic account of masochism is instructive on this point. "Moral masochism," on the one hand, is compatible with "conventional" sexual subjectivity in that it activates the Oedipus complex (38–39). The male subject, in this scenario, oscillates between wanting "to be" the Father and wanting "to love" the Father (43), what Sedgwick has called "slippage between identification and desire" (*Epistemology* 159). These homoerotic tensions within the male subject, Silverman explains, implicate the sexual object choice of the subject (42–43). In other words, the Freudian version of "moral masochism" results in the potential repression of "homosexual" object choice. "Feminine masochism," on the other hand, attempts to "conceal the *homosexual* content of the conscious fantasy" (53), such that "it constitutes a feminine yet heterosexual male subject" (60). Silverman's conclusion is telling in some ways and raises questions in others. The subversive character of feminine masochism, in this account, lies in its ability to avoid the equation of male homosexuality with femininity, as well as its subsequent ability to locate femininity within a conventional heterosexual subjectivity. Yet, doesn't this conclusion perform the very type of inversion *qua* resistance that Tyler warns us about in her essay on masochism? Might we not hypothesize that there is a crucial distinction to be made between male "homoeroticism" and male "homosexuality?"

As a site of modern knowledge, power, and pleasure, Melville's *Billy Budd* performs the masochistic contract in order to produce a "homoerotic" subject rather than either repressing the "homosexual" or reducing his desires to sexual object choice. In so doing, "homosexuality" or sexual object choice is neither obliterated from the texture of modern sexuality nor is it granted unfettered authority. Examining the modes of production that animate the historical-cultural emergence of "homosexuality"—as it is allegorized in *Billy Budd*—we can begin to undermine the ability of sexuality to govern its own scenes of emergence. In short, we can imagine erotic economies as mysterious as they are secretive.

"An inside narrative"

As I turn to the title page of this novella, I realize that my reading experience is already tortured and pleasured. I am struck by the subtitle: "an inside narrative" (*BB* 287). These words do more than merely describe; they invite me into a world of high resolution, seduce me into a series of mysterious events. I submit. I will be reminded of this contract later: "as the story proceeds" (293), "the narration that follows" (293), and so forth. Richard Doyle informs me that, with these words, the promise of a "story," one with a beginning, middle, and end, is broken at the very moment that such a promise is made by the utterance of the word "story" (19). I am bound to be disappointed and disillusioned by this text that calls itself "an inside narrative." I look forward to these failures.

I am located in a strange space between pleasure and knowledge, caught up in the space of invention (Sedgwick, *Epistemology* 99). After all, *this* inside narrative is "no romance." But what is my role precisely? Am I truly "imposed upon," "stripped," "threatened," and "terrorized," as Sedgwick would have me believe (97–98)? Am I really "plunged" into a violent taxonomy, a world of secret identities to decode (97)? Do I not, instead, board the *Bellipotent* as Billy Budd does? And, if so, what is the nature of this crossing, this "abrupt transition" (*BB* 299)? Entering the world of the inside narrative is no simple matter, for the contract emerges problematically. The question: Is the inside narrative demonstrative or persuasive? Is it sadistic force or masochistic contract? Is it taxonomic or economic? I must return to Billy's crossing.

In crossing, I witness a tension between force and contract, between demonstration and persuasion, which are displayed in the body and character of Billy Budd. My attention is now drawn to "a superb figure." Cast as the Handsome Sailor, Billy appears donned in "strength and beauty." I am told, "Such a cynosure, at least in aspect, and something such too in nature, though with important variations made apparent as the story proceeds, was welkin-eyed Billy Budd" (*BB* 292–93). Already my knowledge is troubled, and the narrative horizon promises more. Should I know Billy in his "nature" or in his "aspect," through identity or appearance? Am I being terrorized or seduced by the nascent narrative? I return to the query: How does Billy arrive upon the *Bel-*

lipotent? The initial answers to such questions are not certain, as his arrival performs both a demonstrative power as well as several disruptions of its protocol. Attempting to carry his personals aboard in a large chest, Billy is made to transfer his belongings to a small bag. Waving a sad goodbye to his former shipmates and calling out a final farewell to the *Rights-of-Man,* Billy's display is quickly reprimanded: "'Down, sir!' roared the lieutenant, instantly assuming all the rigor of his rank, though with difficulty repressing a smile" (296–97). Such events bring my knowledge of Billy's arrival into question. I know these performances of apparent demonstrative authority as the lieutenant does, with a repressed smile. Do these disruptions constitute Billy as a knowing and willful agent of subversion? Or rather, does he emerge as an ironic figure through accident and ignorance? "To deal in double meanings and insinuations of any sort was quite foreign to [Billy's] nature" (298). Am I now not drawn into a world of instruction rather than demonstration, a ship affecting Billy's education rather than his repression?

No sooner am I brought into the world of the *Bellipotent,* but my ability to know the events of the story is disavowed, momentarily thwarted, frozen. Melville suggests: "In this matter of writing, resolve as one may to keep to the main road, some bypaths have an enticement not readily to be withstood. I am going to err into such a bypath. If the reader will keep me company I shall be glad. At the least, we can promise ourselves that pleasure which is wickedly said to be in sinning, for a literary sin the divergence will be" (*BB* 304).

I am addressed, as a reader, directly. I am "enticed," seduced. I am entreated, subject to tactics of persuasion, to keep a certain "company." I am promised "pleasure" and "sin." What can I do? . . . I am game.

What takes place in this frozen moment is quite strange. I am introduced, at length and most explicitly, to the players in this drama. Such introductions, however, do not constitute the identity of these players, but, rather, establishes their literary import. Billy Budd, I am told, is "the main figure" in this story (*BB* 302). I make the acquaintance of Captain Vere, it is explained to me, "[i]n view of the part that [he] plays in scenes shortly to follow" (311). John Claggart, "having much to do with the story" (313), is finally brought to my attention. In short, these mysterious figures can only be known in and through the events of the story itself. To know them in this manner is to sign the contract of the narrative— to be seduced. Although I am made aware of history, of 'the Great Mutiny' (303), I am instructed outright, "But with all this the story has little concernment, restricted as it is to the inner life of one particular ship and the career of an individual sailor" (303). My knowledge of these events, of this performance, then, cannot be primarily a metaphoric one, which takes mutiny as a secret to decode through taxonomic means. Rather, I am "restricted" [quite] by the "inner life" of the narrative and its economy of pleasure. I must, therefore, return to the question of this economy and its relations.

It becomes quite plain that the relationship between Billy and Captain Vere operates within an economy of education and persuasion rather than one of demonstrative power. The *Bellipotent* is a masochistic scene of pleasure rather than a site of sadistic predilections. Immediately, Billy is described as "a novice in the complexities of factitious life" (*BB* 299). Further, he is "one to whom not yet has been proffered the questionable apple of knowledge" (300–301). Finally: "Of self-consciousness he seemed to have little or none" (301). In the image of Captain Vere, I witness Billy's foil, for he is the embodiment of knowledge and worldliness (311–12; see also Sedgwick, *Epistemology* 97–100, Sealts, and Stanton). While these starkly contrasting qualities or aspects of character appear to merely suggest a pedagogic relation, such a reading is confirmed in Vere's later "reminiscences" (*BB* 346). Billy Budd had, in fact, "naturally enough attracted the captain's attention from the first" (345). It is here that I encounter the captain's desire to bring the Handsome Sailor into a masochistic contract of education and pleasure. Recalling Billy's breach of military codes of conduct as he bid farewell to his former shipmates, Vere found himself "admiring the spirit that could take an arbitrary enlistment so merrily and sensibly." More significantly, perhaps, "[Vere] had thought of recommending [Billy] to the executive officer for a promotion to a place that would more frequently bring him under his own observation." It is not solely Vere's desire to educate that catches my attention; it is equally what he lacks—force. He is, by all appearances, "the most undemonstrative of men." "Any landsman observing this gentleman," I am informed, "might have taken him for the King's guest, a civilian aboard the King's ship" (309–10). The absence of demonstrative power is so notable that it becomes his signature, "Starry Vere" (310). Thus begins the masochistic narrative.

John Claggart, like his fellow players in this narrative, does not occupy an identity so much as a role within the masochistic economy. Once again, this determination is made through a particular mode of reading: "His portrait I essay, but I shall never hit it" (*BB* 313). But what is the nature of this "essaying?" How am I to know the figure of Claggart? Through "rumor" (314), "the sailor's dogwatch gossip" (315), "gun-deck talk" (316), accounts "exaggerated or romanced" (316)? My knowledge of his position aboard the *Bellipotent,* in contrast to his personal identity, is not "gossip . . . but fact" (316). I am to know him as "master-at-arms." As "master-at-arms," the title itself being overtly instructive, Claggart inhabits a demonstrative and (as we shall later see) sadistic position in the narrative. Although "master-at-arms" was historically conceived as a position of tutelage, its current usage casts Claggart as "a sort of chief of police charged among other matters with the duty of preserving order on the populous lower gun decks" (313).

"Life in the foretop"

Billy and I are educated simultaneously, yet our mastery of the events is equally thwarted, disavowed. We are denied complete authority. Our instruction begins through the spectacle of a gangway punishment, a display of sadistic power, which soon becomes an immediate threat to Billy himself. Bearing witness to "the culprit's naked back under the scourge, gridironed with red welts and worse," Billy resolves, "never through remissness would he make himself liable to such a visitation." The visage of such events leaves him in quite a state of "horror," "concern," "more than vexed," "unconcealed anxiety." When he himself becomes suspect of causing trouble, I am told, "He could not understand it" (*BB* 318). Things aboard this ship are definitely "mysterious" (321).

Dansker, the mastman, soon becomes "wise counsel," a source of knowledge for Billy [and for me]. It is through Dansker's "small weasel eyes" (*BB* 319) that Billy begins to understand the events aboard the *Bellipotent,* and it is through the same eyes that I begin to understand Billy's role in such events. Dansker's perspective—"a quizzing sort of look," "speculative query," and "a certain philosophic interest"—informs me that Billy's presence aboard the ship is an "incongruous" one (319–20). The old mastman draws my attention to the future, to "what might eventually befall a nature like that, dropped into a world not without some mantraps and against whose subtleties simple courage lacking experience and address, and without any touch of defensive ugliness, is of little avail" (319). Dansker's form of address is equally telling. Naming the Handsome Sailor as "Baby Budd," a nickname that stuck, accents the tutelary relation between the two (320). It is through these "small ferret eyes" that Billy learns more fully of sadistic power.

"'Baby Budd, *Jemmy Legs*' (meaning the master-at-arms) 'is down on you'" (*BB* 320). Such begins the education of Billy, incomplete, not nearly satisfying. Remembering that my knowledge of this inside narrative is constructed as much from the literary criticism surrounding it as it is by Melville's words, I turn to Jonathan Yoder's reading to find that Claggart is indeed a sadistic figure. Dansker's warning serves to mark Claggart as a source of demonstrative power. Through the performative and polysemic term "Jemmy Legs," Claggart is associated with mastery, an officer "whom subordinates love to hate," a light cane, a crowbar, and a policeman's club (Yoder 102–3). In fact, doesn't Claggart soon become the very embodiment of phallic power? We are then returned to the events of the story, to "an incident" (*BB* 321).

The "soup scene," taken as a series of homosexual metaphors (Martin, 111–12; Phillips 898; Yoder 103) stages a sadistic dynamic between Claggart and Billy. It is the theater of demonstrative, phallic power in which conduct begets character. Critics tell me that Claggart's "rattan" is a phallic symbol, a representation of his erect penis. But I am also warned against unproblematically mistaking the penis for the phallus (Butler, *Bodies;* Silverman; Tyler). What should I make of the rattan? What is Claggart's role in this scene? I must note the language carefully: "Claggart, the master-at-arms, official rattan in hand, happened to be passing" (*BB* 321). I attend to his status as master of the scene, and recognize that the rattan is classified as "official," relating to his office or position. The object is a phallic instrument indeed, but not necessarily one belonging to male anatomy. Upon first witnessing the "greasy liquid streamed just across his path," the master steps over it, delaying his contact with the fluid. Next: "Pausing, [the master] was about to ejaculate something hasty at the sailor, but checked himself." Once again, a "hasty" orgasm is avoided or "checked." Continuing: "and pointing down to the streaming soup, playfully tapped [Billy] from behind with his rattan" (322–23). Gesturing toward Baby Budd's "soup," the master turns "playful," as if in a game, and taps his slave's buttocks. I witness this mock disciplinary act, Billy's punishment for finishing too soon. But this scene is a fantasy, right? I hear Claggart's "low musical voice peculiar to him at times." I mark his mysteriously placed words, "Handsomely done, my Lad! And handsome is as handsome did it, too!" (322). I now know Billy as Claggart does, as a potential slave, for Billy's recalcitrant conduct becomes his character—handsome is as handsome *does.* The words put the Handsome Sailor in place, in proprietary relation to the master-at-arms, as they name him—"my Lad." These are not affectionate words, but, rather, due to their ironic appearance, they display both "envy and antipathy" (327). For I also see, along with the other sailors, what Billy cannot: Claggart's "involuntary smile, or rather grimace"

(322). With this expression, I am brought into the scene. With it, Claggart puts me and the others in place as well. He is "a superior" and we must respond with "counterfeited glee" to his intended joke. "That functionary," the master of the scene, finally disciplines another. Following a "light collision" with this young man, Claggart displays his phallic power most lucidly. "The official, impetuously giving him a sharp cut with the rattan, vehemently exclaimed, 'Look where you go!'" (322). This staging of sadistic, phallic power is followed by several divergences, delays, suspending the narrative once more.

The first moment of suspense asks directly: "What was the matter with the master-at-arms?" (*BB* 322). A question, I am told, best addressed "by indirection" (324). Sedgwick informs me that this question *can* be answered in and by its very refusal to be answered (*Epistemology* 94–97). In other words, to answer the question of Claggart, to unlock his secrets, I must somehow transform the "mysteriousness" surrounding him into a discrete content. Put another way, "indirection" must become direction; economy must become taxonomy. "Inventing" Claggart (*BB* 323), the narrative takes myriad twists and turns through an epistemological "labyrinth" (324). Turning from an erudite scholar to the Holy Writ, from Plato's discourse on "Natural Depravity" to the gallows and jails, I find that I must "go elsewhere"; I must go to "austere civilization" to explore such a mystery. This mysterious matter appears respectable, for it lacks "vices or small sins," "the sordid or sensual," and "acerbity." It seems, therefore, to embody "the law of reason." The law of rationality, however, ultimately becomes an instrument in its own subversion, in "effecting the irrational" (325–26). These phenomenal dimensions of man are most dangerous because "the method and the outward proceeding are always perfectly rational" (326). Are not the problems of reason and rationality the very problems that define the turn of the century, now embodied in the figure of John Claggart, the master-at-arms? Is he not an invention of pure rationality taken to its extremities, to its limits, to the point of irrationality? Is he not, indeed, a sadistic manifestation of the law of reason?

The second moment of narrative suspense plunges me into the passions that trouble the master-at-arms, passions that trouble reasoning itself. The narrative trajectory and its suspension stage this struggle between passion and reason, which animates the sociohistorical texture of the late nineteenth century. "In the present instance," it is made clear to me, "the stage is a scrubbed gun deck" (*BB* 328). And the passions that dance upon its surface are "envy and antipathy, passions irreconcilable in reason" (327). These incongruent and competing passions are directed at Billy such that his spilling of the soup is taken as a deliberate expression of contempt or "antipathy" toward Claggart (328). I learn this in the third suspended moment. It is this incident that provokes the master-at-arms to more fully punish his slave, providing justification for "a sort of retributive righteousness," for "new experiments" (330). I am, thus, returned to the events of the story.

The next "occurrence" takes place on "a warm night," staging the historical problematics of male agency and their relationship to knowledge. The scene opens, inviting me to gaze upon Billy, "dozing." His body is explicitly inscribed by his lower status as "foretopman" as well as being located spatially in the uppermost deck, "his station" at which he was "at home" (*BB* 330–31). These corporeal inscriptions place him within an economy of demonstrative power in which he lacks masculine agency, for every sailor is "accustomed to obey orders without debating them" (337). More than this, Billy himself is said to possess "an incapacity of plumply saying no to an abrupt proposition" (331). Thus, when he is asked to join the gang of "impressed men," Billy's incapacity becomes manifest in his stutter as he attempts to refuse the proposition before him (332). Such problematics of masculine agency color the same narrative space as Billy's education aboard the *Bellipotent*. The pedagogical nature of the clandestine meeting between Billy and the stranger is doubly marked. The scene begins as Billy is "stirred into semiconsciousness," and "the drowse from his sleep still hung upon him" as he approaches the "retired nook." As he learns of the stranger's intentions, however, Billy awakens, "thoroughly shaking off his drowse" (331–32). Billy also experiences the effects of theatrical lighting as he receives his lessons. As he sleeps, his body appears "as in the shadow of a hillside," and even in the meeting place, the moon and starlight are absent (331–32). It is only when the stranger holds up the bribe—"two small objects faintly twinkling in the night-light"—that Billy sees anything clearly. Or does he? What exactly does Billy know? What do I know? Once again, the divergences from the story paradoxically reveal and conceal the mysteriousness surrounding these events.

Two more suspended moments simultaneously advance and thwart my knowledge of these mysteries. Billy is said to have two tutors aboard the *Bellipotent:* "the sage Dansker" (*BB* 335) and "experience" (336). Yet, neither of these potential sources of knowledge answers the questions that plague Billy's imagination. For instance, Dansker's insistence that the master-at-arms is "down on" Billy provides more "obscurity" than clarity (335–36). "Experience" is equally unsatisfying as a teacher. Hoping to see and thereby know the stranger "in broad day," Billy is struck by the vagueness of his glances and expressions such that he is "now left more at a loss than before" (334). The cohabitation of ignorance and knowledge is followed by "other demonstrations" of Claggart's sadistic power.

Claggart's continual gazing upon Billy Budd renders his sadistic display of power as plainly as one can expect from this narrative. Mizruchi reminds me that "the ability to control what is seen, and by whom, is a sign as well as a source of power" (275). That sight becomes, in a tautological fashion, both a "sign" and a "source" of power should no longer surprise me. Claggart's gaze "lights on belted Billy," "meditates," "catches sight," and "dwells upon" (*BB* 337–38). Such gazing goes unnoticed by Billy; "innocence was his blinder" (338). The contrast here is more than mere theatrics; it reveals "the monomania in the man" (340). These demonstrations set the stage for "something decisive" (340).

"Something decisive"

I am now brought back to the events of the story, events that are carefully staged. Hearing of the possibility of "impressed men" aboard the *Bellipotent,* Captain Vere initially responds to the character of the informer rather than the threat of mutiny. My attention is drawn explicitly, through Vere's eyes, to "Claggart's presence" (*BB* 341). I notice that Vere's countenance is "peculiar" and registers his "distaste" for the informer so much so that Claggart is later taken as "a perjurous witness" (343–44). Once Billy Budd is revealed as the potential mutineer, the story is [once again] frozen for a moment. Vere's "reminiscences" tug at my sleeve and bid me to follow their itinerary. I reflect, as Vere does, on this Handsome Sailor—"a fine specimen," his "nude," sculpted body [on which I can only fantasize], desiring to "bring him under [my] observation." (345–46). As suddenly as I am suspended from the events, I am returned. Upon my return, I find that there has been "a shifting of the scene" (347). We have retired to the privacy of Vere's cabin.

Staging the scene and standing "prepared to scrutinize the mutually confronting visages" of the master-at-arms and Billy Budd (348), Vere's actions position me as a witness to the events. Such events appear before me as the death of the sadist, the demonstration and eventual thwarting of phallic power. The young sailor's reaction to Claggart's accusation makes clear the demonstrative nature of power, for Billy appears "impaled and gagged." Looking into Claggart's eyes, I notice "a phenomenal change": "Those lights of human intelligence, losing human expression, were gelidly protruding like the alien eyes of certain uncatalogued creatures of the deep. The first mesmeristic glance was one of serpent fascination; the last was the paralyzing lurch of the torpedo fish" (349). Vere continues to direct the scene: "Speak, man!" he instructs, "Speak! Defend yourself!" The events now accelerate into a theatre of sadistic force. I am no longer frozen, but sped up, propelled. Billy's body undergoes further torture: his stutter becomes so affected that it "[intensifies] into a convulsed tongue-tie"; I see his "entire form straining forward"; he is in "agony"; his face betrays the feeling of being "buried alive" as he struggles "against suffocation" (349). In spite of Vere's attempts to calm the boy, the words of the captain produce "more violent efforts at utterance" until finally "quick as the flame from a discharged cannon at night, his right arm shot out, and Claggart dropped to the deck" (350).

The death of the master-at-arms, enacting the masochistic contract, serves as a catalyst. Captain Vere is transformed by the event, but I'm not quite sure how. The narrative holds this dimension of the story from me, not as a secret to be disclosed later, but, rather, it is forever a provocative mystery. Here is what I am allowed to see:

> Regaining erectness, Captain Vere with one hand covering his face *stood to all appearance* as impassive as the object at his feet. Was he absorbed in taking in all the bearings of the event and what was best not only now at once to be done, but also in the sequel? Slowly he uncovered his face; and the effect was as if the moon emerging from eclipse should *reappear with quite another aspect than that which had gone into hiding.* The father in him, manifested towards Billy thus far in the scene, was replaced by the military disciplinarian. (my italics, *BB* 350)

Yet this description tells me nothing as to the meaning of Vere's expression; it does not elucidate the changes that have occurred within the captain. Although it appears that Starry Vere is dissembling, I am unsure what lies behind the façade. Perhaps I shall never know. Any knowledge of such mystery is filtered through the musings of the surgeon who comes to examine Claggart's body—it is all invention. The surgeon queries, "Was he unhinged" (352)? Starry Vere's "excitement" and "agitation" seem to indicate a loss of sanity, yet there is no proof. In fact, the narrative tells me that I can never know with certainty: "Whether Captain Vere, as the surgeon professionally and privately surmised, was really the sudden victim of any degree of aberration, every one must determine for himself by such light as this narrative may afford" (353). This being so, I must return to the actual events of the story, to the fate of Billy Budd.

"In the light of that martial code"

The law under which Billy Budd is tried and convicted fully displaces conduct from identity, in the case of the defendant, in the case of the victim, *and* in the case of Captain Vere. The formality of the law inscribes them all. The paradox of the law, its absurdity, appears only in its absolute formal application: "[I]nnocence and guilt personified in Claggart and Budd in effect changed places. In a legal view the apparent victim of the tragedy was he who had sought to victimize a man blameless; and the indisputable deed of the latter, navally regarded, constituted the most heinous of military crimes" (*BB* 354). This necessary reduction of Billy to his conduct does not go unnoticed, for he is "the last man they [the members of the court] would have suspected" (356), and the court must "confine its attention to . . . the striker's deed" (358). Captain Vere reminds the court, "The prisoner's deed—with that alone we have to do" (359). The law equally subjects Claggart to its formalities. The court's decision is made "aside from any conceivable motive actuating the master-at-arms, and irrespective of the provocation of the blow" (358). Official conduct, perhaps, compromises Vere's personage most. I am told, "[T]hough a conscientious disciplinarian, [Vere] was no lover of authority for mere authority's sake" (355). Further: "But a true military officer is one particular like a true monk. Not with more self-abnegation will the latter keep his vows of monastic obedience than the former his vows of allegiance to martial duty" (355). The law takes on an explicitly gendered quality during the trial as Vere proclaims, "But do these buttons that we wear attest that our allegiance is to Nature? No, to the King" (361). The masculinist phallic power that animates this scene predetermines its outcome such that the court, including Vere, "ceased to be natural free agents" (362). Rather than the captain's sadistic and phallic enactment of the law, this decision becomes the law's very subjection of Starry Vere.

The formality of these proceedings is disrupted by yet another by-path, a brief communication between Billy Budd and Starry Vere. Once again, I am left with mere "conjecture" in place of absolute verification, invention in place of discovery (*BB* 366). Although I am not privy to the details of this meeting, I am led to believe that it involved "the passion sometimes latent under an exterior stoical or indifferent" and "what remains primeval in our formalized humanity" (367). In stark contrast to the law's formalities, the "passion" and the "primeval" in men become mechanisms for undermining its absolute power. Such passions are so extremely "rare" that they would be "all but incredible to average minds however much cultivated" (366). In other words, the passions of Vere and Billy are not easily categorized or placed within a convenient taxonomy of sexual subjectivity. They are, instead, "rarer qualities" or erotic econo- mies through which bodies circulate, interact, and transform each other. As Starry Vere exits the chamber, I (along with the senior lieutenant) am pierced by his visage—"the agony of the strong" (367). On the very threshold of life and death, the phallic power of the law is simultane- ously interrogated and upheld, quite literally struck down and enforced with zealousness.

"Behold Billy Budd"

Claggart's funeral and Billy's execution, I am warned, will be narrated in a fashion "less brief" than the events themselves. I am promised even more bypaths, delays, and detours, which (I will soon learn) emphasize the ritualistic, formal, and theatrical character of military ceremony. In fact, not one protocol will be denied. "Strict adherence to usage was observed," from publicly announcing the strange happenings to the master-at-arms being "committed to sea." "Nor in any point," I am assured, "could [military protocol] have been at all deviated from" (369).

The eve preceding Billy's execution, I am instructed to "behold Billy under sentry lying prone in irons" (*BB* 370). Gazing upon his body, be- holding, I both guard and watch. What brings me to this display of power, however, is neither Captain Vere nor my own sadistic impulses, but, rather, the law itself. I appear on a scene of high spectacle whose images remind me of the irony of the law, its absurdity—the execution of the innocent. Under the lanterns, which provide the only light on the upper gun deck, my eyes are confronted with the image of Billy, lying amidst guns mounted on carriages, rammers, and linstocks. Billy's body, while cast as innocent (or at least forgivable) by others in this narrative, has since been tainted by his experiences aboard the *Bellipotent*. His identity is quite different from the outward appearance created by the narrative. "[T]he prone sailor's exterior apparel, white jumper and white duck trousers, each more or less soiled, dimly glimmered in the obscure light of the bay like a patch of discolored snow in early April lingering at some upland cave's black mouth" (370). Although tarnished somewhat by the formality of the law ["a felon in martial law"], Billy remains "essentially innocent" even on the eve of his execution: a "virgin" to experience, taking on "the look of a slumbering child," a "martyr to martial discipline" (371–73). The events of the plot, as well as my knowledge of them, are equally tainted by paradox, for the lanterns by which I see [and know] "pollute the pale moonlight" (371). Experience and law become ironically enough the tools of mystification rather than those of clarity.

As morning arrives, I am lifted from "luminous night" into "the breaking day" and the presence of "a meek, shy light" (*BB* 374). The event is staged to heighten both the visual spectacle and the military rank of those bearing witness: powder-boys and younger tars located on the deck with the topmen gazing down from the balcony (374). Captain Vere is "the central figure" (375), the master of the scene, an embodiment of the law, of sadistic power. Just before the climax of the scene erupts, "at the penultimate moment," I hear Billy's voice. The dramatic character of his voice brings the event to a halt. The words become, in truth, the event, disrupting protocol and ritual. The words are "wholly unobstructed in the utterance," mimic "the clear melody of a singing bird," produce "a phenomenal effect," and create "the spontaneous echo that voluminously rebounded them." These words are "God bless Captain Vere!" (375). To all appearances, this is an act of ultimate submission. I notice Vere's bodily response; he stands "erectly rigid as a musket in the ship-armorer's rack" (376). What I see next renders the scene even more fantastic: Billy's body is illuminated, and "ascending, took the full rose of dawn." The theatrical display of power, suffusing this scene, marks the irony of the law that brought its execution into being. Staging the sadistic economy of power, Starry Vere displays its constitutive paradox.

"Some days afterwards"

All that remains of this inside narrative are bypaths, disavowals of an ending, which plunge me headfirst into the realm of fantasy. I wait for that which will never arrive. The first delay asks after another odd dimension of the execution. Namely, it seeks an explanation for the utter lack of motion in Billy's body upon hanging. An absence of movement remains, however, "phenomenal," "singular," or without any logical "account" (*BB* 376–77). This is, perhaps, one of the most "mysterious" elements of the story, an ultimately unsolvable one. Another bypath follows, returning me to the moments immediately after execution. A sound is heard, one "not easily to be verbally rendered," for its "murmurous indistinctness" and "inarticulate" nature do not allow me to say for certain that this sound is an "involuntary echoing of Billy's benediction" (378). The event of Billy's execution is now so surrounded by fantasy and inexplicable details that I doubt the possibility of any answer.

This mysteriousness is soon swept over by the formality of Billy's sea burial, signaled by "the drum beat to quarters" (*BB* 379). After the men dispersed, the deck was flooded by reports, salutes, "customary morning services," "drum beats," "religious rites," and "orderly manners." In the words of Captain Vere, "forms, measured forms, are everything" (380). The recalcitrance of Billy's corpse, the echoing sounds of "God bless Captain Vere," and the fantastic images of the execution stand as mysteries within the "forms" of sadistic power. They refuse, I find, to be captured or subsumed by the force of the law.

"Ragged edges"

After the "proper" ending of the tale, I am brought to a "sequel" of sorts, and I realize that while "forms are everything," there are lines of resistance—*there are mysteries.* There are loose strands within this historical-cultural texture. There is rebirth in death. There is productive force in repressive power. Such paradoxical spaces exist on the very threshold between fiction and fact: "The symmetry of form attainable in pure fiction cannot so readily be achieved in a narration essentially having less to do with fable than with fact. Truth uncompromisingly told will always have its ragged edges" (*BB* 380–81). A high-resolution narrative indeed! The masochistic ideal of rebirth is embodied in the intoxication of murmur, the secondhand accounts of rumor, and the commemoration of song. It's difficult to get the story straight these days.

Later: "Not long before death, while lying under the influence of that magical drug which, soothing the physical frame, mysteriously operates on the subtler element in man, [Starry Vere] was heard to murmur words inexplicable to his attendant: 'Billy Budd, Billy Budd' " (382). I am told that these words "were not the accents of remorse." Yet, I must consider the source, a member of the drumhead court who was most against Billy's execution. Regret or no, the words uttered by the lips of Starry Vere, on the edges of truth and fiction, on the border between reasoned "forms" and "subtler" passion, display a possibility, a rebirth in the moments before death.

The full irony of the law is equally made apparent in a naval newspaper account, one both "authorized" and "falsified." Subjected further to the taxonomy of the martial law, Claggart and Billy are once more reduced to their conduct aboard the *Bellipotent:* "master-at-arms" and "ringleader," "Englishman" and "alien," "victim" and "criminal," "respectable" and "depraved," "patriot" and "scoundrel" (*BB* 382–83). I am instructed to reject such an account of these events. It is more than merely suggested that this taxonomy is not to be trusted.

Rather, I am to read Billy's body and the site of his execution as a "monument" (*BB* 383). I become a member of the bluejackets, a sailor passing the tale on to future generations. I am not a translator of "secret facts." I undermine the taxonomy of a "naval point of view" at every turn. I become a mysterious subject, not readily subsumed by and reduced to my actions. I create my own possibility. "Ignorant though they were of the *secret facts* of the tragedy, and not thinking but that the penalty was somehow unavoidably inflicted from the *naval point of view,* for all that, they instinctively felt that Billy was *a sort of man as incapable* of mutiny as of willful murder" (384). I am, with Billy, reborn in song, in fantasy. I become "the moonshine" piercing through the port. I become "suspended." I become part of "a sham," a lie, a true fiction. "It is dreaming that I am" (385). As I fall into the cold water, "dropped deep," "I'll dream." "I am sleepy, and the oozy weeds about me twist."

Performative Contradictions and Genealogical Inquiry

The discursive emergence of modern sexuality simultaneously accomplished two things. Historically speaking, homosexuality became an identity—a class of people. Rhetorically speaking, homosexuality became synonymous with secrecy—a means of classification. These two forms of social knowledge were concomitant with what Foucault has called the "repression hypothesis," both a theory of sexuality and a theory of social power. Analysis of this nascent discourse and its performative usages of "identity" and "secrecy" as ideographs has detailed the relationship between social knowledge and social power as it produced modern concepts of sexuality, concepts that remain with us today.

Returning to Melville's *Billy Budd* as well as Sedgwick's reading of its literary texture has uncovered the discursive conditions necessary for speaking about homosexuality in the modern era. These conditions of speaking, the discursive ground upon which rhetorical action takes place, employ and deploy the rhetorical secret, itself composed out of multiple intersecting performative contradictions. For an epistemological world in which "secrecy" stands as a metaphor for "homosexuality," in which a public code represents private essences, is inherently contradictory. As Sedgwick notes, the intensification of "secrecy" in public discourse betrays any claims to actual secrecy; rather, any mention of the secret necessarily discloses its content—homosexuality. As a performative contradiction (a statement whose propositional content contradicts its conditions of speaking), the rhetorical secret sets in motion a series of such contradictions: performing the private in public, inventing ignorance, being enslaved to mastery, forgetting in order to produce knowledge, experiencing pleasure in failing to express pleasure, narrating a story without an ending, telling the truth in fiction.

Locating such contradictions is the first aim of the genealogist/rhetorician. David Halperin explains, "[T]he very incoherence at the core of the modern notion of homosexuality furnishes the most eloquent indication of the historical accumulation of discontinuous notions sheltered within its specious unity. The genealogist attempts to disaggregate those notions by tracing their separate histories as well as the process of their interrelations, their crossings, and, eventually, their unstable convergence in the present day" ("How to Do" 90). Although their coherence is indeed the product of invention, our social identities cannot be rejected outright, carelessly tossed aside, discarded in the name of sexual freedom. Within contemporary American society, for example, people have created sexual identities that appear to be coherent and act *as if* they are indeed coherent. Sexual identity's presumed coherence enables social interaction and in some cases furthers political organizing. Yet, these fictions are built upon a series of historically situated incoherences that can be traced and mapped via genealogical inquiry. For this reason, we must recast our historical line of thought, neither privileging the apparent coherence of male homosexual identity nor ignoring the rhetorical appeal of such coherence, but, rather, continually navigating the space between its coherence and its discontinuous propensities. Genealogy, in its analytics of descent, uncovers the historical events or discontinuous elements—the rhetorical operations—that condition a coherent and apparently stable regime of sexuality. It asks after the historical problems of identity, the ways in which statements participate in and influence particular political operations or "regimes" (Foucault, *Power/Knowledge* 112). Genealogy thus becomes "a painstaking rediscovery of struggles together with the rude memory of their conflicts" (83) in order to "specify the issue at stake in this opposition, this struggle" (87).

In order to better map contemporary U.S. discourse on gay male identity, I situate such rhetoric against the discursive backdrop from which it descended, namely, the modern invention of "homosexuality" in Western societies. I call this production of knowledge-power "the rhetorical secret."

The Essential and the Ethnic

> Emergence is always produced through a particular stage of forces.
> The analysis of Entstehung must delineate this interaction, the
> struggle these forces wage against each other or against adverse cir-
> cumstances.
>
> —Michel Foucault

The social classification of "homosexual identity" is a performative act,
constituting identity by naming itself in public discourse. I have argued
previously that identity is also ideographic, the material of ideology.
"Identity," as a performative ideograph, has taken on two dominant
usages in contemporary lesbian and gay movements: the essential and the
ethnic. In both cases, these rhetorical performances are strategic rather
than merely descriptive, for as rhetorical scholars Smith and Windes have
recently observed, "Identity is forged in combat" ("Identity" 29).

Identity Claims

In the opening pages of *Essentially Speaking,* Diana Fuss declares, "Real
essence is itself a nominal essence—that is, a linguistic kind, a product
of naming" (5). Reopening questions regarding the social-political impact of such naming, Fuss demands historical specificity over general-
ized accusation: "[T]he radicality or conservativism of essentialism depends, to a significant degree, on *who* is utilizing it, *how* it is deployed,
and *where* its effects are concentrated" (20). Put otherwise, claims to an
essential sexual identity are just that—claims—which necessarily take
place within a specific discursive field and are judged within that field.
Claims to an essential sexual orientation demonstrate the rhetorical
character of "essential" identity formation because (unlike the formation of other minority identities) they often provoke controversy. Scientific and public debates on "gay gene theory" illustrate this point quite
well (Brookey, *Reinventing*).

Ethnic models of sexual identity are forged in much the same way. In
response to the constructionist/essentialist debates of the 1980s, Steven
Epstein recommends an ethnic model of sexual identity as an alterna-

tive basis for lesbian and gay activism. Recognizing that social movements must organize around social categories of some variety, Epstein argues that an ethnic model of sexual identity possesses "a clear political utility, for it has permitted a form of group organization that is particularly suited to the American experience, with its history of civil-rights struggles" ("Gay Politics" 20). In fact, Epstein later recognizes, "[T]he 'ethnic' self-understanding is a much looser form of essentialism than, say, a strict genetic or hormonal theory of homosexuality . . . [it] is peculiarly vague about where the essential 'core' of gayness resides" (21). The distinction between essentialism and ethnic models of sexual identity lies in their respective theories of homosexuality's "origin" or cause. Ethnicity, in sum, might be best understood as a strategic essentialism.

Both usages of "identity"—essential and ethnic—remain significant to lesbian and gay political movements today, despite mounting criticism in both academic and activist circles. These ideographic usages of "identity" are historically situated within a specific field of public discourse that provides the necessary conditions for speaking about homosexuality. Smith and Windes conclude, "[G]ay men and lesbians as subjects of discourse can only enter the public sphere if they adopt an essentialized identity" ("Identity" 38). As suggested here, the ideographic term "identity" is restricted by historically situated conditions of speaking, those foundations for the public discourse on homosexuality.

Throughout the twentieth century in America, homosexuality was inscribed within the discursive fields of law, religion, and science. These institutions and their respective modes of knowledge production thus provided the necessary discursive conditions for the social classification of "homosexuality." Put crudely, one could not speak of "homosexuality" outside of these discourses and their rules of engagement. After World War II, however, "legal realism," which coincided with the budding American homophile movement, became the master discourse in which public communication about homosexuality took place and effectively governed the claims advanced within the homophile movement itself (Darsey, "Die Non"). Darsey describes the historical context in which early homophile organizing took place: "The diminuendo of God's 'Thou shalt not . . . ' following the Second World War represents a very real change for sexual mores in general and for homosexuals in particular; the dereliction of natural law allowed for a new ethic of permissiveness . . . Deprived of the authority of religion and science, the law stood exposed as a very fragile creation" (52). Absent the universals of scientific certainty and religious doctrine, legal discourse in America adopted a new orientation toward adjudicating social discord. Within this nascent legal discourse, the concomitant homophile movement articulated civil rights claims.

Federal case law illustrates the ways in which rights discourse continues to restrict the ideographic usage of "identity" in contemporary public discourse. *Bowers v. Hardwick* (1986), in particular, has served as legal precedence until its recent overturning in *Lawrence v. Texas* (2003). Patricia A. Cain, in her legal history of lesbian and gay rights, has tellingly termed post-*Hardwick* case law "litigating around *Hardwick*" (1618). Although the Supreme Court overturned the *Hardwick* decision in *Lawrence,* it did so by simply reevaluating the historical interpretation of sodomy laws in America, rather than reconsidering immutability as the founding criteria for "suspect class" status. In short, the discursive conditions inherent to *Bowers v. Hardwick* remain intact. The *Hardwick* decision (as did the *Lawrence* decision seventeen years later) hinged on the right to privacy and homosexual orientation's immutability, both of which reflect an essentialist usage of the term "identity" (Halley, "Misreading" 358).[1] Insisting that legal questions of "identity" make determinations along the spectrum of mutability and immutability, however, ensures a constant threat to lesbian and gay citizens. Janet Halley explains, "The fluidity of gay identity at one extreme of the spectrum means that it is always threatened with invisibility and political ineffectiveness; the stability of straight identity at the other extreme is so fragile that it encourages defensive, phobic abuses of majority power" ("Politics of the Closet" 180). With these risks in mind, Halley encourages lesbian and gay advocates to turn to the First Amendment (rather than the Fourteenth) as a means of securing political agency, for this foundation for political organizing would provide "a legally authoritative analysis capable of describing not isolated individuals but social interactions—precisely the activities, as we have seen, that constitute public sexual identity" ("Politics" 183).[2] Rather than relying upon the tenuous (at best) and dangerous (at worst) accounts of essential-immutable sexual identity, Halley encourages a heightened scrutiny of the very conditions of public discourse—speech.

This chapter demonstrates how the rhetorical secret, as the dominant structure of thought within the modern discourse on sexuality, reproduces ethnic and essentialist models of sexual identity. Further, the analysis of specific cases will reveal the heteronormative implications that derive from such models. Two cases, a decade apart, stand as benchmarks in the contemporary lesbian and gay movement: *Lawrence v. Texas* (2003) and *Baehr v. Lewin* (1993).

June 26, 2003: *Lawrence v. Texas*

On September 17, 1998, John Lawrence and Tyron Garner were arrested in Houston, Texas, held overnight in jail and fined $200.00 each for engaging in mutually consensual sex in the privacy of Lawrence's home. Because Texas Penal Code, Section 21.06[3] failed to provide a compelling governmental interest in criminalizing oral or anal sexual conduct between persons of the same sex, the fourteenth Court of Appeals in Houston found the statute to be unconstitutional on June 8, 2000. Following significant political backlash and extensive pressure from the Republican Party in Texas (McCabe), the fourteenth Court of Appeals later revalidated the anti-sodomy statute. On March 26, 2003, the U.S. Supreme Court heard arguments in *Lawrence v. Texas,* a landmark case both symbolically and materially. The Supreme Court ruled in favor of Lawrence on June 26, a symbolic expression of equality in this country. Moreover, the High Court overruled the 1986 *Bowers v. Hardwick* decision on the grounds that it had misinterpreted the history of sodomy laws when it upheld Georgia's anti-sodomy statute.[4] The finding in *Lawrence* and the overturning of *Bowers* holds substantive material implications as well. Although anti-sodomy statutes are rarely enforced, they are often evoked to justify other forms of discrimination against lesbian and gay citizens, including: visitation rights, child custody, adoption and foster care, and employment ("Landmark for gay rights"; D. Mason; Robbins, "Showdown").

Paul M. Smith, addressing the Supreme Court on behalf of the petitioners, advanced two constitutional claims: first, the Texas anti-sodomy statute undermined the right to privacy in decisions concerning sexual conduct, and second, it violated the Equal Protection Clause of the Fourteenth Amendment.[5] In the first instance, Smith argued that the right to privacy in sexual decision making has a secure place in U.S. legal history, and that such liberty plays a functional role in citizens' lives.[6] Smith also observed that the Texas statute applied singularly to same-sex couples and thus required the Court to provide a rational basis analysis justifying its discriminatory character. Responding to Smith's claims on behalf of Texas, Charles A. Rosenthal countered that the U.S. Constitution does not explicitly provide a right to privacy; neither has the Supreme Court upheld a right to commit sodomy. Rather, Rosenthal contended, the underlying moral judgment against same-sex sodomy serves to preserve the institution of marriage, families, and the procreation of children and thus the statute did not breach the Equal Protection Clause. These arguments, in all of their complexity, essentially posed two questions to the Supreme Court: 1) Historically speaking, does the U.S. Constitution provide a right to privacy in sexual decision making? 2) Culturally speaking, do anti-sodomy statutes serve a compelling State's interest? Justice Kennedy's majority opinion responded yes to the former and no to the latter.

My interest in these judicial questions, however, extends beyond the Supreme Court's ruling in *Lawrence v. Texas* and even beyond the injustice of anti-sodomy statutes. *Lawrence v. Texas* stands as a paradigm of contemporary American public discourse on sexuality and reveals the means by which heteronormative power takes hold. A critical examination of the legal arguments advanced in this case illuminates the rhetorical constitution of sexual identity in American public discourse. Specifically, normative constructions of sexual identity served as substantive foundations for the legal arguments in *Lawrence v. Texas,* such that the arguments would not have survived without them. *Lawrence v. Texas* (hopefully) strikes a chord of injustice in all of us. Most likely, our first response is one of identification: How would I feel if the police barged into my bedroom in the middle of the night and after witnessing my partner and me engaged in consenting sexual activity, carted us off to jail? In my mind, despite its statistical improbability, this scenario is unjust. In my mind, the Texas anti-sodomy statute was justly declared unconstitutional. In my mind, *Bowers v. Hardwick* was justly overturned. Yet, I contend, the rhetorical construction of sexual identity that achieved these legal changes also restricts our cultural conceptions of sexuality and sexual communities. Invoking the Fourteenth Amendment required proof that Texas's sodomy laws had violated Lawrence's rights to privacy and equal protection under the law. Specific concepts of sexuality formed the underlying premise of these claims: 1) sexual identity must be constructed as "private" rather than public, and 2) sexual identity (homosexual identity, specifically) must constitute a coherent and immutable social classification rather than a contingent entity. The first of these claims required an essentialist homosexual identity while the second demanded an ethnic model of homosexual identity. These two arguments deployed "identity" in distinct, yet complementary ways.

Counterintuitively, the enforcement of Texas's anti-sodomy laws was not about private (homo)sexuality going public. Rather, *Lawrence v. Texas* was a case of public (homo)sexuality becoming private through legal argument, the translation of public codes into private meanings, the public performance of privacy. This performative contradiction is salient in today's political-cultural climate, for as Berlant and Warner explain: "[P]rivatized sexual culture . . . bestows on its sexual practices a tacit sense of rightness and normalcy" (554). *Lawrence v. Texas* displays the rhetorical processes that enable sexual identity to become constituted as private, as essential. Equally counterintuitively, the enforcement of Texas's anti-sodomy laws was not about exposing social and cultural forms of ignorance. Rather, this case demonstrated the rhetorical invention of ignorance, the transformation of pretense into fact, the performance of ignorance. This performative contradiction seems necessary to advance contemporary lesbian and gay politics. To cite once more the passage from Sedgwick's *Epistemology of the Closet:* "Inarguably, there is a satisfaction in dwelling on the degree to which the power of our enemies over us is implicated, not in their command of knowledge, but precisely in their ignorance" (7). Thus, *Lawrence v. Texas* merely constitutes a political wake-up call, a simple reminder to conservative politicians that lesbian and gay citizens remain the victims of discrimination in American society. To overcome social and political discrimination, sexual identity must also come to represent a political constituency, an ethnic minority. These two ideographic usages of "identity"—the essential and the ethnic—and their performative contradictions become evident in *Lawrence v. Texas.*

Right to Privacy: Constructing the Essential

In claiming a constitutional right to privacy, one must first construe sexual identity as "private" rather than public. Identity, in this way, becomes an essential element of personhood. To this end, the rhetorical secret performs specific spatial and temporal relations. The formal structure of secrecy and disclosure, in the first instance, establishes a border between inside and outside, between private and public spaces. Locating sexuality firmly within private spaces, attorney Smith began his oral argument: "[A]mong the fundamental rights that are implicit in our concept of order of liberty, must be the right of all adult couples, whether same-sex or not, to be free from unwarranted State intrusion into their personal decisions about their preferred forms of sexual expression" (Oral arguments 4). Sexuality, construed here as inherently private, became public only through an act of intrusion, a transgression of the border between inside and outside. This border remained self-evident throughout *Lawrence v. Texas* even while the constitutionality of its transgression was being contested. Noting the relative paucity of arrests under anti-sodomy statutes, Smith explained that the protection of sexual expression in private spaces is a morally accepted standard: "Certainly it seems to us there's a significance to the fact that it [sexual conduct] has never been treated as, for example, drug use in the home has been treated. And people do—the police obviously do actively seek to infiltrate homes to find that kind of activity, it's been treated in a categorically different way" (Oral arguments 13). Grounding his position in earlier decisions on sexual liberty, Justice Kennedy reified the borders of private space: "Liberty protects the person from unwarranted government intrusions into a dwelling or other private places" (Opinion 562).[7] Rosenthal claimed exception: "Well, it's our position that the line should be drawn at the marital bedroom, through which we can—through the law enforcement or anyone else cannot pass unless something illegal happens inside that bedroom" (Oral arguments 34). Rosenthal, like Smith and Kennedy, identified the bedroom door as the bastion of private sexual space, despite his claim that the criminal act of sodomy justifies intrusion. Private spaces, in either case, remained the domain of sexuality. *Lawrence v. Texas* thus enacted the rhetorical secret and its performative contradictions in its public performance of privacy.

The privacy of sexual expression also constitutes a temporal relationship between secrecy and disclosure, in which sexual personhood precedes to what Smith called "preferred forms of sexual expression" (Oral arguments 4). Sodomy, in other words, is the transparent communication of one's sexuality, the expression of one's essence, the disclosure of a secret. The two legal claims in *Lawrence v. Texas* echoed this century-old relationship between sexual conduct and sexual identity (E. Cohen, *Talk;* Foucault, *History;* Halperin, "Forgetting"). Claiming that the Texas anti-sodomy statute violated Lawrence's constitutional right to privacy, Smith invoked a right to make decisions regarding sexual *conduct*. Claiming that the statute discriminated against a specific class of citizens, Smith simultaneously established sexuality as a type of *identity*. Justice Kennedy evoked a similar relationship between conduct and identity: "When sexuality finds overt expression in intimate conduct with another person, the conduct can be but one element in a personal bond that is more enduring" (Opinion 567). The logic of *Bowers v. Hardwick,* which declared sodomy as the behavior that defines homosexuality as a class (Goldstein; Halley, "Reasoning"), haunted the proceedings in *Lawrence*. Rosenthal, defending the Texas statute, distinguished the categories of conduct and identity: "[T]here's nothing in the record to indicate that these people are homosexuals. They're not homosexuals if they commit one act. It's our position that a heterosexual person can also violate this code if they commit an act of deviate sexual intercourse with another of the same sex" (Oral arguments 27–28). The rhetorical secret and its invention of ignorance, in this instance, permitted Rosenthal (and the state of Texas) to claim ignorance of the petitioners' sexuality [identity] at the same time he claimed the right to regulate and discipline sexuality [conduct]. Discussing recent shifts in public perceptions, however, Rosenthal observed that American society has become more tolerant of "homosexuals, but not of homosexual activity" (Oral arguments 31). "Homosexual activity" thus functioned as a referent for sodomy, as its stand-in, its equivalent. Discursively speaking, the act of sodomy discloses homosexual identity; yet, paradoxically, in the material world of sexual conduct, anyone can commit the act of sodomy without expressing a specific sexual orientation. Despite this paradox, sexual subjectivity was constituted as a matter of personhood, a matter of privacy, rendered public through either the discursive act of legal sanction or the physical intrusion of private spaces.

Equal Protection: Constructing the Ethnic

In claiming that Texas's anti-sodomy statute violated the Equal Protection Clause, the petitioners constituted sexual identity (homosexual identity, specifically) as a coherent and immutable social classification rather than a contingent entity. Unlike the right to privacy claim, which constituted individual sexual subjectivity, the equal protection argument constructed a class of people, a collective (homo)sexual identity. Yet the rhetorical secret's spatial-temporal relations governed this construction as well: (homo)sexuality's social borders were clearly drawn and its existence remained immutable across time.

Smith evidenced the use of anti-sodomy statutes to justify multiple forms of discrimination against same-sex couples and thus shifted the debate from individual sexual conduct to collective sexual identity: "Here you have a statute that while it—while it purports to just to regulate sexual behavior, has all sorts of collateral effects on people. People in the States who still regulate sodomy everyday they're denied visitation to their own children, they're denied custody of children, they're denied public employment. They're denied private employment,

because they're labeled as criminals merely because they've been identified as homosexuals" (Oral arguments 20). In her concurring opinion,
Justice O'Connor made explicit reference to the "collateral effects"
(Opinion 582) that derive from anti-sodomy statutes. As it must, this
argument constructed a discrete class of people—homosexuals—in order to advance its claim to equal protection under the law. Justice Kennedy spoke similarly of homosexual persons in his judgment: "When
homosexual conduct is made criminal by the law of the State, that declaration in and of itself is an invitation to subject homosexual persons to
discrimination both in the public and in the private spheres" (Opinion
575). The discrete character of "homosexuals," as a classification, was
further supported by rendering it analogous to other minority groups.
Smith reasoned:

> This case is very much like McLaughlin, Your Honor, where you
> have a statute that said we're going to give a special heightened
> penalty to cohabitation, but only when it involves a white person
> with a black person. That interracial cohabitation is different, and
> the State there made the argument we're merely regulating a par-
> ticular form of conduct, and that's a different form of conduct
> than—intro [intra] racial cohabitation. And this Court very clearly
> said no. You're classifying people. And that classification has to be
> justified. (Oral arguments 18)[8]

Smith invoked the rhetorical secret by treating the formation of sexual
communities as self-evident, as a people that preexists its discursive
classification. The classification of a people—labeling, identifying—thus
became a transparent disclosure of sexual identity, the opening of a
thousand closet doors. Ethnicity, it is now apparent, equally requires the
public performance of privacy, simply on a larger scale.

Rosenthal accepted this formation of collective sexual identity, its
transparency, yet rejected the existence of discrimination against homosexual citizens in Texas. Homosexuals in Texas, he contended, are included in a penalty-enhancement hate crime statute and hold public office as open homosexuals (Oral arguments 47–48). Furthermore, the
anti-sodomy statute itself was not discriminatory toward homosexuals
as a class of people: "[T]hey can't be charged as law-breakers for having
that orientation. They can only be charged as law-breakers if they commit that particular act" (Oral arguments 48). Reiterating his distinction
between sexual conduct and sexual identity, Rosenthal contended that

the Texas statute could not be used as evidence of discrimination against a minority population because it merely criminalized conduct that anyone (regardless of their orientation) could commit. In fact, denying charges of discrimination against a class of people *required* the absolute distinction between act and identity, the ability to locate sexuality within the discrete boundaries of the human body, for it provided the ruse, the very disguise that allowed discrimination to take place, undetected. If heterosexual persons were equally capable of committing the act of sodomy, even if the Texas statute didn't prosecute them for committing such an act, then anti-sodomy laws could not be said to discriminate against homosexual persons for merely *being* homosexual. Once more, the rhetorical secret mobilized the claim of ignorance, its invention as a stubborn fact—the state of Texas could not possibly discriminate against homosexuals, for legally speaking, it didn't even recognize that they existed.

The equal protection argument also evoked the rhetorical secret's temporal relation, the immutability of sexuality across time. Attempting a rational basis to the State's interest, the Court asked during oral arguments if there might not be a slippery slope between striking down the Texas law and allowing homosexuals to teach kindergarten, which might subsequently induce children to "follow the path of homosexuality" (Oral arguments 21). Smith responded by making homosexuality and heterosexuality analogous, suggesting that both sexualities are immutable character traits rather than chosen paths. He reasoned ironically, "Well, I—I think the State has to have a greater justification for its discrimination than we prefer pushing people towards heterosexuality" (Oral arguments 21). This distinction between choices in sexual conduct and the immutability of sexuality as an orientation became even more pronounced when other slippery slope scenarios were presented. The Court later expressed concern for the impact of *Lawrence v. Texas* on the legal prohibition of adultery, incest, prostitution, and other sexual choices. Smith concluded, "Well, I can understand a law which says we're going to attempt to channel heterosexuals towards marriage by making them—making it illegal for them to have sex without marriage. I can't understand that law under—under that kind of rational which only regulates same sex couples and says you can't have sex but everyone else has a right to do that" (Oral arguments 25). The first instance, Smith argued, sanctions behavior—sex must take place within the marital bond—while the second instance restricts sexual identity—sex must express a heterosexual orientation. In both situations, sexual identity is an immutable character trait that extends beyond the reach of the law. Adultery is conduct contingent upon choice, while homosexuality is not. Justice O'Connor, recognizing that the Texas statute specifies conduct, explained further that sexual conduct is "closely correlated with being homosexual" (Opinion 583), such that conduct is subordinated to the immutability of orientation, being, or identity.

May 5, 1993: *Baehr v. Lewin*

In December of 1990, three same-sex couples applied for marriage licenses in the state of Hawaii. Their relationships were denied legal sanction. The Hawaii Supreme Court reviewed *Baehr v. Lewin* on May 5, 1993 and held that denying same-sex couples legal marriage went against the Hawaii State Constitution's sex-based discrimination clause (Reske). According to the "strict scrutiny test," the state is required to provide a "compelling interest" to justify legislation that would discriminate against same-sex couples (Arkes, "Gay marriage"). The Hawaii case, a clear catalyst for the legal events to come, would not reach its conclusion until 1998.[9] Meanwhile, a national climate concerning the institution of marriage was emerging.

The recent controversy surrounding same-sex marriage marks the institution, practice, and concept of marriage as a significant site of power and resistance within American culture. In the first instance, the decision to sanction same-sex marriage would extend legal and economic advantages to same-sex couples,[10] which appears to carry the promise of social equality on a broader scale (Dean). In the wake of *Baehr v. Lewin,* however, waves of resistance against same-sex marriage were felt on both national and state levels. What came to be known as the Defense of Marriage Act [DOMA], motivated by the Full Faith and Credit Clause of the U.S. Constitution, bars "federal recognition of gay marriages and specif[ies] that states need not honor such marriages if they are eventually legalized in any other states" (Idelson 1539). Graff observes that DOMA, signed into law by President Clinton on September 21, 1996, creates a "chilling effect" within our legal system, for it can be used "to challenge everything from domestic partnership statutes to lesbian moms' custody rights" (34). DOMA laws have become equally prevalent in state legislatures. By March of 2001, the number of states with statutes banning same-sex marriage had risen to thirty-five.[11]

In addition to marking the legal status of lesbian and gay citizens, the public debates on same-sex marriage also reflect the ways in which "sexual identity" becomes a means of reinforcing heteronormativity. Michael Warner writes, "[T]he campaign for gay marriage is not so much a campaign for marriage as a campaign about the constituency and vocabulary of the gay and lesbian public. The normalizing interpretation of marriage is increasingly established as the self-understanding of the national gay public" ("Normal" 157). The performative and ideographic usages of "identity" within the marriage debates demonstrate what we have suspected all along: essential and ethnic models of sexual identity carry implicit dangers. Since its conception, homosexual "identity" has always been associated with specific sexual activities or modes of conduct. These associations have had substantive rhetorical consequences for the normalization of sexuality in American society. Although the normative association between male homosexual identity and sexual practices [specifically, sodomy][12] can be traced from the epoch in which "the nineteenth-century homosexual became a personage . . . a species" (Foucault, *History* 43) to the U.S. Supreme Court's *Bowers v. Hardwick* decision in 1986 (Babst; Bower; Goldstein; Hunter), queer theorists refuse to mark the historical emergence of the "homosexual" as an identity category fully distinct from sexual conduct or activities (Halperin, "How to Do"; Sedgwick, *Epistemology*). Rather, David Halperin argues, "We need to find ways of asking how different historical cultures fashioned different sorts of links between sexual acts, on the one hand, and sexual tastes, styles, dispositions, characters, gender presentations, and forms of subjectivity, on the other" ("Forgetting" 109). The following traces these linkages as they emerge in the same-sex marriage debates of the 1990s.

Immutability: Enslavement to Mastery

The prohibition of same-sex marriage, according to the primary contention in *Baehr v. Lewin,* functions as "sex" discrimination such that lesbian and gay citizens constitute a "suspect class" under the Fourteenth Amendment. William Eskridge Jr.'s *The Case for Same-Sex Marriage,* reproducing this argument, illustrates the centrality of claims to immutability (ethnic and essentialist models of sexual identity). Eskridge reasons that "sexual orientation" meets the necessary requirements to become a "suspect class," and thus solidifies equal protection for lesbian and gay citizens under the law.[13] Discrimination against gays and lesbians, he argues correctly, serves no "legitimate state goals" (176). Additionally, the prevalence of discrimination against gays and lesbians, and consequently, the need for state protection, is well documented (179–

82). From a judicial model of power, these arguments are compelling. Yet "suspect class" status also requires advocates of same-sex marriage to claim that homosexuality is "immutable" (177–78). Eskridge concludes, "Sexual orientation is a characteristic over which we have little and perhaps no conscious control. In our society it is a fundamental characteristic, pervasively affecting one's social and emotional life. Sexual orientation is part of one's identity—and a more fundamental identity feature for most people than their religion, ethnicity, or profession" (186–87). The "immutability" of homosexual orientation or identity is primary to the Fourteenth Amendment justification for same-sex marriage. If homosexual identity is not conceptualized as such, then advocates of gay and lesbian marriage have no means of claiming the necessary status of homosexuality as a "suspect class." In other words, homosexual identity must be understood as immutable or essential in order to demand the "equal protection" of homosexual persons under the law. In mastering this discourse, one becomes more enslaved to its discursive conditions and less able to launch an effective challenge to its necessary logics.

The immutability of homosexuality, however, is not universally accepted. Claims to immutability in public discourse are inextricably linked to the relations between sexual identity and sexual conduct. As the same-sex marriage debates illustrate, the relationship between identity and conduct is ideologically charged. Claims to immutability are thus embedded within moral judgments and normative prescriptions. Professor Hadley Arkes's position against same-sex marriage effectively reduces homosexual identity to sexual conduct. Unlike the *Hardwick* decision, which reduced homosexual identity to the act of sodomy, Arkes locates homosexual identity in promiscuous sexual activity, a question of quantity, not quality: "[Same-sex marriage] would draw its power from the romance of monogamy . . . But that is not exactly the vision of gay sex. . . . After all, the permissions for this new sexual freedom have been cast to that amorphous formula of 'sexual orientation': the demand of gay rights is that we should recede from casting moral judgments on the way that people find their pleasure in engagements they regard as 'sexual.'" ("Closet Straight" 156). Sexual identity or "orientation" is first a shapeless entity or "amorphous formula," only to be grounded later in sexual activity or "the way that people find their pleasure." Homosexual men are thus constituted solely by their conduct at the very moment they choose to engage in promiscuous sexual activity. The "vision" of "sexual freedom" enables men to choose their mode of sexual conduct and consequently their sexual orientation.

Heterosexual men are equally constituted through their sexual conduct: "In traditional marriage, the understanding of monogamy was originally tied to the 'natural teleology' of the body—to the recognition that only two people, no more and no fewer, can generate children" (Arkes, "Closet" 157).[14] "The [male] body," which fundamentally assumes heterosexual identity in its procreative capacity, is "tied to" the practice of "monogamy," a type of sexual activity. Unlike gay promiscuity, which is a "vision" and a choice, heterosexual monogamy is "natural" and inevitable. Unlike gay identity, heterosexuality is truly immutable. Or is it? Heterosexual monogamy, in this account, is constituted as both cause and effect, both natural and teleological. As Eve Sedgwick has proven in *Epistemology of the Closet,* homosexuality is both universalized and minoritized in modern discourse. Thus, heterosexuality can never be assured and must always find modes of enforcement—some forms more paranoid than others. Marriage, it appears, serves disciplinary functions for heterosexual men as well. Within this disciplinary institution, Arkes suggests that monogamy is a choice that heterosexual men make, yet this choice is not natural because it requires *heterosexual* marriage or "women" to regulate it ("Closet" 155). Even if monogamy, as a mode of sexual conduct, is not immutable, heterosexuality, as a type of sexual orientation or identity, is.

Andrew Sullivan, activist and *New Republic* editor, attempting to master these discursive conditions, becomes enslaved to their logic of identity. In his response to Arkes, Sullivan uses the trope of immutability in order to separate sexual identity from sexual activity:

> [Conservatives] mean by a "homosexual life" one in which emotional commitments are fleeting, promiscuous sex is common, disease is rampant, social ostracism is common, and standards of public decency, propriety, and self-restraint are flaunted. They mean a way of life that deliberately subverts gender norms in order to unsettle the virtues that make family life possible, ridicules heterosexual life, and commits itself to an ethic of hedonism, loneliness, and deceit. ("Conservative Case" 148)

Sullivan then argues that excessive sexual behavior or this type of "homosexual life" is not "necessary" or "inevitable" (148–49). In other words, homosexual identity is separated from sexual conduct altogether, which echoes a larger movement to "redeem gay identity by repudiating sex" (Warner, *Trouble* 42). Furthermore, cultural constructions of sexual identity become completely inconsequential within the context of marriage, for Sullivan conceptualizes "homosexuality" as "involuntary" (148). As he writes later: "[T]hey have no choice but to be homosexual" (153). Although free will or choice cannot influence a man's "orientation" or identity, it can, in Sullivan's estimation, impact his sexual conduct. Same-sex marriage would "construct social institutions and guidelines to modify and change that [promiscuous] behavior for the better" (149). The claim to immutability, in the public debates on same-sex marriage, thus requires a distinction between involuntary sexual identity and choices in sexual conduct. Because of the discursive conditions required by law, this distinction enables moralizing and normalizing judgments on sexual conduct and modes of association in American society. Mastery, in the end, becomes a mode of enslavement.

Promiscuity: Performing the Private in Public

The question of promiscuity, as it emerges in the same-sex marriage debates, performs private sexuality in public. This performative contradiction serves ideological functions such that sexual minorities are forbidden to participate in the only legitimate form of public sexuality— marriage. Considering the historical usage of "public" and "private" as ideological terms that discipline women's sexuality, it should come as no surprise that the contemporary marriage debates participate within a fundamentally gendered discourse. The exclusion of women, lesbians in particular, is required to associate male homosexual identities with specific sexual behaviors [promiscuity], which eventually prevents them from enacting a public sexuality. Male heterosexuality, synonymous with marriage, becomes the only legitimate form of public sexuality.

Performing private sexuality in public, as a means of disciplining heterosexual women, lesbians, and ultimately gay men, occurs on both sides of the same-sex marriage divide. Dennis Prager, for instance, attempts to uphold "a family-based, sexually monogamous society" by associating gay men with promiscuity. He writes, "The male propensity to promiscuity would simply overwhelm most homosexual males' marriage vows. It is women who keep most heterosexual men monogamous, or at least far less likely to cruise, but gay men have no such brake on their cruising natures. Male nature, not the inability to marry, compels gay men to wander from man to man. This is proven by the behavior of lesbians, who, though also prevented from marrying each other, are not promiscuous" (66–67). Prager's "family-based, sexually monogamous society" is, in essence, a society of men. Within such a society, which presupposes a reduction of all sexual activity to phallic penetration (Smart 161), heterosexual women are not granted any sexual desires or erotic practices. They remain simply a mechanism to "keep most heterosexual men monogamous." Similarly, lesbians serve as evidence, proving the inherent link between gay male identity and promiscuous sexual conduct, and their own sexual conduct is irrelevant, insignificant. It is the absence of sexual behavior that constitutes lesbian identity in this heteronormative discourse—they are "not promiscuous." Jonathan Rauch's essay, which affirms same-sex marriage due to its ability to "domesticate men," also erases the sexual activity of women: "Of course, women and older men don't generally travel in marauding or orgiastic packs" (177). When Rauch praises the disciplinary effect of marriage, we must remember that he reduces same-sex relations and activities to those of men. For instance, "Surely [keeping them off the streets and at home] is a very good thing, especially as compared to the closet-gay culture of furtive sex with innumerable partners in parks and bathhouses" (178). These instances demonstrate the consistent moralistic denigration of "promiscuity" within same-sex marriage debates. Performing private sexuality in public produces this normalizing discourse.

Performing private sexuality in public and the moralizing of promiscuous sexual conduct, in the final instance, crystallizes images of gay men that are frequently evoked in the age of AIDS—images of death. Eskridge's argument for same-sex marriage deploys the trope of "erotic domestication" to such an effect. He warns, "It should not have required the AIDS epidemic to alert us to the problems of sexual promiscuity and to the advantages of committed relationships. In part because of their greater tendency toward bonding in committed pairs, lesbians have been the group least infected by the virus that leads to AIDS and have emerged in the 1990s as an unusually vital group" (9). "Promiscuity" and "committed relationships" are mutually exclusive: one is a "problem," the other is an "advantage." Lesbians become further (hetero)normalized by this discourse because their committed relationships have prevented the AIDS epidemic from significantly infecting their population.[15] This exclusion of women, as we have already witnessed, is necessary for the rhetorical condensation of male homosexual [identity] and promiscuity [act]. Most important, the invocation of AIDS within the marriage debates rhetorically constitutes the gay male body and its promiscuous activities as harbingers of death.[16] The constitution of gay male identity within the same-sex marriage debates cites historically situated ideographs such that: *male homosexuality* = *promiscuity [HIV transmission]* = *death*. Due to the binary form of these ideographic equations, gay male promiscuity easily becomes a foil for heterosexual reproduction.

Procreation: The Invention of Ignorance

The rhetorically charged association between heterosexuality, procreation and monogamy exists within a symbolic order, yet its modes of invention are born out of ideological commitments, not hard facts about sexual practice. James Wilson's "conservative" response to Andrew Sullivan, for example, first locates his grounds for equating "heterosexual marriage" [identity] with "procreation" [act] in scripture: the Torah links "sex to procreation the highest standard by which to judge sexual relations" (159). Heterosexual marriage, in its ideal or symbolic form, serves procreative purposes. Although Sullivan argues that heterosexual couples practice adultery and sodomy in addition to monogamous procreative sex, Wilson counters that Sullivan forgets "the distinction alive in most people's minds between marriage as an institution and marriage as a practice" (160–61). Heteronormativity thus privileges the symbolic or "institutional" conceptions of marriage over the social practice itself. Wilson's position also finds its theoretical foundation in "natural law," the presumption that the human body is inherently a heterosexual body, which links monogamy and procreation to the heterosexual subject. Wilson explains, "natural-law theorists respond much as would the [conventional] average citizen—never mind 'utility,' what counts is what is right. In particular, homosexual uses of the reproductive organs violate the condition that sex serve solely as the basis of heterosexual marriage" (161–62). The "natural" body assumes a fundamentally heterosexual identity as certain organs are classified as "reproductive." The "homosexual" body is also reduced to specific "uses" of the body or practices [sodomy, most likely]; it becomes a body whose identity is equally determined by its actions. But how does Wilson accomplish these rhetorical condensations of identity and act? In the face of Sullivan's argument that sterile (nonprocreative) heterosexual individuals are permitted to enter the institution of marriage, Wilson responds, "[P]eople, I think, want the [heterosexual] form [of marriage] observed even when the practice varies; a sterile marriage, whether from choice or necessity, remains a marriage of a man and a woman" (162). When Wilson and other "natural law" proponents oppose same-sex marriage for procreative reasons, they are isolating and privileging the symbolic over the material practices of married individuals.

In response, the "pro" side of the marriage debate merely grants primacy to materiality, to the hard facts of sexual practice. Those who associate heterosexuality with procreation and monogamy simply don't know "the facts." They are, fundamentally, ignorant, lacking knowledge. Daniel Maguire, Professor of Moral Theology, for instance, attacks what he terms "biologism," the creation of moral principles based entirely on "basic biological facts." He reasons, "The penis and the vagina do enjoy a congenial fit, and the species' need for reproduction relies on that. But sex rarely, in any lifetime, has to do with reproduction, and not even heterosexual persons are limited to coitus for sexual fulfillment" (58). This statement isolates the material practices of "sex" from their symbolic dimension ("congenial fit"), and thereby, dismisses the rhetorical significance of the symbolic within the marriage debates (not to mention the production of heteronormativity in general). Maguire also echoes Sullivan's position on "sterility" in order to repudiate the necessary link between heterosexual marriage [identity] and procreation [act]. "Reproductive fertility," he writes, "is not the essence of genuine marriage. Even in the Roman Catholic tradition, sterile persons are permitted to marry . . . even fertile heterosexual persons do not have an obligation to have children" (62). Dismissing the symbolic dimension of sexuality forecloses a resistive understanding of the constitutive relationship between sexual acts and sexual identities because it denies the ideographic character of these equations. Ideology thus becomes ignorance rather than invention.

The heteronormative appeal to procreation produces the invention of ignorance. Immediately after acknowledging heterosexism's "emotional" element, which contributes to "*much* of the opposition" to same-sex marriage, Eskridge explains, "There is little I can say to such people, for visceral distaste is not susceptible to argument based on reason and facts" (87). Eskridge resolves not to deal with the emotional dimensions of the same-sex marriage debate. He offers: "The only strategy for persuading such persons is to urge them to work through their homophobia with a therapist" (183). The insistence on participating in a purely "rational" discourse leads Eskridge to deny the constitutive relation between sexual acts and sexual identities, in particular, the ideological link between marriage and procreation. Eskridge, as do most advocates of same-sex marriage, responds to the procreative argument against same-sex marriage with "reasons" and "facts." Eskridge reasons that if couples who are sterile or impotent, postmenopausal women, couples using contraception, and women who receive abortions are permitted to marry, then homosexuals should be given that right as well (96–98). Based on the evidence, Eskridge contends, "In today's society the importance of marriage is relational and not procreational" (11). This characterization extends beyond a merely descriptive mode of discourse and becomes prescriptive: "My normative argument will be that the dominant goal of marriage is and should be *unitive,* the spiritual and personal union of the committed couple, and not *procreative,* the production of children by the couple" (91). Eskridge's discourse creates a fundamental conceptual break between erotic acts and sexual identities, and thereby, forecloses a critical engagement that might explore the ways in which heteronormativity is constituted on the very border between procreation and heterosexuality, sodomy and homosexuality, or promiscuity and homosexuality. Ideological invention becomes simple ignorance, easily corrected and redirected by pure facts and reasoning—knowledge.

Queer Collectivity and an Ethics of Identity

To clarify, ethnic and essential conceptions of sexual identity are not inherently problematic, and, as in these cases, might even be beneficial to the aim of social justice. Put simply, American citizens should not be thrown in jail and fined for their sexual conduct. Moreover, American citizens should be treated equally under the law. The rhetorical secret, however, also substantively limits our conceptions of sexual identity within legal discourse. In the terms of the rhetorical secret's performative contradictions, mastering the discourse of essentialism and ethnicity equally enslaves queer citizens to ideologically charged ways of thinking and knowing the world. Contemporary legal discourses on homosexual identity, like its historical predecessors, perform (and thereby regulate) private sexuality in public and invent (and thereby promote) social forms of ignorance.

Genealogical inquiry, in its analysis of historical emergence, examines the current staging of ideological forces such that discourse invents forms of knowledge and enacts regimes of power. Contemporary legal discourse, for example, invents male homosexuality via the rhetorical secret such that gay men must present and represent themselves as private rather than public, as a unified, ethnic minority rather than a normative, diverse subculture. Although constituting sexual identity and conduct as matters of private life is necessary to claim certain civil and civic rights, such as protection from unjust incarceration and equal access to governmental services, these claims carry normative implications as well. Although countering social ignorance about the presence of heteronormativity and homophobia in American society is vital to ending various forms of discrimination and prejudice, it does not critically examine the normative production of heteronormative ideologies.

First, claiming a right to privacy in sexual matters might easily be (mis)construed as a *social responsibility* for queer citizens to remain private—in a word, closeted. If private spaces are the proper locale for sexual expression, then aren't public demonstrations of sexuality taboo? If sexuality is a matter of individual personhood, then why share it publicly with others? The lesbian and gay movement, Michael Warner observes, has recently conformed to the regulations imbedded in "institutions of privacy" (*Trouble* 168). Warner explicates, "These tacit rules about what can be acknowledged or said in public are as much a closet as any" (182). Second, claiming equal protection for a class of people called "homosexuals" presumes (even requires) the essential sameness, the immutability, of those who fall under that classification. While this formulation of sexual collectivity provides legal recourse, it fails to explore the ethical dimensions of queer life, the dynamics of self and other that take place within sexual subcultures. Creating equal citizens of this country is a noble endeavor, yet this objective often leaves a residue of heteronormativity *within* queer communities. Janet Halley, in a critique of racial analogies within lesbian and gay politics, writes: "[*If*] advocacy constructs identity, *if* it generates a script which identity bearers must heed, *if* that script restricts group members, then identity politics compels its beneficiaries. Identity politics is no longer mere or simple resistance: it begins to look like power" ("Like Race" 43). For these reasons, the unspoken rules of public sexuality must be scrutinized, not presumed. This project moves toward an ethical model of sexual identity that would expand contemporary gay identity politics and collective interaction beyond the ethnic and the essential.

3

Semen and Subjectivity

> [O]ne must set aside the widely held thesis that power, in bourgeois,
> capitalist, societies has denied the reality of the body in favor of the
> soul, consciousness, ideality. In fact nothing is more material, physi-
> cal, corporeal than the exercise of power
>
> —Michel Foucault

On February 6, 2003, *Rolling Stone* magazine printed a shocking story.
Interviewing a young gay man named Carlos, the magazine reported:

> Carlos is part of an intricate underground world that has sprouted,
> driven almost completely by the Internet, in which men who want
> to be infected with HIV get together with those who are willing
> to infect them. The men who want the virus are called "bug chas-
> ers," and the men who freely give their virus to them are called
> "gift givers." While the rest of the world fights the AIDS epidemic
> and most people fear HIV infection, this subculture celebrates the
> virus and eroticizes it. HIV-infected semen is treated like liquid
> gold. (Freeman 46)

The story is shocking because the practices of "bug-chasing" and "bare-
backing" [deliberately having anal sex without a condom] seem incomprehensible after decades of HIV prevention and education.[1] For other
reasons, the story is quite conventional, almost predictable: the sexual
practices of gay men are once again pathological; HIV infection is once
again a death sentence; health officials and gay activists are once again
dismissive of the impact. Although most of the article's controversy
seems to lie in the accuracy of its statistics indicating the scope of the
problem (Howard and Yamey; "Quick Hits"), the cultural phenomenon
that has been termed "bug-chasing" once again raises questions about
the nature of sexual identity, the formation of sexual communities, and
the ethics of HIV prevention.

The HIV/AIDS crisis in America, and the fields of knowledge in
which it emerged, undeniably influenced the formation of gay male
communities, their social-sexual practices, and their ethics. Unlike the

mythic monolithic gay male community, based on a unified gay male identity, which often reductively translates into "white middle-class forms of same-sex relations" (C. Patton, *Fatal Advice* 143), gay male communities emerge out of complex perceptions and multiple identifications, including race (Crawford et al.; Diaz) and geography (Mills et al.). Dowsett et al., in their critical ethnography of three distinct gay communities in Australia, argue: "[C]ommunities are not simply aggregations, nor are they merely collectivities, tribes, groups, region or areas . . . Communities are sophisticated, cultural processes of active and collective human endeavour in distinct and changing circumstances" (220). Contingent, local constructions of "community," however unstable and fluid, remain central to any ethical and effective response to the HIV/ AIDS crisis (Altman, *Power and Community;* Deverell and Prout; Dowsett et al.; Gatter; Ross and Williams; Silvestre) because changing behavioral norms within any sexual community requires collective identification with "risk."[2] J. Blake Scott explains, "Facilitation of queer identification involves helping people who see their normality as protection recognize risk in the contexts of their lives" (116).

In this chapter, I critique the ethics of monogamy that appears, due to its promise of sexual normalcy, to protect various gay male communities from HIV infection; instead, I advocate an ethics of fluidity, which conceptualizes HIV as an ally rather than as an enemy. In so doing, I advance the following claims. First, the HIV/AIDS crisis in America engendered historically situated problematics of sexual identity and social power to which queer theory responded. Second, the Western discourse on male subjectivity and its synecdochic relation to semen constituted a necessary conceptual backdrop against which the rhetorical construction of the gay man as a scapegoat for HIV/AIDS appeared. Third, both scientific and popular discourses then produced this scapegoat and its subsequent material effects through three distinct, yet interdependent narratives: epidemiology, immunology, and virology. Fourth, reworking the rhetorical trope of synecdoche enables different relations between the male body, power, and sexual identity, which become rhetorical resources for collective action and community formation in the age of HIV/AIDS.

Queer Theory and the HIV/AIDS Crisis in America

Queer theory emerged in academic circles in the early 1990s,[3] as the HIV/AIDS crisis in the United States was entering its second decade.

This historical coemergence was by no means accidental (Escoffier; Jagose; C. Patton, *Sex and Germs;* Seidman, *Difference*) as it derived from the necessary link between gay politics and AIDS activism (Gamson; Padgug and Oppenheimer). Eve Kosofsky Sedgwick explicates, "[T]heory is important with this disease, because the self-evident categories that we had before don't work with this virus" (qtd. in Barber and Clark 1). The HIV/AIDS crisis, in other words, made manifest competing notions of sexual identity and social power, evidencing the ways in which such theories impacted people's very lives. Cultural constructions of identity, for instance, are intricately woven into the social institutions and public policies that respond to the HIV/AIDS crisis. The knowledges and structures of understanding that are produced by epidemiological research, for example, are tailor-made for policymaking and institutional forms of heteronormative power because they create subjects—"gay men," "HIV-positive," and so forth—who can be identified and monitored (Waldby). Much like HIV is said to reside in its host, heteronormative concepts of sexuality and identity have inhabited the responses of every social institution and have infected every public policy.[4] While the institutional effects of heteronormative power are clear, I contend that heteronormative power is equally manifest in the everyday ethics of collective gay life.

This chapter, through a series of textual analyses, lays bare the historically situated ideological struggles that engender contemporary narratives about HIV transmission and the social-sexual practices in gay male communities. These ideological contests revolve around what Lee Edelman has termed "the cultural fantasmatics of agency" (*Homographesis* 96). The problem of masculine agency, as it circulates within HIV/AIDS discourse, is inherent to the relationship between semen and male subjectivity, for as John Paul Ricco eloquently notes, "Semen is a key term in libidinal economies, precisely because it has the potential to defy the limits of strict definition (proper spaces), to subvert meanings, and put into question the logic of identity and signification" (60).[5] Rhetorical associations between semen and male subjectivity, which provide a necessary foundation for understanding the rhetorical and ideological representations of semen in HIV/AIDS discourse, exist throughout Western culture.

Between Agency and Fluidity: A Cultural-Historical Narrative

In the Western imagination, semen has always been defined by what it *does,* what it accomplishes; its essence, its identity, pivots around the actions that it takes. Simple enough, except that semen conducts itself in a paradoxical fashion: in the first instance, semen has always been an agent, and, in the second, semen has always been a fluid. This inherent contradiction, between agency and fluidity, does not paralyze the construction of cultural and political meanings around semen and male subjectivity, but rather, it mobilizes such meanings to respond to historically situated problems and thus facilitates material consequences. In short, the tension between agency and fluidity becomes a rhetorical resource for power relations of gender and sexuality in Western culture. Understanding how this rhetorical resource operates in the HIV/AIDS crisis in America necessitates a map of its discursive foundations. I will rehearse the synecdochic relation between semen and male subjectivity, the symbolic interchangeability of container and thing contained, during two key historical periods in Western culture: ancient and modern.

Varied problematics of masculine agency serve as the historical conditions for symbolic associations between semen and male subjectivity. These discursive roots run deep in Western societies. David Halperin explains, "[T]he 'sexuality' of the classical Athenians, far from being independent and detached from 'politics' (as we conceive sexuality to be), was constituted by the very principles on which Athenian public life was organized" (*One Hundred Years* 31). More simply: "The social body precedes the sexual body" (38). In this case, Halperin is speaking of Greek pederastic practices in which male-male erotics are perceived as an expression of domination and social status rather than the more modern formulations of "homosexual" identity. The active, penetrating male body represented the body of the Athenian citizen—"free, autonomous, and inviolable" (Halperin 98). These symbolic connections between male subjectivity, sexual conduct, and social agency cannot be divorced from the philosophical discourse on semen in ancient times.

The pleasures associated with expending semen were closely tied to the ethics of Greek life and the problem of masculine agency (Foucault, *Use* 75). Philosophical discourse of the time reflected a concern with self-governance, moderation, and man's immortality, echoed in the writings of Plato, Hippocrates, and Aristotle. Foucault crystallizes these accounts: "The sexual act extracted from the body a substance that was capable of imparting life, but only because it was itself tied to the existence of the individual and claimed a portion of that existence. By expelling their semen, living creatures did not just evacuate a surplus fluid, they deprived themselves of elements that were valuable for their own existence" (*Use* 130).

If semen appeared to possess a certain agency (a capacity to "impart life" and thus create immortality), its agency was neither inherent nor essential; rather, semen only acquired agency through the "existence of the individual." The movement of semen was thereby subordinated to the will of the male subject. Yet semen was also acted upon in ways that permitted it to cross the border between the inside and the outside of its container—semen was "extracted," "expelled," and "evacuated." It was indeed "a surplus fluid," crossing the borders of the body, threatening the agency of man from the inside out.

Roman civilization shifted the problematic of masculine agency in two ways: 1) marriage became thematized as a reciprocal relation between partners, and 2) political power was no longer a matter of being born into the authority of civic life, but a question of being positioned within a social network (Foucault, *Care* 71–95). The medical discourses of the time, in their characterizations of semen, represented these concerns. For cultural and political reasons different than those found in ancient Greece, the Roman discourse on male sexuality was equally caught between the agency of semen and its dangerous fluidity, between its ability to transcend man's mortality and its ability to temporarily violently seize and exhaust the body. Aretaeus's *On the Causes and Signs of Acute and Chronic Diseases* exemplifies this tension. In its reproductive agency, semen was thought to provide "health, strength, courage, and generation" (qtd. in Foucault, *Care* 112). In the act of pleasure, however, the male body experienced "[s]pasms of all the nerves, and tension of all the tendons, groins, and perineum, inflammation and pain of all the genital parts" (qtd. in Foucault 114). Galen, a medical contemporary of Aretaeus, more dramatically depicts the expenditure of semen from the male body: "[A]ll the parts of the animal find themselves robbed of their vital breath" (qtd. in Foucault 109). The synecdochic relation between semen and the male body in ancient discourse is undeniable and represents larger political and cultural anxieties surrounding masculine agency.

At the turn of the twentieth century in Europe, the male body was classified within the discourse on sexuality, which responded to the problematics of agency that were facing European middle-class men, or what George Mosse has termed "the perils of modernity" (23): the declining birth rate and threats to economic sovereignty. This anxiety over masculine agency, however, was distinct from its ancient predecessors in that it now required a mastery of "subjects" rather than merely a mastery of "conduct." The rhetorical resonance between the social-sexual body and the physical body was equally present in medical texts and popular accounts.

Twentieth-century psychoanalysis, for example, responded to the problematics of middle-class, masculine agency by translating the fluidity of the male body—semen—into the phallocentric logic of solids. In order to become a proper social-sexual subject, the male body was required to reconcile its own fluidity and recapture its agency by spinning a procreative tale. In her critical reading of psychoanalysis, Luce Irigaray asks rhetorically: "Isn't the subjection of sperm to the imperatives of reproduction alone symptomatic of a preeminence historically allocated to the solid (product)?" (113). Somewhere between fluidity and solidity, semen simultaneously threatens and engenders masculine, phallic agency. Semen's rebellious character, therefore, must be cast out, projected onto abject bodies. Women are thus discounted as legitimate subjects through the psychoanalytic idealization of the penis-as-phallus (Irigaray 110).

In its construction of masculine agency, the modern regime of sexuality produced two additional abject bodies: the masturbator and the homosexual (Foucault, *History* 105). These bodies were harbingers of decline in modern civilization, corporeal warnings that became legible in their synecdochic relation with semen. The masturbator, a foil to the sexually reproductive and economically productive middle-class male, appeared in pedagogical lectures, sermons, and medical pamphlets. The masturbator "[personified] the violation of normative expectations for 'productive' or 'industrious' middle-class male behavior [making money]," and became, in essence, "the embodiment of anti-social impulses" (E. Cohen, *Talk* 61). In his reading of Henry Maudsley's 1868 paper on masturbation, Cohen concludes, "By depicting the masturbator as the negation of 'the highest mental endowment of mankind,' Maudsley personifies him as the 'degeneration of mankind' in its most threatening form" (63). The masturbator, a subject defined by his conduct, thus became a sign of degeneration and death. The "homosexual" embodied these fears in the Victorian narrative of sexuality. Oscar Wilde's body—both in judicial and literary terms—was prototypical, and fostered the "extinction of man" narrative in modern discourse (Sedgwick, *Epistemology* 127–30). Ed Cohen's close reading of newspaper accounts demonstrates the role played by the Oscar Wilde trials in producing the normative public imaginary on male homosexuality. Moreover, Nunokawa argues that Oscar Wilde's *The Picture of Dorian Gray* [1891] constituted the "deathbed image" as "the gay signature" in the modern era (316). The rhetorically potent association between homosexuality and man's finitude relied upon medical and legal discourses on "sodomy" (often a code word for homosexual anal intercourse), which characterized the rectum as a "failed vagina" (Hanson 337), a "grave" for phallic agency (Bersani, "Rectum" 222). While substantively different from ancient Western discourses, the modern regime of sexuality also conceived semen as synecdochic for the male body. Although these rhetorical figures set the stage for the HIV/AIDS crisis in the United States, their relationship has been dramatically altered in the process and formed historically specific relations of heteronormative power.

The Politics of AIDS Science

In the United States, the gay male body has become a (if not *the* central) scapegoat for the HIV/AIDS epidemic, widely depicted as "sexually voracious and murderously irresponsible" (Crimp 244). The heteronormative ideological performances that have made possible the gay scapegoat and its very real-world effects have taken place in and through public discourse. Discourse is more than merely the means by which particular ideologies take hold in society, for it is equally the material evidence that ideologies exist at all. Discourse is the repository or host in which ideology resides. Heteronormative ideology, in the case of HIV/AIDS, is communicative, a discursive virus that reproduces itself in public policy, medicine, law, mass media, etc. The ideological nature of HIV/AIDS discourse is precisely "a plague of discourse" (Edelman 79), "an epidemic of signification" (Treichler 11). These conceptualizations of HIV/AIDS discourse are more than mere metaphors; they mark discourse as a material space in which ideological contests occur and take effect.

Scientific and popular narratives of HIV transmission have mobilized the synecdochic relation between semen and male subjectivity in ideologically charged ways, casting gay men as scapegoats for the HIV/AIDS crisis in the United States. Synecdoche, the interchangeability of container and thing contained, enables this interchangeability between cause and effect (Burke, *Philosophy* 25–26). Much like its ancient and modern predecessors, semen is rhetorically linked to images of life and death. In HIV/AIDS discourse, however, death is no longer effected by semen's *absence,* its excessive expenditure, or its failure to result in human reproduction. Rather, it is now semen's *presence,* its capacity to host and transmit HIV that functions as an agent of death. Yet the figural and ideological aspect of the scientific discourse on HIV transmission often remains invisible (Edelman, *Homographesis;* C. Patton, *Inventing*). The public discourse on HIV/AIDS repeatedly denies the rumors of their illicit affair, continually casting AIDS politics and AIDS science as mortal enemies rather than as passionate lovers. Narrative frameworks enable ideological relations to enter scientific explanations undetected and remain unquestioned.[6] Specifically, semen's ability to function as synecdoche for male subjectivity has reproduced heteronormative power relations within the medical and popular discourse on HIV/AIDS, yet these effects of power rarely appear strange or out of place. In rereading mutually reinforcing HIV transmission narratives, I document the figural nature of medical-popular discourse, its particular time-space relations of heteronormative power, and its ethical implications for queer life.

An Ethics of Monogamy

Throughout the HIV/AIDS crisis, the sexual body and the social body have performed a discursive seduction in which the human body serves as a handy metaphor for American society, what Waldby has termed "the body politic" (1). Two genres of medical discourse performatively (re)produce this figural relation between the medical body and the political body. Epidemiology ultimately "isolate[s] the causal variables of the disease in question" (Oppenheimer 51), and has thus located the gay male body as the origin of the AIDS epidemic in America. Immunology, on the other hand, invents the human immune system as the central command post in a war against disease and illness. In the instance of HIV/AIDS, this military operation takes place "in the drama of the T-cell and its 'perversion' by HIV infection" (Waldby 60). The medical war against HIV in the human body instantly becomes a social-political war against those bodies that play host to the virus. These two medical discourses have spun a rhetorically potent, heteronormative narrative, which shapes the ways in which we respond to the AIDS crisis and those most affected by it.

The epidemiological narrative of AIDS in the United States retroactively constructed the gay male body as a scapegoat.[7] The chronology of AIDS cases, in part, located gay men as the origins of AIDS in America, and thus positioned them as the agents responsible for the spread of AIDS within what has been termed the "general [heterosexual] population."[8] This temporal structure was embedded in early medical theories of the disease, such as the "homosexual lifestyle" hypothesis (Oppenheimer 56–59), early names for the illness, such as "GRID" or Gay-Related Immunodeficiency (Treichler 27), and early modes of describing infected populations, such as "risk group" (Grover 27–28). These theories, names, and modes of description were eventually condensed into a single body—Patient Zero—and entered the popular imagination through a well-intentioned journalistic bestseller. Randy Shilts's *And the Band Played On,* the tale of Patient Zero, was an epidemiological narrative in popular form, one of origins and truths whose press release reads: "What remains a mystery for most people is where AIDS came from" (qtd. in Crimp, "Promiscuity" 241). Yet Patient Zero's story quickly became a morality tale about urban gay male communities and sexual conduct. Nunokawa explicates, "The story of Dugas singlehandedly infecting an entire community with HIV serves to narrate his status, in Shilts's novelization, as reflection of that community" (313). Epidemiology's temporal structure has thus constituted gay men as *agents* of death. This construction of gay men, however, is not limited to the cultural imagination surrounding HIV infection; it also motivates social policy, such as the FDA prohibiting "men who have had sex with men since 1977" from donating blood (a policy that remains in place today). The blood ban, explains Jeffrey Bennett, represents "a performative act of community building that is intimately linked to notions of citizenship and nationalism" (255). Moreover, "the image of the gay man in relation to blood and nationhood is always already condemned to failure" (256).

The rhetorically charged association between HIV infection and death required yet another temporal relation, what Erni has called "the structure of morbidity" (37), embedded in the immunological narrative of HIV and its war against the T-cells. The clinical narrative established stages of HIV infection, measured the decreasing concentration of T-4 cells over time, and charted what scientists call "'the balance of power' between HIV and the immune system as they shift during the course of infection" (Erni 71–73). The temporality of the HIV/AIDS narrative effectively mobilized epidemiology's model of causality and immunology's militaristic metaphors to create a scapegoat, an enemy.

The epidemiology of AIDS has been equally structured by spatial relations, multiple variations of *inside/outside,* which have provided a rhetorical bridge between epidemiology's social-sexual analysis of AIDS and immunology's analysis of the T-cell. That both discourses are structured spatially has enabled multiple ideological associations to congeal. Positing the concept of "risk groups," AIDS epidemiology has necessarily constructed its other—the "general population." As a normative category, "the general population" presupposes the ideological contents of its borders: heterosexuality, the family, the nation, and the species

(Grover 23; Watney 75; Hanson 335; Yingling 297).[9] The social-political body of AIDS, spatially organized around these categories, easily became interchangeable with the medical body of AIDS, for the very concept of disease is also founded upon the structuring of inside and outside. Sontag observes, in *AIDS and Its Metaphors,* "[T]here is a link between imagining disease and imagining foreignness. It lies perhaps in the very concept of wrong, which is archaically identical with the non-us, the alien" (48). Reflecting upon the FDA's blood ban, Bennett eloquently crystallizes, "In the eyes of the state, homosexuality is foreign, but domestic. It is present everywhere, but without a history or a home" (69). Homosexuality, in other words, has become a specter that haunts American society and culture as it is located both inside and outside diverse social categories—family, nation, species. As such, homosexuality requires mechanisms to police it.

This spatial structuring of disease simultaneously operated within the immunological narratives of HIV/AIDS to produce a militaristic discourse. Waldby's analysis of metaphors used to depict T-4 cells and their function within the human immune system summarizes: "T cells have the ultimate responsibility in the body for the determination of self/non-self distinctions, because they are equipped in various ways to 'see' the difference between 'self' antigen and 'foreign antigen.' This recognition capacity prevents the immune system attacking 'self' cells, and ensures that its activity is directed against 'foreign' organisms" (63). It was through scientific discourse's spatial metaphors that the social body and the medical body became synonymous in the HIV/AIDS crisis. War has been declared on both fronts; the gay male body has thus become an enemy to both the general population and to himself.

Citing the figural tropes that first emerged in epidemiology and immunology, a similar war against the other has been declared within gay male communities. Heteronormativity, a discursive virus, has invaded contemporary debates on the social-sexual practices of gay life in America and replicated an ethics of monogamy, which advocates responding to the other as an enemy. In an ecological investigation of the AIDS epidemic, which identifies those sexual behaviors that enable HIV transmission within gay male social networks, Gabriel Rotello writes: "HIV truly strikes us where we live. Its means of transmission—sex—is the very thing that to many of us defines us as gay men, drives our politics and our erotics, gives us our modern identity, provides the mortar of much of our philosophy and community, animates much of our lives" (5). Calling for "transformative change," his *Sexual Ecology* advocates both consistent condom use *and monogamous sexual relations* as correctives to the HIV/AIDS epidemic within gay male subcultures.[10] To advance this agenda, Rotello repeatedly casts his argument as science, not politics: "what I seek to explore here is how gay behavior itself interacted with HIV to contribute to the epidemic. I will try to look at AIDS as an ecological rather than as a political or social event" (2).

Grounded firmly in a scientific discourse and eschewing its own politics, *Sexual Ecology* constitutes the other-as-enemy. Yet science, as we have already established, relies on political-social metaphors to make claims about disease. In Rotello's spatially structured description of the AIDS epidemic, this metaphoric relation between the social body and the medical body turns bellicose: "[This book looks] at the means by which an invader was able to roll like a Trojan Horse into the center of our home. An ancient adage is 'Know your enemy.' Most of us in the age of AIDS have thought of the enemy as HIV itself. We have generally failed to recognize that an equal if not greater enemy is the complex set of conditions that favor HIV's transmission" (4). These conditions, the greater enemy, are the promiscuous sexual networks that compose gay male subcultures, which are contrasted to "the sexual ecology of middle-class Western heterosexuals" (4). Heterosexual monogamy, it turns out, becomes a rhetorical specter that haunts the entire argument. Rotello's ecological analysis echoes early epidemiological research in that it is guided primarily by heteronormative ideology and an ethics of monogamy rather than by empirical data. Just as AIDS epidemiology ignored heterosexual cases in order to advance the "homosexual lifestyle" theory (Oppenheimer), Rotello asserts: "[AIDS] is not producing a self-sustaining heterosexual epidemic in the middle-class, mainstream American population. True, there are growing cases of what is sometimes called 'heterosexual AIDS,' but virtually all of these cases occur when HIV is passed from IV drug users to their sexual partners and children" (5). By excluding heterosexual cases, the war on AIDS is effectively transformed into a war on gay culture itself.

War, by definition, also requires the enemy, now clearly identified, to possess collective agency. Rotello's ecological narrative, while relying on the temporal structures provided by conventional epidemiology, diverges ever so slightly from its scapegoating rhetoric. Gay male subcultures remain the origin of AIDS, a "core group" that generated and sustained the disease due to the nature of their collective network of sexual activity. Historicizing gay male sexual practices, *Sexual Ecology* traces the ideal of "sexual freedom" to the formation of gay urban subcultures following WWII and the subsequent public openness of these subcultures produced by the gay liberation movement. The ethics of "sexual freedom" and its sexual ecology become causal agents, factors that produced the epidemic proportions of HIV/AIDS. Opposing activist claims that AIDS was simply a "historic accident," Rotello contends, "Multiple concurrent partners, versatile anal sex, core group behavior centered in commercial sex establishments, widespread recreational drug abuse, repeated waves of STDs and constant intake of antibiotics, sexual tourism and travel—these factors were not 'accidents'" (89). Although the concept of ecological "core groups" appears to scapegoat gay men, Rotello cautions against "attempts to distort that concept to demonize" (49). "Core groups," we are asked to remember, is a purely scientific term with no political implications. Gay male subcultures are thus responsible, yet not necessarily guilty, for the emergence and spread of AIDS in America. The logic that constructs such a fine distinction is simple: scapegoating requires guilt and guilt requires knowledge. Rotello recalls, for instance, early defense strategies against scapegoating, "We argued that the vast majority of HIV-infected gay men were stricken before anyone knew about the epidemic" (277). Today, however, we do know and with this knowledge comes full responsibility—and guilt.

The contemporary ethics of monogamy finally requires an epistemological shift, a return to identity. In the first instance, Rotello denounces the condom code's exclusive focus on sexual conduct. Although idealizing monogamy and essentializing sexual identity are dangerous for safe-sex education and HIV prevention (C. Patton, *Fatal Advice;* J. Blake Scott), this discourse contains ethical implications as well. In order to disentangle sexual conduct from sexual identity, Rotello attacks what he calls the "condom code" of HIV/AIDS prevention, for it is "a simple mechanical analysis of the connection between the biology of HIV transmission and the sexuality of gay men [which] ignores or glosses over the fact that a whole network of behaviors created, and continue to sustain, epidemic conditions in the gay population" (184). We should, as a gay male subculture, adopt monogamous sexual practices *in addition to condoms* because condoms *alone* have not worked to prevent the spread of HIV/AIDS within our community. Around 1993, a "second wave" of HIV/AIDS emerged within the gay male population. Although Rotello acknowledges the complex, multifaceted character of these new HIV cases, the "second wave" is primarily attributed to the failure of the condom code. He surmises, "[W]hile the code undoubtedly succeeded in keeping many individuals uninfected, it does not appear to have succeeded for the overall gay population" (134).[11] And although the difficulty in sustaining *any* kind of transformative cultural change is recognized, Rotello remains wedded to a "holistic approach" to HIV prevention. For example, "[T]he strategy of monogamy alone has the same kind of drawbacks as the strategy of the condom code alone: unrealistic reliance on just one isolated factor of risk, when in fact the real problem is multifactorial. But those who dismiss monogamy as a strategy fail to consider the long-term consequences of maintaining a culture of promiscuity" (207). The ethics of monogamy, a practical-scientific solution to HIV infection rather than a cultural-political orientation, is bound up in a rhetoric of identity and, as we shall see, a rhetoric of war.

Shifting fully from conduct to identity, Rotello identifies HIV-positive gay men as the new enemy, an other that threatens gay male subculture from within. Perhaps any discourse on HIV prevention necessarily narrates a defense of the self. Perhaps it is impossible to speak about "risk" without identifying the other that poses the threat. I will later advocate alternative narratives of HIV prevention that take gay male subcultures out of a war-based rhetoric, narratives in which the other represents an ally rather than an enemy. Within the ethics of monogamy, however, AIDS' other remains an enemy, and this enemy is now HIV-positive gay men rather than HIV itself. The condom code, Rotello reasons, creates "a position of self-defense" for those who wish to avoid HIV infection (108). Later, he continues, "This self-defense strategy is fine as far as it goes, but it addresses only half of the prevention equation. The other half concerns those who are HIV-positive, and who ought to have an absolute responsibility to protect others" (193). This statement constitutes sexual relations as a matter of "defense" and "protection," further entrenching gay male subculture within a rhetoric of war. The ethics of monogamy, in so doing, performs an epistemological shift from conduct to identity. This is evident in Rotello's mandate to take the HIV-test and know one's serostatus (108). The responsibility of HIV-positive gay men to prevent further infections thus requires additional knowledge, the knowledge that they are HIV positive. Such knowledge is produced within yet another scientific narrative—virology and its logic of identity.

HIV and the Logic of Identity

HIV stands as the center of AIDS epistemology, forever replicating its logic of identity in both scientific and popular discourses; it has become "a constitutive paradigm for virtually *all* understanding of AIDS" (Erni 67). This viral epistemology constructs the identities of both HIV and its host via the rhetorical trope of secrecy and disclosure, what I have been calling the rhetorical secret. Temporally, the rhetorical secret performs a teleological narrative, a story that tells the Truth. Spatially, the rhetorical secret performs a synecdochic narrative, a story that associates insides and outsides. These performances of identity occur on both the micro level, between HIV and its host cell, and the macro level, between the host cell and the HIV-positive body in which it lives.

As Cindy Patton remarks, the scientific search for HIV was essentially a "detective narrative" (*Inventing* 70), and thus possessed a teleological structure. The viral narrative of AIDS inherits this structure from molecular biology, in which "the genome as 'text' makes Revelation possible. It inscribes the genome within a hermeneutic of disclosure, one that allows the Truth to be unveiled as a secret text that has been waiting to be read all along" (Doyle 62). Constituting human genes as "texts waiting to be read," as secrets to be disclosed, has enabled narrative resolution [*telos*] and the coherence of identity. Cindy Patton's description of the scientific search for a retrovirus demonstrates the replication of this genetic metaphor within AIDS discourse:

> Most viruses are chunks of DNA—the basic genetic material in all cells. Retroviruses are RNA, a component which works with DNA in cell-division processes. In retroviruses, replication happens backwards: instead of going from DNA through RNA to produce daughter DNA, the retrovirus begins with RNA and then an enzyme called reverse transcriptase acts on the RNA to produce DNA. Once inside a host cell, the HTLV-III/LAV [eventually called HIV], for example, produces this DNA, which penetrates the core of the host cell and attempts to integrate itself at certain points in the host cell's DNA. If successful, the retrovirus's transcribed RNA is ever after part of that cell's genetic code. (*Sex and Germs* 46–47)

As a retrovirus, HIV reproduces itself within the host cell such that their identities become the same, such that they communicate their identities in precisely the same genetic language. Virology, as a teleological narrative, claims to have revealed this identity, transcribed and transparent, in HIV's genetic recoding of the host cell's DNA. This reproduction of identity also requires agency, penetration, and integration, in order to associate inside and outside, to establish a synecdoche in which the contained [HIV] and its container [host cell] become interchangeable. Temporally and spatially, the rhetorical secret inscribes HIV and its host cell within the logic of identity or sameness.

The logic of identity is replicated on the macro level, engendering a synecdochic relationship between the host cell and the HIV-positive body. Patton affirms, "[S]erostatus has become part of the identity of gay men involved in urban gay communities" (*Inventing* 39). The presence of HIV within the host cell has become an identity for the entire body through a nominalist rhetoric: "He is HIV positive" or "I am HIV positive." Gay men have become "the voice of the virus" because they now find themselves "living under the sign of HIV" (C. Patton, *Inventing* 52). The formation of "HIV positive" as a transparent code, an unequivocal sign, a coherent subject position is "anchored by the mobile metaphor of the HIV antibody test" (100). The HIV antibody test becomes a primary mechanism for establishing the synecdoche between HIV and the gay male body. The logic of identity, however, is never as absolute as it appears, for the rhetorical secret also requires us to forget. We must forget that the HIV test locates antibodies rather than the retrovirus itself; we must forget that the Western blot HIV test does not detect antibodies until after a three-month "window period"; we must forget that the ELISA HIV test is highly sensitive and can produce false positive results; we must forget that these ambiguities are often resolved by the individual's membership in a "risk group" (see Waldby 126–31). In short, we must forget that the synecdochic relationship between HIV and the gay male body is just that—a relation produced in and through discourse.

The Fluidity of Identity

Although HIV is often read as an enemy that invades communities, bodies, and cells, its synecdochic capacity also enables a different reading of difference in which the other becomes an ally. Burke clarifies, "Polar otherness unites things that are *opposite to* one another; synecdochic otherness unites things that are simply *different from* one another" (*Philosophy* 78). Synecdoche, in the very act of producing coherent identities, is founded upon otherness. The other that resides at the core of identity, however, is not an enemy, but, rather, an ally, for synecdoche, like semen, lives between agency and fluidity, between coherence and instability, between identity and difference. Synecdoche, Edelman impresses, simultaneously establishes the "coherence of identity" (*Homographesis*

50) and "refutes the positional stability of inside and outside" (70). In the medical narrative of HIV transmission, semen plays this dual role, encouraging us to reread HIV as an ally rather than an enemy. This re-reading of HIV will require a radical shift in our ethical responses to the AIDS crisis and those individuals and communities that have been affected.

To begin, HIV inhabits the synecdochic relation between semen and male subjectivity in scientific research. An article on the presence of "drug-resistant HIV" or HIV mutations within the blood and semen of male bodies, for instance, relies upon and reinforces the synecdochic relation between semen and the male body to advance its claims.[12] The article opens: "Research on AIDS has hinted that HIV can evolve along distinct lines in an infected man's blood and semen" (Seppa 279). HIV thus becomes doubly located: in blood and semen, as parts of the male body, and within the male body, as a whole, for a man is infected with the retrovirus. The brief article repeats this doubling of HIV-infected semen and blood and the HIV-infected body. For instance, "viral mutations [drug-resistant HIV] emerge in the blood but not in the semen of some men [and] the opposite also occurs." Later, "not all of the mutations arose on parallel tracks in blood and semen." Finally, "seven [out of eleven men] had viral substrains in their semen that were different from those in their blood." HIV and its mutations are located within the boundaries of semen (and blood), thus constituting the identity of semen as "HIV-positive." The article simultaneously confirms the presence of HIV in the male body as a whole, evoking the figure of the "infected" man. In medical discourse, HIV becomes the mark of identity for both semen and the male body as it unites them in synecdoche. The fluidity of semen, however, disrupts the tidiness of such rhetorical associations. Semen and the male body are not merely containers for HIV; they are equally vehicles for its transmission.

Although this article initially confirms the status of semen as a container, it simultaneously undermines the absolute coherence of these boundaries as semen becomes a vehicle for the transmission of HIV. "If men are sexually active and pass it [drug-resistant HIV in semen] on, the next person will have that much more difficulty benefiting from the [anti-HIV] drugs" (Seppa 279). As in Western discourse more generally, semen functions as a vehicle, acted upon from the outside: "If men are sexually active and pass it [drug-resistant HIV in semen] on . . . " Semen thus becomes a vehicle for HIV transmission, an action initiated by the male body. Although agency seems to be forever initiated from the outside, from the body acting upon its interior contents, agency cuts both ways in HIV transmission. When semen shifts back from vehicle to container, agency shifts back from outside its borders (the male body) to inside (HIV itself). HIV, as a discursive figure, enables this shift, for "it" is passed on through sexual activity, yet, more important, "it" is what takes effect. As the above statement concludes, "the next person will have that much more difficulty benefiting from the [anti-HIV] drugs." Drug-resistant HIV or "it" ultimately becomes the causal agent, for the function of semen is determined by the inside at the same moment that it is mobilized from the outside. The production of HIV as a causal agent thus transgresses the borders between inside and outside, bringing the male body's containment into question. Following the performative constitution of semen as a vehicle for HIV transmission, the otherness of semen and the male body multiplies.

This tension between semen-as-container and semen-as-vehicle engenders a causal relationship, for the act of containing HIV is suspected to increase the infectiousness of semen (Anderson et al.).[13] We might theorize, therefore, that the very containment of HIV within the seminal border increases the probability that this border will be traversed. We might conclude: *to contain is to transmit.* In examining factors that affect the capacity to detect HIV-1 in semen, Anderson et al. suggest the causal link between these two functions. Semen is first characterized as a vehicle, "Epidemiologic studies indicate that transmission of HIV-1 via semen to sexual partners occurs with varying degrees of efficiency" (2769). The article later addresses the "sexual transmission of HIV-1 by men." The capacity of semen to transmit HIV-1 from one body to the next is enabled, thus far, by the male body. Anderson et al. then constitute semen-as-container: "sexual transmission of HIV-1 by men is presumed to result from the presence of HIV-1 in semen." The potential to transgress masculine, phallic agency lies in this paradox of cause and effect— to contain is to transmit. Although these statements gesture toward a transgressive conceptualization of semen, fully acknowledging its fluidity, we must further interrogate the implications of this study. Does the medical gaze fully penetrate the borders of semen to "detect" HIV? Is the force of the gaze compromised or limited in any way? Is the causal relation between the presence of HIV and its transmission confirmed? Or is this transgressive avenue ultimately thwarted?

The study by Anderson et al. presents two problematic elements: detection and infectiousness. The detection of HIV-1 in semen is not pure, but, rather, depends upon other factors. Detection of HIV-1 in semen appears to be enhanced by immunosuppression or low T-cell count, and adversely affected by zidovudine therapy or AZT treatments (2772). Due to these difficulties in detecting HIV-1, it is impossible to confirm its presence in semen, which troubles semen's status as a "container" for HIV. The method of observation also impacts claims about HIV's infectiousness, which problematizes semen's role as a "vehicle" for HIV transmission. For instance, "Polymerase chain reaction is the most sensitive viral detection method available, but it does not measure the infectious potential of the HIV detected; at present, detection and quantification of infectious HIV is best achieved by culture" (2773). Anderson et al. reason, "While our study did not measure HIV-1 transmission, it is reasonable to assume that if the titer [concentration] of HIV-1 in semen were reduced by zidovudine therapy, infectivity would also be reduced" (2774). Hypothetically, AZT treatments might decrease the amount of HIV-1 in semen, and thereby, decrease its potential for transmission. This statement tentatively supports the transgressive logic that to contain is to transmit, for it reasons that the inverse is true: *not* to contain is *not* to transmit. Or even more specifically: to contain *less* is to transmit *less*. We must remember, however, that the presence of AZT therapies is positively associated with a lower detection of HIV-1 in semen. Therefore, we do not know if this occurs because the amount of HIV-1 present in semen has been decreased, or if HIV-1 is present, but simply not detectable. The article must, then, avoid an absolute certainty that AZT reduces or eliminates HIV-1 from semen: "men who are receiving zidovudine therapy cannot be assured that they do not have infectious HIV-1 in their semen" (2774). Consequently, we must turn elsewhere if we are to locate the transgressive statement—to contain is to transmit.

Gilliam et al. improve the ability to detect HIV-1 in semen and reduce the uncertainty of HIV-1's infectiousness in semen. The article concludes, "We believe that these data resolve the uncertainty raised by several studies [including that of Anderson et al.] that gave conflicting results regarding the effect of antiretroviral therapy on HIV-1 shedding in semen" (57). Gilliam's essay provides the conditions for transgression because it more directly links the containment of HIV-1 in semen to its infectious potential or its capacity to transmit. In fact, the aim of Gilliam's study is identical to that of Anderson et al., except that it measures the impact of reverse transcriptase inhibitor therapy, rather than the efficacy of AZT, in reducing the amount of HIV-1 in semen (55). Although the Gilliam article appears to be more aggressive in reporting their findings, significant uncertainties in their conclusions echo those in Anderson et al. For instance, "No definitive correlation of virus level in semen with infectiousness can be made, although several observations support the hypothesis that reducing viral levels in transmitting fluids reduces infectiousness of that fluid" (59). And later, "Our results suggest that antretroviral therapy, by decreasing levels of HIV-1 in semen, may lower the infectious inoculum of treated men and possibly reduce the likelihood of sexual transmission to uninfected partners" (59).

Here, our analysis must turn from questions of HIV-1 concentration *levels* and toward the relation between the *presence* of HIV-1 in semen and its infectiousness, which generally implicates the causality between containment and transmission. Gilliam et al. contend, "[U]nderstanding the factors that contribute to the shedding of HIV-1 in semen is an important step in elucidating the biology of HIV-1 transmission (54). Gilliam's study attempts to account for contributing factors to transmission of HIV-1 through semen, such as the concentration of HIV-1 in semen. Although the results do not provide a definitive answer on that particular factor, the act of shedding HIV-1 itself, the capacity to "pass virus in certain body fluids under certain conditions" (C. Patton, *Sex and Germs* 44), confirms our transgressive equation: *to contain is to transmit.* The presence of HIV-1 in semen creates a possibility to transmit, shed, or pass that virus through the boundaries of its container. This transgressive formula is not unique to the relationship between HIV-1, semen, and the male body, for sperm, as a figure in the discourse on fertility and reproduction, functions in a similar manner.[14] Yet, as Irigaray's critique of psychoanalysis has illuminated, semen's role in human reproduction is more easily translated into an economy of solids rather than testifying to the fluidity of male corporeality.

An Ethics of Fluidity

Dominant scientific narratives on HIV transmission, those found in epidemiology, immunology, and virology, employ a notion of "identity" governed by the rhetorical secret and its performative contradictions. HIV/AIDS science, for example, is a powerful means by which private sexuality is represented in public discourse. HIV/AIDS science also portrays itself as a panacea for ignorance rather than a product of rhetorical invention. HIV/AIDS science thus performs a particular way of knowing the world. Scientific knowledge of "HIV," however, also requires a great deal of forgetting: early epidemiological categories of "general population" and "risk group" essentially forgot heterosexual cases of HIV/AIDS; the HIV test often forgets that it actually locates HIV antibodies, that it includes a three-month "window period" and that it sometimes produces "false positive" results; the public frequently forgets that HIV is transmitted through sexual conduct rather than by those with specific sexual orientations. Scientific knowledge must also forget its figural tropes: immunology's war metaphors and virology's synecdoche. In so doing, science ultimately forgets its inherent politics— its modes of rhetorical invention.

Genealogical analysis of historical emergence examines the current staging of ideological forces such that discourse invents forms of knowledge and enacts regimes of power. Inventions of male homosexuality in medical discourse, much like those enacted in law, materialize heteronormative ideology in two ways. First, public discourse is the very evidence of ideological commitments in American society; discourse is thus material in that it is the only means of observing ideology in action. Second, law and medicine perform these ideological commitments upon human bodies; discourse is thus material in that it mobilizes ideology to act. Genealogy, as a mode of rhetorical scholarship, maps these incorporeal and corporeal performances of ideology. Medical discourse on HIV/AIDS materializes heteronormative ideology in both the practice of medicine and the communities it addresses.

The rhetorical secret imports its normative conditions into the public discourse on HIV/AIDS and impacts gay life and queer collectives. The HIV/AIDS crisis signals the dawn of a different ethics for gay life, a different mode of responding to difference. Jeffrey Nealon defines ethical inquiry as "a linkage of theoretical necessity with concrete response" (2). The ethics of monogamy, heterosexual and homosexual, has proved to be problematic on both counts. The ethics of monogamy, as theory, renders sexual conduct as private conduct, safe-sex as a matter of individual responsibility. The ethics of monogamy, as praxis, is an ineffective model of safe-sex because it invests in "policing individual change" (C. Patton, "Visualizing" 381), identifying "risk" with nonnormative sexual identity categories. As Cindy Patton so eloquently crystallizes, "[Q]ueer sex had to be *made* safe while heterosexual sex *was* safe until queered" (*Fatal Advice* 97). In the ethics of monogamy, those who perceive themselves as "normal" often fail to identify with risk and thus fail to respond effectively to the presence of HIV in American society. HIV transmission is further privatized when HIV serostatus becomes a simple question of information, when the HIV test becomes the sole arbiter of safe-sex. HIV serostatus, from this theoretical base, is thus invented as a matter of ignorance. Relying on the HIV test as pure information, however, is a dangerous way to make decisions about sexual conduct, for it is indeed a product of rhetorical invention, wrought with heteronormative associations and interpretive claims. Mastering this scientific discourse, as Rotello and other gay activists have done, has further entrenched gay male communities within heteronormative power relations via a substantively flawed ethics of monogamy. Mastering the scientific logic of identity is thus a mode of ideological enslavement.

Finally, the ethics of monogamy conceptualizes HIV and HIV-positive citizens as enemies rather than as members of a community. This rhetorical invention institutes yet another performative contradiction within contemporary discourses on male homosexual identity: *allies are performed as enemies*. This performative contradiction derives from the tension between masculine agency and fluidity, between the male body as container and the male body as vehicle. Reading scientific texts on semen and HIV transmission has illuminated the inherent fluidity of the male body, suggesting a radically different conceptualization of male subjectivity and masculine agency than that found in epidemiology, immunology, and virology. In light of our inability to fully distinguish between corporeal containment and corporeal transmission, the other necessarily becomes an ally rather than an enemy. Waldby similarly concludes, "HIV infection represents a particularly serious and extreme form of this marriage of the viral and the human" (19). Unlike the ethics of monogamy, an ethics of fluidity bears witness to this marriage of other and self with solemnity. In his critique of contemporary identity-based politics, Nealon writes, "Identity is always a question of response, of difference, of alterity." The vital ethical question, for Nealon, becomes a matter of effect, a matter of "responding to the specific emergence of alterity" (170). Gay male communities, like all forms of community in America, find themselves responding to the otherness of HIV. These responses are embodied in concrete sexual practices and norms that take hold within the specific dynamics of each community. Imagining the otherness of HIV as an ally, a material presence within our communities with which we must interact, enables us to respond ethically and effectively.

4

Experiencing the Erotic

> It was against the background of this cultivation of the self, of its themes and practices, that reflection on the ethics of pleasure developed in the first centuries of our era.
>
> —Michel Foucault

Over a decade ago, Frank Browning described gay life as a "culture of desire," writing: "What began for me as a tour of the state of gay 'culture' under the profound stress of AIDS has, along the way, turned into an odyssey of personal and communal desire—desire not only in its limited physical sense, but desire for community, identity, and moral purpose" (9–10). Now, in the twenty-first century, gay male culture remains Odyssean. We are still journeying home after the war. We are still writing our collective history. We are still searching for ourselves. Perhaps none of this is strange. What is strange, however, is the nature of our travels, our epic, our quest. Our contemporary collective identity, as gay men, is marked not by remembering erotic and communal desire, but rather, by forgetting these dimensions of gay life. We are now marked by a desire to be private and a desire to be normal, by the drive toward the essential and the ethnic.

The homoerotic is a site of controversy, for the salience of eroticism within gay male subcultures gives birth to the concern that gay male identity and collectivity is too often reduced to its sexual component. While I do not intend to reproduce such an oversimplification of gay experience here, the pendulum has indeed swung to the other extreme. Gay and lesbian social movements, Michael Warner observes, have adopted de-eroticization as a political strategy and attempted to "redeem gay identity by repudiating sex" (*Trouble* 42). I am more than merely asserting the presence of erotic desire within gay male communities, a rather banal claim by itself. I explore, instead, how contemporary performances of gay male eroticism produce ethical forms of collective identity, alternatives to the predominant essentialist and ethnicity models of LGBT politics.

I document and interrogate the rhetorical performances that seduce gay male communities into these modes of being and advocate a necessary corrective—an ethical model of sexual collectivity. In recuperating the erotic, I argue, we can reformulate collective gay male identity in necessary ways. "Identity," the central ideographic term in contemporary queer politics, takes on two dominant usages—essentialism and ethnicity. Although these usages often serve important functions in community formation and collective action, they also carry a normative burden, one that reinforces heteronormativity rather than challenging its effects of power. I map these rhetorical performances in Michelangelo Signorile's *Life Outside* and its disciplining of eroticism within gay male communities. Privatizing the erotic becomes the primary rhetorical means by which such discipline operates, how heteronormative power takes hold. As a corrective, I insist that homoeroticism is a public form of expression, first and foremost. Through phenomenological inquiry, I illuminate the ways in which the erotic might lead us to reconsider the ethical dimensions of identity formation and collective interaction. Essentialist and ethnic accounts of sexual identity, in their dominance, have created both theoretical and practical blind spots for queer activism. The rhetorical performances of "identity" as essential and ethnic often discipline (even eclipse) another dimension of sexual collectivity— the erotic.

Privatizing the Erotic

Michelangelo Signorile's *Life Outside* illustrates how the essentialist and ethnic usages of "identity" discipline the erotic, and thus deserves critical attention. As both a prolific and highly controversial activist figure within the gay male community (Simmons; Wieder), Signorile's writings are ideal for a critique of heteronormative discourse. *Life Outside,* upon its release, topped the bestseller lists in the *Lambda Book Report,* and reviews in the gay and lesbian press typically praised Signorile's warning about the excesses of hypermasculine gay male culture (Greaves; Kevles; Pela). *Life Outside,* in documenting what Signorile calls "the cult of masculinity," materializes our desire to be private and our desire to be normal, thus performing essentialist and ethnic models of gay community. We can witness, in its rhetorical reflection, these ideological performances of "identity."

Life Outside largely casts gay identity and homoeroticism as private matters rather than public forms of expression and association. Signorile's method, conducting personal interviews about individual lives, as well as his social-political aim, the deprogramming of circuit life, privatize the erotic. Signorile further separates private life from public spaces and collective interaction through his primary categories of analysis: "Life Inside" and "Life Outside." Yet he deploys these categories differently than most writings on gay life, in which "inside" is associated with the private and "outside" with the public. In Signorile's argument, "Life Inside" refers to the circuit scene [public, community life] while "Life Outside" refers to private relationships that exist outside of this scene. *Life Outside* further troubles these conventional categories in discussing its social-political aims. Advocating life outside the circuit, Signorile hopes that gay men will come out of the closet and "live their lives openly in nonurban locales" (xxviii). Living "normal" lives within committed sexual relationships initially appears to express gay male sexuality "openly" in public. Yet, upon closer inspection, "life outside" paradoxically makes gay male sexuality disappear by rendering it private. In describing the deprogrammed gay man, Signorile cites therapist Michael Shernoff, praising gay men who are "virtually indistinguishable from their heterosexual neighbors . . . more like Middle Americans . . . living their lives like the rest of Americans, but they just happen to be homosexual" (229). The desire to live life outside of the closet [in public] thus entails a desire to be normal [just like heterosexuals], which renders homosexuality indistinguishable from heterosexuals [invisible].

Gay male identity, in this rhetorically charged vocabulary, finds two opposing forms of expression: one public, the other private. Signorile describes the public, hypermasculine, homoerotic gay scene in individualistic terms. Hypermasculine gay men are "circuit queens" (33), "narcissistic," "hedonistic," and "self-absorbed" (10), whose social practices are said to display a "fast and furious appetite" (26), "awash in hedonism, excess, and hot, masculine bodies" (61). When these individual traits form social norms within the circuit scene, the personal interviews testify, low self-esteem is often the result (*Life Outside,* Chapter One; see also, Mann). The "deprogrammed" gay man, depicted as "more mainstream and traditional" (179), appears in sharp contrast to the "circuit queen." Signorile defines the deprogrammed gay man not only by *who* he is, but also by *where* he is. Recognizing the growing trend of gay men moving away from the urban gay ghettos and into the suburbs, Signorile privatizes sexuality and sexual identity in significant ways. Migrating to the suburbs, the deprogrammed gay man ultimately *blends in* even though he is *out* to his family and neighbors. Signorile's essentialist narrative concludes: "The deurbanization of homosexuality has perhaps only just begun. And many of these men express needs and desires in life that are just as simple and traditional as the heterosexual people they grew up with: In interview and surveys, many of these men said their main priority was to meet someone, fall in love, and settle down" (206). These types of relationships, what Signorile calls "postmodern monogamy," enable gay men to experience true relational intimacy in a way formerly prohibited by the circuit scene (240–52). Although he acknowledges the significance of community and camaraderie, the gay ghettos' beneficial by-products, "life outside" becomes an alternative to the cult of masculinity, "a blueprint for all gay men to follow in the future" (180). The derivatives of deprogramming, thus far, are solely individual ones—increased self-esteem and greater interpersonal intimacy. A successful and satisfying gay life is indeed a private life. As alternatives, these behavioral shifts within gay male subcultures are framed as individual choices rather than ethical norms within a community. I am not suggesting by this critique that gay men do not have these desires and needs, or that they shouldn't have them. It is to say, however, that when the essentialist account of sexual identity becomes the rhetorical lynchpin in a polemical argument, we are asked to forget that sexuality is public and collective as well as private and individual.

Is it? The desire to be private is also rhetorically associated with the desire to be normal. *Life Outside,* for example, evokes an ethnic account of gay male identity such that gay male collectivity requires an ethic of monogamy, thus creating heteronormative effects. Hypermasculine eroticism, in this account, erroneously becomes a direct causal factor in HIV infection, for the social pressures of circuit culture and its hypermasculine standards "have in part *created* a breakdown in safer sex among many men on the scene . . . [and] we are seeing the *resulting* serotransmissions that are *contributing* to the AIDS epidemic in the gay population" (my italics, xxii). The excesses of hypermasculinity—its corporeal musculature and promiscuous erotic practices—are effectively translated into causes of death, thus regulating gay men's social-erotic practices. After HIV/AIDS emerged in gay male communities, gay life, gay sex, and gay relationships changed. Signorile narrates, "Fearful for their lives many men settled into relationships, lowered their number of partners, or stopped having sex altogether" (61). Adopting the HIV/AIDS crisis's conventional language, monogamy becomes synonymous with safety and protection from HIV. Signorile later observes, "[M]any gay men in the urban ghettos were affected in this way by AIDS [made changes in their sexual conduct] and settled into relationships, monogamous and otherwise" (227). In this idealization of monogamous relations, HIV/ AIDS becomes a threat to those who don't normalize their sexual activity. This disciplinary warning is then made explicit: "But cohort studies tracking the epidemic show that significant numbers of gay men in the major cities not only appear to be engaging in sex with multiple partners, but are doing so frequently and often unsafely" (227). Although *Life Outside* initially distinguishes between unsafe sex and multiple sexual partners (the former increases risk of HIV infection while the latter *by itself* does not), these two behaviors are later conflated in such a way that "safe-sex" ceases to be a category of sexual behavior and promiscuity becomes a highly problematic synonym for unsafe sex practices.[1] Signorile summarizes, "we all know that multiple-partner sex and non-monogamous relationships among gay men are alive and well in the urban centers" (228). Hypermasculine excess is thus deemed "unsafe." Gay men, consequently, must become obedient to the ethic of monogamy.

The ethic of monogamy's rhetorical power lies in its formal quality rather than in its scientific accuracy. To take hold in our collective consciousness, it depends upon the rhetorical secret and its performative contradictions. Specifically, HIV serostatus must be invented as a type of ignorance, a secret identity to be disclosed. Rather than using an HIV test, itself a problematic diagnostic method, Signorile adopts a more informal means of establishing HIV serostatus: hypermasculinity. The physical body itself, its musculature, becomes a mechanism of disclosure, a signifier for the virus. Recounting the emergence of circuit culture in the early 1990s, Signorile portrays hypermasculinity as a ruse, a simulacrum of physical health, one that disguised the awful truth of gay male subcultures. He writes:

Exploiting the fear and anxiety, the gay porn industry, centered on the West Coast, helped define the ideal further: the corn-fed, youthful, hairless, white, muscle man-boy with a healthy California tan. He was every bit a man, and he was disease-free. The irony of this of course—beyond the fact that at the time perhaps as many as half of all gay men in some large cities were infected with HIV, no matter how healthy they looked—was that many men who came close to being the ideal were taking dangerous illegal steroids to get that way, drugs that made them anything but healthy. (68–69)

The hypermasculine body, through a narrative of disclosure, tells us its truth, confesses its illness. The erotic must remain private rather than public in order to avoid this fate. The erotic must be disciplined.

Signorile's criticisms constitute a significant relationship of knowledge-power in our present times. *Life Outside* enacts the rhetorical secret and its performative contradictions on the stage of contemporary gay male culture, thus materializing and reproducing heteronormative ideology. As a key instance of public discourse aimed primarily at a gay male audience, it further illustrates how the rhetorical secret promises the mastery of a discursive regime at the very moment it enslaves our community within a normalizing and disciplinary rhetorical culture. Moreover, the desire to be private and the desire to be normal mobilize essentialist and ethnic forms of gay male "identity" such that gay male communities understand themselves in ideologically charged ways—"identity" produces knowledge. Yet, as is true of the rhetorical secret, this knowledge requires forgetting. These current constructions of gay male identity, materialized through the rhetorical secret, inherently ask gay men to forget the public, collective, and erotic dimensions of our lives. Instead, I ask that we recuperate these elements of gay life in order to conceptualize a "queer ethics."

Performing the Erotic in Public

Signorile's *Life Outside* demonstrates the rhetorical means by which hypermasculinity and homoeroticism are disciplined within gay culture. The rhetorical secret, its performances of essentialist and ethnic identity, addresses a gay male collectivity and in that address calls it into being. Yet this form of gay male collectivity remains merely an aggregate of individual, private identities, thus reinforcing heteronormative modes of subjection and producing material effects of power. In contrast, I contend that gay male identity, hypermasculinity, and homoeroticism are better understood as fundamentally public phenomena, constituting a dynamic collective experience.

Hypermasculine imagery circulates throughout the American urban landscape, evokes erotic desire by occupying public spaces, creates an awareness of gay male identity, and risks being disciplined or punished by heteronormative society. Hypermasculine images, for instance, have proven quite lucrative in mainstream advertising, upscale photographic art, wall posters, postcards, and deluxe coffee-table volumes (Bronski 98; Dutton 321–29; Harris 160–78) due primarily to the presumption of "the pink dollar," the perception that gay men have available a large amount of disposable income (Bordo 179–82; Bronski 138–57; Edwards 113–14).[2] Hypermasculine bodies, when viewed in this context, are frequently understood as homoerotic forces penetrating straight culture and society. Put otherwise, hypermasculinity functions as a code for homoeroticism in heterosexual public spaces, as an imagistic "open secret."[3] Hypermasculinity, prevalent in contemporary advertising and professional bodybuilding, are often read in this way. Some have celebrated the emergence of homoeroticism in mainstream cultural forms for its ability to parody heterosexual masculinity (Healey; Simpson 150–63) while others perceive its assimilation into mainstream culture as "subcultural suicide" (Harris 5). As an open secret, hypermasculinity always risks betraying its homoeroticism and must, therefore, adopt a paranoid, homophobic discourse to purge itself of homoerotic meanings and dissuade audiences/viewers from homoerotic interpretations. Bodybuilders, for example, transform erotic desire (their desire *to have* other men sexually) into identification (the desire *to be like* other men physically) (Parsi 112; Simpson 23). Companies employing hypermasculine figures to market their wares involve similar paranoid strategies to disavow any potential homosexual meanings. Due to the hypermasculine male body's dangerously homoerotic appeal, advertisers locate that body within a strictly regulated heterosexual context (Bronski 105–6). Marky Mark's *Calvin Klein* underwear ads in the early 1990s indicate such regulation and discipline. As Marky Mark's body approached iconic status within gay culture, his public appearances continually rearticulated his heterosexuality: a "you can look but don't touch" attitude (Simpson 150–62). The cultural lesson is clear: homoerotic *desire* must always transform itself into homosocial forms of *identification*.

Hypermasculine body images not only "speak about" homosexuality within heterosexual culture; these visual spectacles also "speak to" gay male communities. Such imagery has been a notable presence within gay, urban spaces since the 1970s, originally cast as gay reformism because the Gay Clone aimed to discredit conventional stereotypes of effeminate gay men (Humphries; M. Levine, *Gay Macho*).[4] In the 1980s, hypermasculine bodies and imagery took on new meanings within gay male communities. Edmund White reminds us that in the age of HIV/AIDS, "The body becomes central, the body that until recently was at once so natural (athletic, young, casually dressed) and so artificial (pumped up, pierced, ornamented). Now it is feeble, yellowing, infected —or boisterously healthy as a denial of precisely this possibility" (214).

Cover image for *Hotspots,* an Atlanta-based gay magazine. Reprinted with permission of the publisher. Photograph by Raymond Vino, (c) 2003.

The gay press still traffics heavily in hypermasculine imagery today—from national magazines like *The Advocate, Out,* and *Genre* to local gay newspapers and magazines. The dissemination of hypermasculine body images clearly brings gay male communities into being. Ron Long notes that contemporary gay male culture is "very much centered on the pursuit of the beautiful body—both the pursuit of other men's bodies and the pursuit of a beautiful body for oneself" (20). The centrality of this pursuit, the simultaneous desire *to be* and *to have* a hypermasculine body is evidenced, in part, by the emergence of a specifically gay gym culture within the past decade (Arning).[5] This is not to say, however, that erotic desire is the only force responsible for creating gay male collectivity. Desire for identification, social equality, friendship, and long-term relationships are other foundations for community. Yet same-sex erotic desire remains central to the constitution of gay male identity in contemporary America. Due to their salience in public culture and their powerful rhetorical capacity, hypermasculine images stand as a significant constitutive discourse, one that enables us to further thematize the rhetorical formation of gay male collectivity in contemporary urban America.

Table 1 Hypermasculine Images: Production and Reception

	PRODUCTION: Mainstream media	PRODUCTION: Gay media
RECEPTION: Identification	Assimilation: Homosexuality assimilates into heterosexual masculinity	Individual impact: Hypermasculinity produces trends of low self-esteem and steroid use
RECEPTION: Desire	Parody: Homoerotic imagery parodies heterosexual masculinity	Collective impact: Hypermasculinity creates communities based on eroticism and sexuality

If hypermasculinity does in fact represent an open secret, a public code for private homoeroticism, its rhetorical force relies upon differing modes of production and reception. The ability to read hypermasculinity as a sign of homoeroticism and thus recognize the audience's homophobic, homosocial, and homosexual identifications are largely influenced by *where* the image is located (mainstream media forms or gay media forms) and *how* the image is digested (identification or desire). As the preceding discussion suggests, hypermasculine imagery simultaneously operates as homosexual assimilation into "straight" society and as a parody of that society; it creates identification among gay men while constituting collective identity through erotic desire (see Table 1 above). To develop an ethical notion of gay male identity, I focus attention on the rhetorical dimensions of hypermasculinity in gay media forms and their public reception by gay male viewers. Specifically, when hypermasculine and homoerotically charged images appear in local gay media, their presence creates communities based on erotic desire and sexuality.

Erotic Desire, Queerness, and Ethics

To advance an ethical model of gay male identity through the consideration of hypermasculine, homoerotic imagery in gay media forms requires reflection upon three dimensions central to modern male homosexuality—erotic desire, queerness, and ethics—and their connection to one another. Historically speaking, the emergence of male homosexuality in the late nineteenth century exhibited a tension between taking pleasure in expressing homoerotic desire and finding pleasure in the inability to do so. Melville's *Billy Budd,* as a key literary example of that tension, illustrates the necessarily masochistic pleasure found in engaging homoerotic texts: the pleasure in failing to fully express pleasure. Likewise, photographic images possess a masochistic character, for they are located at what Roland Barthes has termed "the *limit* of meaning" ("Rhetoric" 32). Images, Barthes explicates, demonstrate "a loss of equivalence characteristic of true sign systems" (36). True sign systems, whether discursive or imagistic, are a chimera, a performative contradiction, for they claim relations of equivalence even though their conditions of production and reception engender fundamentally contingent relations between the sign and what it represents. The contingency imbued in images makes gazing a responsive act in which rhetorical and ideological contests take place. Erotically charged images, more specifically, display the gap between self and other, between identity and difference inherent to all symbolic expressions of pleasure.

Representing homosexuality in public discourse today continues to perform the ideological tension between identification and desire, a tension evident in the public vocabulary of contemporary sexual politics. Legal debates regarding sodomy laws (*Lawrence v. Texas*) and same-sex marriage (*Baehr v. Lewin*), for example, remind us that rhetorical and ideographic uses of "identity" in contemporary lesbian and gay politics often mobilize our collective desires to be private and to be normal. "Queer," in contrast, marks the performative contradictions within the identity politics model of lesbian and gay activism, signaling identity's non-identity, its other. Historian David Halperin explains, "Queer is by definition *whatever* is at odds with the normal, the legitimate, the dominant. *There is nothing in particular to which it necessarily refers.* It is an identity without an essence" (*Saint* 62). By questioning identity's status and its ability to fully represent its object, queer thus directs our attention toward how myriad differences between self and other are fundamental to collective life. Hypermasculine images, as a mode of constituting gay male identity through media forms, provide access to a gay collectivity derivative of erotic desire, the desire to be public and to be different. Erotic desire is thus essentially queer in that it produces a different collective ethos, an ethos responsive to difference. Casting gay male identity as erotic and queer, I argue, suggests an alternative to the essentialist and ethnic conceptions of gay male identity and collectivity.

Because erotic and queer dimensions of gay life announce the presence of difference as a fundamental element in collective association, this alternative model foregrounds gay life's ethical dimensions. The HIV/AIDS crisis, for instance, makes ethical considerations vital to cultural participation and political action. The performative contradictions that ground scientific discourse on HIV transmission reconfigure our understandings of identity (semen as both container and vehicle for HIV), agency (semen as both solid and fluid), and ethical perspectives (gay men as both allies and enemies). Eschewing these contradictions, translating difference back into identity or sameness, can produce fatal results. The HIV/AIDS crisis suggests that the body is the ground for ethical thought, for it is the stage upon which these contradictions play out.

Queer Ethics

Gay scholars, following Foucault's later interest in ethics,[6] have recently turned to gay life and its modes of public expression as sources for ethical thought. Deriving ethical questions from gay life re-creates the tension between identification and desire that inhabits all public expressions of male homosexuality. These ethical models thus articulate the historically situated problems of our present time and suggest ways of challenging the heteronormative ideology made material in and through our cultural artifacts. I begin with Richard Mohr's ethical considerations in *Gay Ideas*.

Working through hypermasculine iconography, Mohr develops an ethical perspective grounding the ideals of democracy and equality in gay male culture. "Hypermasculine pairings," he suggests, "provide a model for the background sense of equality—mutual respect—on which all other values of democracy depend" (195). Yet Mohr's examples and metaphors for equality reveal two performative contradictions: 1) resisting heteronormative power enacts traditional forms of masculine agency; and 2) pursuing the ideal of equality enacts social inequalities.

Mohr's challenge to heteronormative and masculinist power derives from hypermasculine images. The sadomasochism in Tom of Finland and Robert Mapplethorpe's photography, for instance, are said to challenge heterosexist associations between male sexuality and penetration by destabilizing conventional relations of agent/non-agent. Masochism, as our earlier analysis demonstrates, does not eliminate the categories of active/passive, agent/non-agent, but, rather, it transgresses heteronormativity through the fluid and interchanging repetition of these roles. In this sense, gay sadomasochism undermines traditional masculine agency through its own ironic performance. Yet Mohr, in his critique of Guy Hocquenghem's (1972) treatise on gay relations, argues that gay male anal sex is untenable as an ethical model because (unlike gay S&M) it remains stuck in an active/passive binary thus requiring "the loss of human agency altogether" (205).[7] Mohr's critique of Hocquenghem's ethics thus exposes sameness as the requirement for human agency in his own ethical model. Anal sex, in its formal structure of agent/non-agent becomes a metaphor for failed ethical communication: "On Hocquenghem's model, the individual does not become equal with other individuals; rather, the individual simply disappears, disappears into a cloud-like existence of 'communication,' but communication in which, at least oddly, there are no hearers or speakers" (205). This passage reveals the philosophical ground upon which Mohr builds gay ethics. Mohr's vision, despite disclaimers to the contrary, is an individualistic one, a masculinist one, a heteronormative one for sameness or equality remains the unquestioned prerequisite for human agency.[8]

Mohr's ethical vision is clarified through the concept of "mutual respect." Democracy in practice, Mohr observes, does not always live up to its ideal—equal dignity for all. "Homosexual relations," in contrast, "create and sustain just the right balance between self and other to provide the mutual respect needed to model democracy" (203). "Mutual respect," as the fundamental condition for democratic ethics, presupposes a "balance between self and other." As if on a scale, they would measure the same weight. This version of equality collapses social differences into a model based on sameness, one which is both untenable and undesirable. Yet Mohr's selection of examples suggests that life's inequalities are never far away. In fact, his ability to erase power and inequality appears solipsistic, lacking a foundation for judgment. Michelangelo's Battle of the Lapiths and Centaurs serves as one such example. Mohr writes, "In these orgies, everyone by turns does everything to everyone; the differentiations of doer and done, top and bottom, dominant and submissive, remain as instrumentalities of sex acts but are stripped of moral or political hierarchy" (209). This analytical twist suggests that power and difference aren't power and difference after all; they are, rather, equality and sameness.

Michael Warner's gay ethics, developed in *The Trouble with Normal,* is built upon a different principle, sexual autonomy. Warner's notion of "sexual autonomy" is not a theoretical throwback to the mainstays of liberalism and individual freedom, however. He explains, "So sexual autonomy requires more than freedom of choice, tolerance, and the liberalization of sex laws. It requires access to pleasures and possibilities, since people commonly do not know their desires until they find them" (7). For Warner, sexual autonomy requires the production of "new freedoms, new experiences, new pleasures, new identities, new bodies . . . variation" (12). Sexual autonomy, in this vision, is public rather than private. In order to achieve sexual autonomy, Warner advocates embracing our "shame" as gay men. Rather than social stigma, which attaches to social categories of identity, shame is a judgment on activity and conduct. Gay culture, through its rhetorical use of "identity," has privileged the former while denigrating the importance of the latter. As Warner observes, "[To] have a politics of one without the other is to doom oneself to incoherence and weakness. It is to challenge the stigma on identity, but only by reinforcing the shame of sex. And unfortunately, this has been the choice not only of individuals, but of much of the official gay movement" (31). The HIV/AIDS crisis exemplifies the necessity for this change in perspective on gay life: "Careful reflection on public health has led most people who work with HIV prevention to conclude that an accessible sexual culture is a resource, not an enemy" (210). Sexual culture, the erotic, is thus the ground upon which a queer ethics might be built.

Building on Foucault's work, Mark Blasius crafts a similar vision for gay life. Power and difference are not excised from gay life, but rather, are seen as necessary dimensions of freedom (30). Identity, then, is not our savior but the most powerful constraint on gay life. Blasius argues, "[L]esbian and gay politics is 'identity politics' in the specific sense that it involves reversal, sometimes ironically, of procedures within our culture by which people are subjected and attributed an identity" (40). The undoing of identity is an important aim for gay persons because, as Foucault and Blasius recognize, identity is as much an apparatus of power as it is a source of agency and freedom. Blasius explains, "It is not *state* power that is primarily at issue, and it is precisely in governing us through regulating our 'self' and its relations with other 'selves,' in what seems most 'private,' that the power exercised through sexuality is most effective" (86).

Blasius advocates "ethos" as the best way to articulate freedom and gay life, preferring the concept of "ethos" over "sexual preference or orientation," "lifestyle," "subculture," and "community" (180). These other terms and concepts, while benefiting lesbian and gay politics in some ways, leave gay life saddled with damaging political and cultural baggage. "Sexual preference" and "lifestyle," for example, maintain a psychiatric model that has historically characterized lesbians and gay men as social deviants (183). "Subculture" and "community," though more positive in tone, carry negative connotations as well. "Subculture," for instance, suggests that it automatically and inherently deviates from the normal (199). "Community," when referring to lesbian and gay people, constitutes a utopia, literally existing nowhere. Community, in its singularity, is misleading because it rests upon the notion of sameness rather than invoking the differences that proliferate in queer life. Consideration of a queer ethics thus begins in public life, grounds itself in the body, and attends to differences between self and other. Queer ethics thus begins in the erotic dimensions of gay life.

A Phenomenology of Gay Identity

As an alternative to the essentialist and ethnic conceptions of gay male identity and collectivity, I advocate an "ethical" model. Rather than simply replacing essentialist and ethnic modes of subjection with more and/or different identity categories, an ethical model calls the practice of sexual subjection itself into question. Kath Weston's recent critique of gender studies challenges the frequent reliance on non-binary forms of classification, the extended counting of multiple genders and multiple sexualities (e.g., "the third sex"), in the quest for social resistance. Instead, Weston argues, resistance to the inequalities produced by discursive systems of gender and sexuality resides in "fleeting moments of displacement" (45). The erotic gaze is such a moment, for it shatters the very notions of identity and non-identity. Questioning "identity" as a rhetorical resource for non-heterosexual citizens opens up future possibilities for ethical thought and collective action.

The erotic, as a source of resistive power, is neither a different mode of sexual classification nor a strategy of lasting social change. Rather, the erotic gaze opens up onto brief segments of time in which the modern regime of sexuality is rendered unintelligible, in which subjects and objects are left without their disciplinary maps. In his treatise on eroticism, Georges Bataille describes the erotic as "the deliberate loss of self," "the disequilibrium in which the being consciously calls his own existence in question" (31). Bataille goes on to argue that such moments cannot be captured through scientific inquiry, for science merely results in further codification and thereby devalues the erotic from the outset (37). The radical nature of eroticism, its ability to transgress the borders between subject and object, is best revealed through an analysis of what Bataille calls "inner experience." Phenomenological inquiry maintains the erotic as a fleeting moment, as a force that displaces heteronormative discourse's disciplinary inscriptions.

Phenomenology, as a philosophical discourse, describes "the experience of truth" (Merleau-Ponty, *Phenomenology* 395). Yet the phenomenological word, M. Merleau-Ponty clarifies, is not "the reflection of a pre-existing truth, but, like art, the act of bringing truth into being" (xx). Elizabeth Grosz provides a similar reading of Merleau-Ponty: "Experience is not outside social, political, historical, and cultural forces." Rather, it is directly invested in "the production of knowledge" (94–95). Additionally, phenomenology provides insight into the other side of human subjectivity, the moments before we are reinscribed into relations of power, the fleeting moments of resistance. Merleau-Ponty explicates, "We have the experience of an *I* not in the sense of an absolute subjectivity, but indivisibly demolished and remade by the course of time" (219). The larger context of Merleau-Ponty's work suggests that these processes of demolition and remaking are political ones, and, I argue, rhetorically charged operations.

Despite Foucault's critique of phenomenology [of Merleau-Ponty, specifically] in *The Order of Things,*[9] phenomenology and genealogy are compatible in that they both conceive a subjectivity that is at once historical, philosophical, and political. In *Phenomenology of Perception,* Merleau-Ponty describes the perceptual experience as such: "The *person who* perceives is not spread out before himself as a consciousness must be; he has historical density, he takes up a perceptual tradition and is faced with a present" (238). Rather than a Cartesian *cogito* [pure consciousness], the subject is a historical being, situated in time. Scholars of philosophy also recognize this compatibility between phenomenological and genealogical methods. Rudi Visker suggests: "Such, then, might be our issue (in both sense of the word); to grow (into) such a room by outrunning those signifiers ("Foucault," "Merleau-Ponty") between which we were supposed to choose, until their shadows leave their bearers and mingle with the echo of voices it would be pointless to try to identify" ("Raw Being" 111). Nick Crossley goes as far as to conclude that Foucault's genealogy possesses a "phenomenological dimen-

sion" (192). Both Merleau-Ponty and Foucault challenge Cartesian philosophy and its central tenet—the mind/body binary, refusing to resolve
the apparent dualism between subjective/objective, idealism/realism,
transcendental/empirical (R. Cohen, "Merleau-Ponty" 329–30, 335;
Merleau-Ponty, *Phenomenology* 13–51; Visker, "Raw Being" 113), and instead locate new ground for rethinking subjectivity. This challenge to
Descartes holds that the experience of perception is "a non-thetic [non-
positing], pre-objective, and preconscious experience" (Merleau-Ponty,
Phenomenology 242). Put otherwise, phenomenology locates its project
between the binary intersections created by empiricism and transcendentalism.

Beyond the claim that Merleau-Ponty and Foucault are not as methodo-
logically hostile to each other as it might first appear, each thinker
provides analytical tools that are lacking in the other, creating what
Crossley terms a "phenomenology of power" (133). In the first instance,
Foucault's analytics of disciplinary power supplements Merleau-Ponty's
theory of social politics in significant ways. Although both conceptualize a contemporary politics beyond the judicial model of power, Crossley explains, "[Merleau-Ponty] does not analyze the politics of our 'ways
of loving, living, and dying,' nor does he provide us with adequate means
of doing so" (103). Foucault's genealogical method clearly enables such
an analysis of disciplinary apparatuses of power, yet falls short of locating resistances within disciplinary regimes of power. Merleau-Ponty's
concepts of "perception" and "intersubjectivity" constitute a resistive
toolbox of sorts (Crossley 188), providing a method of staging and articulating resistance. In fact, *Phenomenology of Perception* argues that the
aim of phenomenology is not merely to "practice philosophy," but to
"realize the transformation which it brings with it in the spectacle of
the world and in our existence" (62). These processes of transformation
inhabit the possible rather than the necessary, and are thus rhetorical
actions—partial, incomplete, and contingent operations within the spectacle of the world.

A phenomenological concept of visual "perception" transforms the
conventional Cartesian relationship between self and other, subject and
object into a *mutually* constitutive one (Merleau-Ponty, *Phenomenology*
214–19). In other words, we can avoid the trappings of imagining either
a transcendent subject or an empirical object. Crossley explains, "[P]er-
ception should be conceived of as an originary act that brings both seer
and seen into being" (11). Visker takes Merleau-Ponty's thought even
further, for visual perception eats away at the transcendent subject's very

coherence. In response to Merleau-Ponty's comparison between perception and copulation, Visker asks, "For isn't a copulation precisely that experience of almost losing myself in the other and yet at the brink of fusion losing hold of him in the uncontrolled movement of my spasms" ("Raw Being" 120)? Alphonso Lingis theorizes this exteriorization of the self, this "almost losing" of identity through the excessive musculature of bodybuilders (*Foreign* 43–44). Exposure and exhibitionism render corporeal borders as sites of reception. Perception, in other words, inhabits "that vital borderline which divides our exterior from our interior, endorses our separateness and our form" (Lingis, *Foreign* 79). "The skin of the other extends before me not as the membrane that contains his or her substance in a depth structure exposed to my comprehensive hold nor as the sheath that holds him or her at a distance from me, leaving me master in my own space; it extends before me its anxiety and pain" (Lingis, *Foreign* 177). Phenomenology performs this destabilization of body image, creating a site for rhetorical invention.

Merleau-Ponty's concept of "the flesh" disrupts the coherence produced by disciplinary apparatuses of power and thus creates a site of possibility (*Visible* 133). The flesh, to begin, is reversible. Merleau-Ponty, in this way, conceives of the flesh as a "means of communication" between the seer and the thing (*Visible* 135) *and* a "formative medium" for the seer and the thing (147), rather than the conventional Cartesian "bifurcation" of the seer and the thing (141). Richard Cohen explains, "Subject and object [seer and thing] are not two opposed domains to be somehow united, they are both aspects of the same flesh: the flesh seeing itself, turned upon itself, overlapping itself, folded upon itself, reversible" ("Merleau-Ponty" 331). The visual perception of corporeal images takes place in a space in which neither transcendent subject nor empirical object are granted privilege. Rather, who is seeing [subject] and what is seen [object] are historically situated relations that are open to interrogation; neither can be taken as predetermined in the rhetorical process. Such a predetermination would constitute the seer and the thing as coherent or realized. Merleau-Ponty holds instead that the flesh is "always imminent and never fully realized" (*Visible* 147). Because the flesh is reversible, it also involves "transitivity" or "influential cross exchanges" (Cohen 332), which do not flow unilaterally from the Cartesian rhetorical agent. The act of perception, instead, creates opportunities for mutual influence between the seer and the seen, what Merleau-Ponty calls "a style of being" (139) or what Foucault has called the "aesthetics of existence" (*Politics* 47–53). These rhetorical exchanges take place on a "horizon" of thought (*Visible* 148, 153–54), a landscape that is constantly changing and altering the relationships between seer and thing, between subject and object. In the same moment, on the same horizon, it is possible to create a new "style" of response, and thereby, alter the perception. The flesh, therefore, is a constitutive site, a rhetorical exchange between "identity and difference" (Merleau-Ponty, *Visible* 142), or "an ongoing process of coherence and deformation" (R. Cohen, "Merleau-Ponty" 334).

Merleau-Ponty's concept of "intersubjectivity" or the "situated self," derived from his concept of the flesh, illuminates [some might say corrects] Foucault's theory of subjectivity. Rudi Visker clarifies: "To be sure, what is at stake here is not the attempt to reduce discourse to existence, or existence to discourse, but to find in their mutual intrication some indication of what it could mean for us to be those subjects who take up positions we did not ourselves generate" ("Raw Being" 126). The site of "mutual intrication," the site of intersubjectivity, might first appear contradictory within a Foucauldian genealogy. Such a contradiction, however, relies upon a misreading of Foucault on subjectivity as well as a failure to recognize Foucault's presupposition of an "intersubjective" subject. Although the subject is brought into existence by discourse, s/he does not lose all recourse to agency. Rather than eliminating the humanist subject, Foucault merely "brackets" this dimension of contemporary subjectivity in order to follow other questions of power (Butler, *Bodies* 8–9; Crossley 155, 159–60, 165). By appropriating Judith Butler's work on performative speech acts and its relation to processes of subjection, I have already extended the idea that agency is simultaneously limited and enabled. The discursive formation of the subject is not a deterministic operation (Visker, "Raw Being" 111–15), but rather a contingent and rhetorical one.

Furthermore, Foucault presupposes a subject that is compatible with Merleau-Ponty's thematization of intersubjectivity, in which human agency and corporeal coherence are conditional rather than absolute. Merleau-Ponty's concept of a tacit *cogito* refers to "myself experienced by myself . . . But this subjectivity, indeclinable, has upon itself and upon the world *only a precarious hold*" (*Phenomenology* 403–4). In other words, the agency presumed by the Cartesian *cogito* is, in reality, contingent and unstable. It is only when we take the leap of faith to an absolute agency that we can act *as if* our agency is not precarious, but guaranteed. Likewise, the "virtual body," rather than being fully coherent, is "a system of possible actions" that is "defined by its task and situation" (*Phenomenology* 250). These two phenomenological concepts are ultimately linked to the processes of perception, the visual interaction with an other. Crossley explains: "[S]ubjects belong to each other by belonging to a common visible world . . . perceiving subjects open onto each other and are thereby engaged with each other. To see the other . . . is not to have her as an object of thought or contemplation, although this is possible . . . It is to be involved or engaged with her in a non-objectifying [non-empirical], non-intellectualising [non-transcendental] manner" (27). This intersubjectivity is thus "mediated" (Merleau-Ponty, *Phenomenology* 203), or constituted though processes of negotiation. In other words, the intersubjective world is a space created *between* self and other; it is a site of rhetorical invention. The rhetorical character of intersubjectivity is further suggested by its radical contingency (Crossley 46).

In contrast to objective biology, physiology, and psychology, phenomenology "describes a body in the first person" (Lingis, *Foreign* 47).[10] Alphonso Lingis conceptualizes this body through the figure of Yukio Mishima: "[The self] displaced its locus onto the surfaces. He does not feel the ridges and reliefs of his musculature from within, out of his visceral ego, but contemplates them on the surfaces of mirrors and feels them in the cool breeze on their glistening sweat. The self had become a surface self, a self no longer in inwardness but in distension, exposure, and exhibition" (*Foreign* 84). The male body's identity becomes exposed to elements of otherness. Its [transcendent or empirical] interior is no longer sacred, no longer an origin. Otherness becomes a visual, perceptual experience; it is the extension of an imaged body toward an other. The body is seen and felt, in a mirror and on a breeze. Its muscles and contours glisten outward. The surface of the body, its corporeal and imaged borders, does not protect itself, but rather invites the influences of an other. It "receives into itself the forms and forces of an other" (*Foreign* 86).

The phenomenological gaze equally disrupts the subjective and corporeal borders of the viewer, creating yet another indeterminate space: "The eyes and the hands and the voice of another appeal imperatively; their movements facing me can address an appeal to me because they summon me, putting me in question. The eyes of the other slide across my paths and axes of organization; they are not simply ignorant of them, they disturb this order, question it, put demands on it" (Lingis, *Foreign*

172). The imaged or perceived body, as an exhibition or an extension into perceptual space, becomes a rhetorical site. The body acquires its rhetorical character, not through its confirmed subjective borders and presumed agency, but, rather, it appeals *in being perceived* by an other. The rhetorical capacity of the body requires the senses of an other. It demands perception. It is fundamentally constituted by the other, for his eyes, hands, and voice "summon" or invite that other body—me. An invitation functions to "question" my own subjective and corporeal boundaries. The invitation is neither a text nor a language, but, rather, a perception of an imaged other. The image "slides across" or transgresses the borders that "organize" my body. It is a spectacle that alters me as a subject and as a body.

Perceiving an imaged body is potentially erotic, rather than merely disciplinary. Homoerotic gazes thus disrupt the subject/object binary, necessary condition of heteronormative relations of power. "Subject" and "object" no longer make sense in an erotic gaze. New possibilities, different perceptual experiences of the gay male body are now available. The muscular gay male body is disindividuated through an act of exhibition, opening the body to the gaze of others, and a movement toward light. Responding to this image of muscular contours within the discursive regime of sexuality, which might be thought to constitute or inscribe the identity of a gay male body, is fundamentally heteronormative, for it reduces corporeal musculature to a sign or code for sexual object choice. The coherence of this code is simultaneously authenticated in its very articulation. Although such discursive practices confer secrecy upon the surface of the body, these borders or muscular contours might also become sites for transgression. Rather than revealing the secrets of the subject, erotic gazing interacts with the "mysterious." Merleau-Ponty makes the claim: "We may say, if we wish, that [the world and reason] are mysterious, but their mystery is what defines them: there can be no question of dispelling it by some 'solution,' it is on the hither side of all solutions" (*Phenomenology* xx). The mysteriousness of the world is felt in the act of perception: "As I contemplate the blue of the sky I am not *set over against* it as an acosmic subject; I do not possess it in thought, or spread out towards it some idea of blue such as might reveal the secret of it, I abandon myself to it an plunge into this mystery . . . my consciousness is saturated with this limitless blue" (Merleau-Ponty 214). This mysterious quality pervades both perception and subjectivity; it is the site of resistance that resides in the space between the gaze and the spectacle.

Advertisement for "The Number" appearing in *David Atlanta*.
Reprinted with permission of "The Number."

Experiencing the Erotic

Shadows invade the contours of his body inch by inch, transforming all
that is hard into supple curvature. His body does not disappear into the
darkness, thwarting the desire of my gaze. We are not plunged into the
night, forced to rely on other sensory perceptions to meet one another.
Shadows now direct my gaze, guide its desire across his imaged body.
His imaged body is no longer contained within itself, a surface protect-
ing him. A firm outline becomes a sketch, a suggestion, a hint. The force
of the body becomes an appeal.

Shadows cast his eyes inward, eyes that might otherwise assert power
as they gaze out toward me. A reflection of light against his mouth creates an opening, a passageway inside. I am summoned. I become no-
madic. The passageway is not a habitat of secrets, waiting to be let out,
to see the light of day. Secrets protect and are protected. They conceal
and are concealed. Secrets are a fortress. The passageway, rather, becomes
a home for my gaze. It invites me to stay for a while, to become his body.
I am drawn toward his shoulder, which is eclipsed by his forearms rest-
ing lightly atop a wooden rod. Following his collarbone along its ridges
until I am swallowed up, I return to his body again and again, losing

myself within its contours. As a shine glistens across the hardness of his torso, the sharp edges fade into the musculature of his bicep and under the curvature of his pectoral. I am swept up in a sensation of pleasure as my gaze creeps along the shadows of his body. I arc and lower myself into the coloration of his nipple—tracing the outer, darker lines that encompass this flesh, sliding into a field of gray, reaching the whiteness as it pierces out of his body. I continue to follow my gaze.

Light splashes and spills, creating small ridges on the surface of his stomach. I dip myself into these spaces and explore their softness, wriggling between the tautness of his abdominal muscles. I pause for a moment atop his oblique, a mound of membranes and fibers extending outward, inviting me to rest. A beacon of light insists that I return to the exposure of his body; my time is both limited and infinite. The forces of gravity and desire pull my gaze swiftly downward and I fall into the cavernous recesses of his navel. Its roundness abates the sense of my own body and erases all perception of boundaries. I am both lost and found, astray and at home. I am neither held captive nor am I an agent explorer. My gaze seeks out the contours of another, and the contours etch multiple paths along the musculature of his body. Light beckons me once again. I climb out and rest upon the firm borders of his abdomen, exhausted by my own desire. I continue to follow my gaze.

Downward, gliding, the smooth, pale skin provides no resistance to the sweeping movement of my eyes. They coast over the flatness until they perceive a tuft of hair, its soft bristles boldly asserting their presence. I locate grooves that arch downward toward a quiet radiance. Reflections of light on both sides constitute this path. I travel through the shadows of a canal, its liquids evaporated for now, allowing my passage. I disappear as I gaze into the night. Darkness envelops my gaze, gradually, but surely. The terrain of his body, its borders, does not evaporate into thin air. His body remains. Only now, it becomes a space of experimentation. I continue to follow my gaze, endlessly.

Facing the musculature of his back, shoulders, and arms, which are framed by thin slivers of light and the stitching of his T-shirt, I am confronted by a body that craves violation. My gaze attends to the erotic imperative of his body, extending itself in my direction. His arms become strands of muscle and fiber, pulling themselves taught and extending outward, twisting as if they are the intertwining braids of a rope. The T-shirt ripples down the tapering edges of his back, creasing and folding upon itself as it responds to the contours of his body. The excess material rests on top of his buttocks, their symmetry accented by light

Photographic image from Hans
Fahrmeyer's *Between Men*.
Reprinted with permission of
Hans Fahrmeyer

reflecting off of their surface. Shadows collect along the slopes of muscle
and between his legs. My violation of his body does not occur here,
responding to an invitation lurking in the mysteriousness of his orifice,
for it has already occurred. My erotic gaze violates the certainty of his
extended arms, his tapering back, his protruding buttocks. His body desires this violation, demands it.

His eyes pierce me; they seek me out and pull me near. I become an
erotic body as I enter into the view of an other. His gaze constitutes my
perceptible being, for it responds to the contours of my own body. I am
violated, and within this violation, because of it, I violate. The violations
of my gaze, of his gaze, do not engender subjects and objects. We do not
play those games; we deny the viability of those rules. Our bodies become imperative to each other, for they seek out, appeal to, and demand
an erotic response. We coalesce.

Richard Dyer is not fundamentally mistaken when he concludes: "a
hard, contoured body does not look like it runs the risk of being merged
into other bodies" (152). Susan Bordo is not necessarily off the mark
when she asserts, "[men] tend to present their bodies aggressively and so
rarely seem truly exposed" (30). We must, however, respond to these im-

Advertisement for "ManHunt.net," appearing in *David Atlanta*, an Atlanta-based gay magazine. Reprinted with permission of Online Buddies, Inc.

ages differently. We must do away with a discourse of semblance, codes, and translation. We must respond directly to the imperatives, the mysteries of the hypermasculine body, rather than to what it "looks like" and how it "seems." Let us insist that the contours of the male body always "run the risk." Let us contend that the flesh of the male body, open to the light and gaze of an other, is "truly exposed." Bataille beautifully depicts the radical force these fleeting, erotic moments: "We are faced with the paradox of an object which implies the abolition of the limits of all objects, of an *erotic object*" (130). Let us echo the words of D. A. Miller (1992), who responds differently to the hypermasculine musculature of the gay male body: "[The hypermasculine body] displays its muscle primarily in terms of an *image* openly appealing to, and deliberately courting the possibility of being shivered by, someone else's desire. Even the most macho gay image tends to modify cultural fantasy about the male body if only by suspending the main response that the armored body seems developed to induce: if this is still *the body that can fuck you, etc.,* it is no longer—quite the contrary—*the body you don't fuck with*" (*Bringing Out* 31). The wholeness and coherence of his body is shattered at the instant my gaze invades his contours, when light meets the armor of his arms, shoulders, chest, stomach, and legs. His body reasserts its identity in the moment that he fucks me with his eyes. Our bodies are no longer individuals. They are possibilities and capacities that extend into the future. Hypermasculinity appeals to, courts, and craves the erotic desire of my gaze. The firmness of his gaze, the sturdiness of his posture, the hardness of his musculature, and the smooth surface of his skin constitute a hypermasculine imperative that both engenders and contests the identities of our bodies.

The circulation of hypermasculine body images in urban America opens up these spaces of transgression. Social-cultural meanings, the relations of heteronormative power and the moments of resistance towards which they gesture, are never predetermined, never guaranteed. Phenomenological gazing does not thrust us, **he** and **I,** outside of historical time and place. We become, through the responsive act of gazing, the very site of cultural-political mediation.

Toward an Ethical Account of Identity

Essentialist and ethnic accounts of gay "identity" often eclipse the fundamental difference between self and other that we experience through the erotic in its most basic form. The rhetorical secret, as a form of knowledge-power, enacts its performative contradictions within gay male communities as well as in more mainstream public discourse. Hypermasculine images, a key instance of homoeroticism in both mainstream society and gay subcultures, operate as a public code for private homosexuality, circulating homoeroticism in public spaces. Both mainstream and gay viewers, however, inscribe heteronormative knowledge upon hypermasculine bodies, thus disciplining gay erotic culture in specific ways. Mastering heteronormative understandings of sexual identity ultimately enslaves us to their logic. Yet, as examining the rhetorical secret has taught us, knowledge always requires forgetting. Reducing sexual identity to notions of private personhood, we forget that gay male identity is primarily forged in public through a sense of collectivity. Reducing the nature of sexual collectivity to political organizing for the purpose of claiming rights and social privileges, we forget the heteronormativity that often accompanies such political gains.

In the genealogical project, an analytics of descent enables the rhetorician to uncover the struggles and contradictions that ground social and cultural forms of identity. Mapping the historical emergence of identity, the rhetorician witnesses the particular staging of forces that produce social knowledge and enact corporeal effects of power. Genealogy's third objective—critique—raises questions about possibility, futurity and social change. Regarding the "specific intellectual," Foucault writes, "The intellectual no longer has to play the role of an advisor. The project, tactics and goals to be adopted are a matter for those who do the fighting. What the intellectual can do is to provide instruments for analysis, and at present this is the historian's essential role" (*Power* 62). Genealogy, then, is a "history of thought" where "thought" constitutes a social response to historically situated, material problems (During; Rajchman). If genealogical critique represents the convergence of history and politics, knowledge and power, then how might such a critique mobilize new "thought," new responses to our contemporary problems? How does the genealogist–rhetorician avoid charges of "relativist," "determinist" and "transcendentalist" as s/he performs the critical functions of inquiry?[11] Philosophers and historians gesture toward Foucault's ethics as a potential answer (McNay; Schwartz). Mapping the shift from genealogy to ethics, Thomas McCarthy witnesses Foucault's incorporation of "strategic" power into his line of thought: "Both the ethical subject and the strategic subject are now represented as acting intentionally and voluntarily—within, to be sure, cultural and institutional systems that organize their ways of doing things . . . This model now enables us to make sense of the possibilities of resistance and revolt which, Foucault always insisted, are inherent in systems of power" (459). William Connolly, in his response to Foucault's ethics, asks, "But how can this combination of genealogical disturbance and noble sensibility ever establish itself securely in a self or a culture at any particular time?" (377). He replies, "It cannot" (378). We might best conceive of such resistances, Connolly suggests, as "at best always coming to be" (378). Genealogical critique leads us to questions about ethics, the ethics of gay male culture specifically.

The desires to be private and to be normal erase crucial ethical questions that impact sexual collectivity. Still living within the cultural landscape of the HIV/AIDS crisis, we must recognize that sexual identity and collectivity are anything but private and normal. The ethics of monogamy, espoused in the name of safety, enables us to forget that eroticism and sexuality are, at their core, public and queer. We must remember that erotic desire and communal desire are woven together in the fabric of gay culture and that they demand an ethical account of identity. Recuperating the eroticism of gay male urban culture, we must reconsider our relations between self and other by exposing the fundamental differences that form our notions of identity and collectivity.

5

Coming Out as Contagious Discourse

> If interpretation were the slow exposure of the meaning hidden in
> an origin, then only metaphysics could interpret the development
> of humanity. But if interpretation is the violent or surreptitious
> appropriation of a system of rules, which in itself has no essential
> meaning, in order to impose a direction, to bend it to a new will,
> to force its participation in a different game, and to subject it to
> secondary rules, then the development of humanity is a series of
> interpretations. The role of genealogy is to record its history.
>
> —Michel Foucault

Urvashi Vaid, the former executive director of the National Gay and
Lesbian Task Force, claims, "[A]ll the gains we've made derive from the
fact that more of us live out of the closet today" ("After Identity" 28).
These words betray the significance of secrets, their rhetorical force,
their capacity to oppress, and their capacity to liberate. In this final
chapter, I turn to the rhetorical secret in its most prevalent social and
political form—coming out of the closet—to identify the true conditions of speaking about homosexuality in American society: its public
character, its inventiveness, and its normative enslavement to discourse.
Yet the rhetorical secret continually undermines these conditions of
speaking, rendering coming out as merely disclosing one's private sexual
identity, simply countering societal ignorance, demonstrating one's mastery over social discourse. We have witnessed the normative consequences of this thinking as it directs the contemporary public discourse
on gay male identity. Coming out, as the rhetorical secret's most proud
accomplishment in American society, thus provides the most obvious
site in which to rework these performative, ideographic usages of "secrecy" and "identity." Coming out is arguably the most significant rhetorical practice for queer politics due to gay visibility's powerful social
influences in contemporary American culture. But what rhetorical presumptions and philosophical conditions mobilize, proliferate, and even
require this strategy for liberation? Are these foundations sufficient to the
task of fully theorizing coming out's rhetorical force? I contend that
they are not.

Coming Out as Identification

What's Wrong with Visibility Politics?

Under the visibility politics model, coming out requires a rhetorical abstraction, thereby divorcing the rhetorical secret from its concrete, material situations. Briefly surveying contemporary LGBT activism will illustrate how visibility politics enacts the rhetorical secret and its performative contradictions in its very formulations of identity and power.

Visibility politics' first premise holds that the closet, passing, or secrecy is primarily responsible for the oppression of gay men and lesbians. Michelangelo Signorile's opening words in *Queer in America* evidence how pervasive the public repression of private homosexuality is thought to be: "By promoting a system that rewards the closeted with money, power, prestige, and fame—and that shuts out and destroys the uncloseted—heterosexuals in power [the press, the government, and the entertainment industry] unconsciously make closeted gays act as role models for all other gays. The message coming from the top down is *If you want to make it, kid, just stay locked in the closet*" (xvii). Visibility politics thus reduces the disclosure of sexual identity to a simple exchange of private information, effectively erasing its social conditions.

Sexuality's disclosure thus performs the private in public.

Knowledge and power, in this political model, become negative forces rather than productive ones, for this model causally links lacking knowledge to a lack of social power.

Sexuality's secrecy thus invents heteronormative claims of ignorance.

Responsibility for the repression of homosexuality extends to gay and lesbian persons as well. Victoria Brownworth, for example, has argued, "[E]very gay man and lesbian who 'passes' oppresses me further and reaps the benefits of my activism while hiding" (48–49). The second premise behind visibility politics compliments the first: while secrecy is equated with power, the simple disclosure of lesbian or gay identity becomes synonymous with liberation. Visibility, pure and simple, is cast as unfettered resistance to homophobia. Positing mere visibility as unqualified subversion has also produced the practice of "outing," the ethical implications of which are neither clear nor unanimous within LGBT political circles (see, for instance, Gross, *Contested;* Mohr, *Gay Ideas;* Signorile, *Queer*). Urvashi Vaid confesses her own ambivalence toward the practice: "I cannot ethically rationalize the coercive aspect of outing . . . On the other hand, I share the urgency felt by proponents of outing about the need for a new gay community ethic about the closet" (*Virtual*

32). When coming out (at all costs) serves as the key to overcoming heteronormative power, social liberation derives from learning and mastering the public vocabulary of visibility, the discourse of identity and secrecy.

Sexuality's enslavement to discourse is thus mistaken for mastery over that discourse.

The abstractions inherent to today's visibility politics enable non-heterosexual citizens to remain blind to the rhetorical secret's normative implications. Bernstein and Reimann have recently observed, "LGBT people often embrace white, middle-class, straight, suburban American norms in the ongoing quest for acceptance" (5). The ultimate paradox of this normalization, Bernstein and Reimann note, is requiring every queer person to come out while ignoring the immense difficulties faced by queers of color and/or those from lower- to middle-class backgrounds. Public knowledge of homosexuality effectively erases social differences such as race, class and gender.

Sexuality's knowledge thus requires forgetting.

Considering coming out's disparate and conflicting derivatives, I contest this oversimplification of the cultural politics facing queer individuals and communities today. Reducing cultural politics to visibility casts coming out as a mode of identification achieved by exchanging information about one's private identity. Coming out, I contend, is more than the mere exchange of information. At its core, coming out is a social act, a complex and nuanced rhetorical practice—a matter of invention.

Coming Out / Coming In

Although today we frequently understand coming out as a means of creating identification between non-heterosexual and heterosexual citizens, its social practice has historically constituted community forms among non-heterosexual citizens. Between World War II and the 1969 Stonewall riots, self-identifying as "gay" or "lesbian" meant forging group consciousness and organizing for political change. The Mattachine Society, for example, "focused on mobilizing a large gay constituency and welding it into a cohesive force capable of militancy" (D'Emilio 63). Rather than simply addressing heterosexual audiences, coming out was first a rhetorical act directed at other non-heterosexual citizens.

Coming out's dual function, its ability to rhetorically address gay and straight audiences, first emerged through gay liberation activism during the post-Stonewall epoch. "Gay liberation philosophy," Annamarie

Jagose explains, "was committed to a radical and extensive transformation of social structures and values" (40). To this end, gay liberation simultaneously deployed "identity" as a rhetorical resource and employed coming out as a rhetorical practice. Donn Teal's *The Gay Militants,* for instance, documents the political and cultural strategies of the Gay Liberation Front between 1969 and 1971. Despite conflicts over political organizing, between those committed primarily to the New Left and those who were solely pursuing homosexual liberation, GLF members shared one common ground: "They had shed, or were shedding, all vestiges of homosexual shame, wanted to live in the light. They were ready for a confrontation with anybody who might challenge or even delay their right to do so" (Teal 35). Coming out, as a rhetorical practice, both avowed a "public" homosexuality in one's political strategizing and connoted being an "open" homosexual in one's personal life (36).

Through books, leaflets, gay newspapers, and consciousness-raising groups, the concept of "Gay Pride" emerged. Franklin Kameny, a prominent homophile leader, wrote: " . . . it is time to open the closet door and let in the fresh air and the sunshine; it is time to hold up your heads and look the world squarely in the eye as the homosexual that you are" (qtd. in Teal 62). Likewise, Craig Schoonmaker prompted in the *Homosexual Renaissance,* "Homosexuals can effectively demand respect from others only if we first respect ourselves—*as* homosexuals. That requires that we admit to ourselves that we are homosexual; that we affirm it, understand it, *realize* it in all its implications: I am homosexual. Say it! aloud: 'I am homosexual'" (qtd. in Teal 63). Coming out, in this sense, involved a self-awareness of one's identity more than it implied the public disclosure of one's sexuality to non-homosexual others. Gay male consciousness-raising groups during this period demonstrate further the cultural and political significance of in-group identification. A consciousness-raising group pamphlet distributed in New York in 1970 illustrates this aspect of coming out:

> We as men are struggling with our eagerness to dominate and ego-trip by being aware of the needs of others in the group, and struggling with our tendency to intellectualize by speaking from our experience. We are also learning what has been forbidden us—to relate to one another with respect and love. [Consciousness-raising] provides a format in which this potential can develop and operate. We use it to discover our identity as gay men, to recognize our oppression in a straight society, and to seek a collective solution to mutual problems. (qtd. in Teal 145)

Forming one's sexual identity through consciousness-raising emerged as in-group communication and thus represented a collective consciousness rather than merely an individual mode of being and acting in the world. Coming out in this fashion served crucial psychological and social functions, especially when one considers the historical and cultural context in which it took place, for as one gay male consciousness-raising group notes: "We have been defined by the churches, by psychiatrists, by sociologists and, generally, by our sector in society which is not homosexual. Through the process of consciousness-raising, we have begun to define *ourselves*" (qtd. in Jay and Young 296).

Coming out's distinctive rhetorical role in gay liberation, its formation of group consciousness and collective experience, was strongly influenced by the movement's objectives. Gay liberation, Urvashi Vaid reminds us, emphasized "living gay and lesbian lives" rather than changes in public policy (*Virtual* 63).[1] Gay liberation, put otherwise, promoted a cultural revolution rather than merely political reformation. In this paradigm for social change, coming out and gay culture are inextricably linked as they share the need for in-group identification. Laud Humphrey's *Out of the Closets,* published in 1972, explains the importance of in-group identification for gay persons: "Next to passing . . . involvement in the gay subculture is the second most common means for homosexuals to ease the burden of censure to which they are subjected. There they find the facilities and training needed for making sexual liaisons, support from those who experience the same discrimination, and a system of norms and values that help provide meaning and justification for stigmatized behavior patterns" (140). John Knoebel, in one of the most widely read books of the time, testifies, "As I continued to go to GLF meetings and meet gay people, I listened to what they said and saw a viable way to live as a gay person. I accepted my new identity. I had come out in the movement" (302). Knoebel's words, embodying the voice of gay liberation, locate the rhetorical practice of coming out within gay collective spaces. Coming out thus addressed gay audiences in an act of identification.

Gay identity and coming out were symbolically associated with and materially performed in gay-identified public spaces—the gay bar scene and what became known as the "gay ghetto." Gay bars, while providing the most viable option for meeting other gay people in the early 1970s, were equally a site of oppression. Materially speaking, police raids of gay establishments were common in large urban settings (D'Emilio; Teal). Symbolically speaking, gay bars were perceived as an oppressive industry, representing the power of heterosexual society. One article in a gay periodical articulated, "GLF must demand the complete negation of the use of gay bars, tea rooms, trucks, baths, streets, and other traditional cruising institutions. These are exploitative institutions designed to keep gay men in the roles given to them by a male heterosexual system" (qtd. in Teal 40). Likewise, the "gay ghettos" simultaneously represented freedom from straight oppression and its enactment (Teal 39). Were "gay ghettos" an invention of safe spaces for non-heterosexual citizens? Or were they merely another type of closet for homosexuals to inhabit? These controversies within the GLF movement do not betray an inherent contradiction between the radical reinvention of social norms and assimilation into straight culture, for the GLF remained committed to the former. Instead, these debates within the gay community demonstrate a distrust of straight culture and its establishments. Gay liberation was simply questioning its method of cultural articulation and communal practice. Craig Schoonmaker, in an article championing gay separatism or gay nationalism, illustrates the commitment to gay culture: "[W]e must become the majority. I don't mean that we should wage an aggressive campaign to convert people to homosexuality . . . but rather, that we should designate certain geographical areas for demographic takeover by homosexuals" (qtd. in Teal 291). Schoonmaker's initial justification is political—to create a voting constituency. Later in the essay, however, his rationale for gay separatism turns cultural: "Exclusive homosexuality is *not* sick. Nor is it sick to want to live in a gay neighborhood, work with gay people, socialize with gay people—even with gay people of the same sex. Heterosexuals do not think it is a sickness to live, work, and socialize with only (presumed) heterosexuals—they think the whole world IS heterosexual, and they're very happy that's the case" (292). Based on these historical documents, as instances of public discourse on homosexuality and identity, we must understand coming out as a cultural articulation of in-group consciousness and a material practice of community building. Coming out is thus a rhetorical practice that produces various forms of identification. Yet coming out also performs relations of desire.

Coming Out as Desire

Contagion and Homosexuality in Public Discourse

The debate surrounding gays in the military further demonstrates the political and rhetorical force of "coming out" and "outing," especially its capacity to produce paranoid reactions within a heteronormative society (Butler, *Excitable;* Diane Miller, *Freedom*). The closet's phobic, paranoid structure is most acute in the military context, Sedgwick argues, for "men's manipulability and their potential for violence are at the highest possible premium, the *pre*scription of the most intimate male bonding and the *pro*scription of (the remarkably cognate) 'homosexuality' are both stronger than in civilian society" (*Epistemology* 186). Within such intense male homosocial bonds, this paranoid way of knowing derives from pronounced "slippages between identification and desire" (159). Although anti-gay violence is by no means confined to the military, the military context best illuminates the correlation between paranoid epistemologies of male homosocial desire and antigay violence, evidenced by the highly publicized murder of Private Barry Winchell, for instance. On July 5, 1999, in the barracks at Fort Campbell, twenty-one year old Winchell was beaten to death in his sleep with a baseball bat by Pvt. Calvin Glover (Hackett). Although divergent explanations for Glover's actions abound, few dispute the role played by Winchell's sexual identity and the events leading up to his murder. Fellow soldiers and Sergeant Kleifgen concur that Winchell was harassed daily for three months preceding his death by members of his platoon. The harassment (which included calling Winchell a "faggot") began shortly after Justin Fisher (Winchell's roommate) outed him, disclosing Winchell's relationship with a drag queen from Nashville. On July 3, just two days before the murder, Glover was publicly humiliated by losing a fight to Winchell during a platoon party. Glover's disgrace was, of course, doubled by the fact that a "faggot" had beaten him in the fight. Glover's defense of his masculinity and heterosexuality amplifies the paranoid and phobic character of his attack. Rather than constituting a mode of identification (like gay consciousness-raising), coming out (or being outed, in this case) operated within a paranoid scheme, for Winchell's public sexuality threatened to expose the desire lurking within male-male social bonds.

In critically examining debates surrounding gays in the military, Judith Butler specifies the ways in which explicit self-declarations of homosexuality ("I am a homosexual") within the context of the U.S. military are conceived as contagious discourse, a notion that becomes part of the rationale behind President Clinton's "Don't ask, don't tell" policy. Specifically, Butler traces the path this self-declaratory statement takes such that speech [sexual identity] becomes sexual conduct, "doing precisely that which it says" (*Excitable* 107). Such logic, Butler acutely observes, does not produce censorship writ large, but, rather, it determines the conditions of speaking on homosexuality (104–5). These conditions of speaking are worth elaborating as they also influence the discourse on homosexuality outside of the military context.

Butler's critique of the military debates distinguishes two conceptualizations of coming out: that belonging to the military and that grounded in lesbian and gay activism. The military concept presents coming out as sexual conduct through three propositions: 1) coming out is not a report, but a "happening"; 2) coming out creates a relationship through which the audience is "implicated in the 'homosexuality'" that is uttered; and 3) the name constituting coming out functions as "contagion" by transmitting "homosexuality" to the audience (*Excitable* 113–15). This conceptualization of coming out regulates discourse, Butler explicates, through a "paranoid and pathological reduction" of discursive sexual identities to sexual acts (a reduction common to modern discourses on sexuality). She then contrasts the military version of coming out to that of LGBT politics: "The declaration that is 'coming out' is certainly a kind of act, but it does not fully constitute the referent to which it refers" (125). In other words, the paranoid reading of coming out erroneously equates a declaration of sexual identity with actual sexual conduct.

Butler argues that we need to avoid (at all costs) closing the gap between discourse and desire, exhausting the meaning of homosexuality, or having the "last word" on homosexual identity, for doing so disallows future "democratic rearticulations" of homosexual identity. In order to prevent these foreclosures, Butler recommends that "one of the tasks of a critical production of alternative homosexualities will be *to disjoin* homosexuality from the figures by which it is conveyed in dominant discourse, especially when they take the form of either assault or disease" (my italics, *Excitable* 125). Rather than detaching from heteronormative discourse in order to resist its rhetorical appeals, I contend, we must engage such figures in order to disrupt their heteronormative rhetorical functions and rearticulate their modes of thought. In other words, we might conceptualize coming out as contagion, not in the homophobic manner of the military policy on homosexual self-declaration, but as a means of rearticulating and altering homophobic-heteronormative discourse.

If, for Butler, the happening or event-ness of coming out and the ways in which others are "implicated in" homosexuality via coming out constitute "pathological reductions," we might inquire into how such events and implications also enable us to "[enter] into [their] chain of

Table 2 Coming Out: Production and Reception

	PRODUCTION: Heterosexual society	PRODUCTION: Homosexual subculture
RECEPTION: Identification	Visibility politics: Coming out assimilates homosexuality into heterosexual society	Consciousness raising: Coming out (speech) constitutes collective political identity
RECEPTION: Desire	Paranoid: Coming out produces violent prohibitions on homosexuality	Contagion: Coming out (bodily action) constitutes collective forms of identity

performativity" (*Excitable* 122), a task Butler embraces earlier and elsewhere, but then appears to abandon. In the end, coming out is fully reduced to speech, an expression of identification, thus prohibited from taking corporeal form, a bodily expression of desire.

Coming out's rhetorical force, its multiple and sometimes contradictory identifications, depends upon differing modes of production and reception (see Table 2 above). As indicated above, coming out simultaneously operates as homosexual assimilation into "straight" society and as the articulation of a unique subculture or community; coming out produces paranoid reactions within straight society and (as I suggest below) constitutes forms of gay male collectivity founded on erotic desire. To develop further an ethical vision of gay male identity, I focus attention on coming out's rhetorical dimensions in gay male autobiography and its reception by gay male readers.[2] Specifically, making male homosexual identity public through coming out narratives engenders corporeal experiences of desire.

Deleuze and Guattari's ethical discourse on becoming encourages us to incorporate coming out's corporeal dimension into our analysis of its rhetorical force. This shift from textual meanings to corporeal experience invites us to enter heteronormative discourse as contagious agents. In what ways might coming out create relations rather than reductions? Deleuze and Guattari, articulating a theory of becoming, conceptualize the subject as a potential site of contagion or alliance with the other rather than as a site of imitation or identification. Conceptualizing coming out as becoming produces a different kind of subjectivity than those constituted by both the military and conventional gay and lesbian politics. Coming out, as a rhetorical practice, is more than merely the disclosure of sexual identity, a question of identification. Coming out, I contend, is equally a corporeal experience, a matter of desire. Taking Deleuze and Guattari's formulation of becoming as grounds for rhetorical theory and critical practice, I suggest new ethical responses to the modern regime of sexuality and its contemporary existence.

Modernity, Sexuality, and the Rhetorical Secret

The modern emergence of sexuality, a sexuality that remains today, is inextricably caught up with notions of secrecy and disclosure. The rhetorical secret, as I have shown, presumes that sexual identity is a private phenomenon that can be known through simple acts of disclosure in order to claim social agency, and these presumptions form the discursive conditions necessary for speaking about sexuality and identity in contemporary society. These abstractions first emerged within the modern articulation of homosexuality. In different ways, Foucault's *History of Sexuality* and Deleuze and Guattari's *Anti-Oedipus* demonstrate how modern sexuality's discursive grounds emerged alongside capitalist modes of production, and how these conditions for speaking were instantly operations of establishing and maintaining social power. These different yet compatible histories of sexuality also suggest alternative conditions for speaking, possibilities for resisting the modern regime of sexuality.

Sexuality's power, its rhetorical prowess, lies in its ability to create desire as private property, as the domain of the individual subject. Foucault locates sexuality's privatization in the confession, a primary tool in modern psychiatric practice: "[I]t is in the confession that truth and sex are joined, through the obligatory and exhaustive expression of an individual secret . . . The confession is a ritual of discourse in which the speaking subject is also the subject of the statement; it is also a ritual that unfolds within a power relationship, for one does not confess without the presence (or virtual presence) of a partner who is not simply the interlocutor but the authority who requires the confession" (*History* 61). The rhetorical secret's performative contradictions are present in Foucault's account, for the confession or disclosure of one's sexuality claims to be expressive of private desire and constitutive of one's subjectivity. Yet, Foucault also evidences sexuality's inherent publicity, inventiveness and enslavement, the true conditions of speaking as a sexual subject. Deleuze and Guattari, in their materialist psychiatry, argue similarly: "[Freud's] greatness lies in having determined the essence or nature of desire, no longer in relation to objects, aims, or even sources (territories), but as an abstract subjective essence—libido or sexuality. But he still relates this essence to the family as the last territoriality of private man—whence the position of Oedipus" (*Anti-Oedipus* 270). Through Oedipal mythology, desire is ultimately displaced onto the psychic, removed from the social sphere of production in which it circulates (*Anti-Oedipus* 114). Resisting modern sexuality requires a rupture in this model of private sexuality (which operates as an apparatus of power), thereby disassociating desire and lack. Foucault writes, toward the end of *History of Sexuality:* "The rallying point for the counterattack against the deployment of sexuality ought not to be sex-desire, but bodies and pleasures" (175). Deleuze and Guattari conclude likewise: "[A]ssuredly, perversions, and even sexual emancipation, give no privilege as long as sexuality remains confined within the framework of the 'dirty little secret'" (*Anti-Oedipus* 350).

Both thinkers, in different ways, recognize the modern shift in power from operations of repression to mechanisms of production and sites of knowledge, which privatized social forces through subjection. Eugene W. Holland has recently observed that both Foucault and Deleuze and Guattari highlight the historical shift from sovereign/despotic power to disciplinary/civilized power, locating this shift in the emergence of "man"—the subject of modern discourse (85–86). Deleuze and Guattari theorize these modern forms of power in relation to the forces of capitalism while Foucault focuses on disciplinary forms of power that inhabit specific institutions (Holland). The modern individual, while common to both accounts, is characterized differently. Deleuze and Guattari's individual remains singular (nonspecific) while Foucault's is specific. Peter Hallward explains, "The singular recognizes no limits. The specific, on the other hand, exists only in the medium of relations with others, and turns ultimately on the confrontation of limits" (93). Deleuze and Guattari do not present singular power as transcendent or deterministic, but, rather, as an immanent force (Hayden 68). Hallward explicates the consequence that this distinction has for resistance: "Singularity tends toward a radical plentitude. If we cannot say that the singular abhors a vacuum, it only allows space for one only insofar as it opens an unpredictable path for another vector of its own ongoing self-differentiation. The specific, on the other hand, always *eventually* confronts the empty horizon of its extension; what is *beyond* the specific is only the void, pure and simple" (99). For Deleuze and Guattari, the outside of thought is plentitude, multiplicity, or the virtual, while, for Foucault, the outside of thought is entirely void, empty. In the end, however, this becomes a question of priority rather than one of incompatibility. Paul Patton summarizes, "The difference between Deleuze-Guattari and Foucault would then turn on the question of whether theoretical priority is accorded to power or to desire" (*Deleuze* 74). While Foucault's genealogies specify mechanisms of power, Deleuze and Guattari emphasize forces of desire, which serve both modes of stratification [normalization] and avenues of new connections, new possibilities (*Thousand* 165–66).

Distinguishing Deleuze and Guattari's treatment of the individual from Foucault's marks different conceptions of social resistance and ethical thought that emerge from such a distinction. Connecting power and production, we might conclude, does not automatically result in identical notions of resistance. Observe Foucault's statement in *History of Sexuality:* "Where there is power, there is resistance, and yet, or rather consequently, this resistance is never in a position of exteriority in relation to power" (95). In contrast, Deleuze posits: "[T]he final word on power is that *resistance comes first,* to the extent that power relations operate completely within the diagram, while resistances necessarily operate in a direct relation with the outside [the virtual, the event] from which the diagrams emerge" (*Foucault* 89–90).[3] Challenging Foucault's articulation of resistance as a mode of "counterattack" (*History* 157), Deleuze and Guattari give primacy to "lines of flight, which are not phenomena of resistance or counterattack in an assemblage, but cutting edges of creation and deterritorialization" (*Thousand* 531). "Counterattack," it appears to Deleuze and Guattari, relies too much on a sense of negation, harking back to a Hegelian dialectics, the object of Foucault's critique (Conway). Working from Nietzsche's "will to power," yet in contrast to Foucault, Deleuze maintains an explicitly normative approach to power and resistance (P. Patton 49), which enables Deleuze and Guattari to provide a mode of advocacy that appears lacking in Foucault's method (Crossley; Hallward).[4]

Deleuze's attempt to avoid a dialectic approach to social-political resistance, similar to Foucault's, involves a move to ethics. Deleuze and Guattari locate their ethical project in the philosophical task of inventing concepts, whose first principle states, "Universals explain nothing but must themselves be explained" (*Philosophy,* 7). Like Foucault, Deleuze and Guattari advocate an ethical thought that questions rather than presumes universality as the grounds of knowledge. In so doing, ethics opens up "new possibilities for affecting and being affected" (P. Patton, *Deleuze* 75). Social agency thus becomes situated historically and materially. Turning to *A Thousand Plateaus,* Paul Patton describes Deleuze and Guattari's work as an ethics of "critical freedom, where 'critical' is understood not in the sense that relates to criticism or judgment, but in the technical sense [that] relates to a crisis or turning point in some process. In these terms, a critical point is an extreme or limit case; a point at which some state or condition of things passes over into a different state or condition" (83). This ethical stance posits a social agent that differs from the liberal model in which the individual subject remains unchanged. Ian Buchanan further characterizes Deleuze and Guattari's ethics as "transcendental/empiricist," in which the fundamental question is: "how must man be composed that he can be reinvented?" (83). In Buchanan's reading, the relation of the subject to his/ her environment is the key problem. Conventional transcendentalism constitutes a subject who remains unable to be affected by the environment, while classic empiricism leaves the subject without agency. Thus, for Deleuze and Guattari, explains Buchanan, "the subject is constituted in the given but is able to transcend the given" (85). Deleuze and Guattari, in their biophysical ethics, give critical rhetoricians tools for judgment, a means of avoiding the trappings of historical determinism and historical relativism.

In this final chapter, I claim that the starting point of gay male subjectivity is not the individual, but, rather, moments of social crisis that change the conditions of subjectivity: coming out and HIV/AIDS serve as prime examples. Counter to the performative contradictions embedded in the rhetorical secret, biophysical ethics insists that social agency is at once public rather than private, a matter of invention rather than mere disclosure, and entails enslavement rather than mastery.

Immanent Secrets

Rethinking coming out as a resistive rhetorical practice demands that we conceptualize the rhetorical secret differently. Contrary to our discussion thus far, the rhetorical secret's abstract form (secrecy/disclosure) does not *inherently* result in mere information exchange. Deleuze and

Guattari, in *A Thousand Plateaus,* experiment with the secret, demonstrating its social dimensions, its capacity to become an event.

Most conventionally, the secret appears as content, as information to be exchanged in discourse: "In short, the secret, defined as a content that has hidden its form in favor of a simple container, is inseparable from two movements that can accidentally interrupt its course or betray it, but are nonetheless an essential part of it: something must ooze from the box, something will be perceived through the box or in the half-opened box" (*Thousand* 287). In this state, the secret functions as a thing, as a possession. If we conceptualize the secret as content, we focus on its movement, how it is moved, and to what effect. The movement of the secret is "essential" to and "inseparable from" its existence. Even when the secret is disclosed or "betrayed," the box itself is inconsequential, unimportant. The secret itself, *a thing,* moves and is perceived by an other, which makes the secret what it *is.* The secret may "ooze" or slip through the edges of the box; it may be "perceived through" the walls of its container; or it may peek out from an opening in the box. Regardless, these movements constitute the secret as content, as a specific and discrete thing. The secret, as a result of becoming a secret, acquires an identity. The movement of the secret does not change or alter its identity. On the contrary, the movement of the secret stabilizes its identity. The secret remains the same regardless of where it is or how it got there. *It is a thing.*

The second state of the secret is a threshold. It shares qualities with the secret-as-content and the secret-as-immanence (its third state), drawing each concept of the secret toward the other. "The secret, as secret, must now acquire its own form. The secret is elevated from a finite content to the infinite form of secrecy" (Deleuze and Guattari, *Thousand* 288). The form of the secret, its transition from inside to outside, from secrecy to disclosure, becomes a means of altering the secret itself. The secret becomes immanent through its "infinite" or abstracted form. "We go from a content that is well defined, localized, and belongs to the past, to the a priori general form of a nonlocalizable *something* that has happened" (288). When a secret takes an abstracted form, its thing-ness or identity is authenticated; it becomes "something that has happened." The form of secrecy and disclosure verifies the secret; it makes the secret function as if it were true. We ignore the social character of the secret, neglecting to inquire into its qualities. But abstraction also opens a space for transgression, in which both content and form disappear.

What happened? "[T]he answer is necessarily that nothing happened . . .

The news travels fast that the secret of men is nothing, in truth nothing at all" (Deleuze and Guattari, *Thousand* 289). As a happening, an event, the secret is no longer "a thing." *It is no thing. It is, rather, a happening.* The secret transforms itself into an event through its abstracted form. "The more the secret is made into a structuring, organizing form, the thinner and more ubiquitous it becomes, the more its content becomes molecular, at the same time as its form dissolves" (289). The secret, which is "made" conceptually into a form, spreads, thins itself out, and encounters us everywhere. This continuous making and remaking of the secret changes the secret; it also enables social agents to make the secret differently. The secret is no longer a thing. The secret becomes "molecular;" it becomes particles. It is an event or happening. It has a capacity to change, to mutate. In becoming an event, in becoming molecular, the secret exists "where the imperceptible, the clandestine with nothing left to hide, has finally been perceived" (290). We encounter, here, neither the secret as content nor the secret as form, for there is no thing "left to hide." There are no more things, simply events. Things can be perceived and authenticated. The secret, in contrast, is imperceptible when it becomes an event. We perceive the imperceptibility of the secret; we encounter an event without borders, without an identity. We become-secrets. "Some people can talk, hide nothing, not lie: they are secret by transparency, as impenetrable as water, in truth incomprehensible" (290). When the secret becomes an event, the subject is transformed. In the act of talking, of telling or creating a truth (not at all lying), no thing is hidden. Yet the secret is not merely information. Rather, the subject becomes a cipher—a mystery. The subject is "impenetrable as water," for the subject is not a thing. "In truth," in the act of talking truthfully, in that space of discourse, the subject is incomprehensible. The subject is perceivable, yet unknowable.

Becoming-Homosexual

We encounter a becoming-homosexual in Allan Gurganus's autobiographical story, "He's One, Too." As a mode of becoming-homosexual, coming out creates a "zone of proximity" or a site in which "something" (*no* thing) is shared (Deleuze & Guattari, *Thousand* 273). Becoming-homosexual disrupts the binary form of identity logic (Doel; Hayden) thus entering into a politics of difference (P. Patton, *Deleuze* 29). Paul Patton, however, warns us of wrong turns in rhizomatic thought: We are not "overthrowing" identity (29), speaking of difference as "opposition"

(32), or "privileging" difference over unity (39–40). Rather, becoming-homosexual produces alliances that are distinct from relations that are produced by information exchange. The members of the alliance exist only in the act of sharing something. These conceptual implications are best isolated in literature. Deleuze contends, "Writing is a question of becoming, always incomplete, always in the midst of being formed, and goes beyond the matter of any livable or lived experience" ("Literature" 225). The literary process thus "[invents] a people" through experimentation (228).[5]

1957: Getting Caught

Gurganus writes, "In Falls, North Carolina, in 1957, we had just one way of 'coming out.' It was called getting caught" (40). On its face, Gurganus's coming out story describes a rather simple occurrence of information exchange—"getting caught." A thirty-three year old businessman and father of three (Dan) is *caught* (by the police) making sexual advances to a young man (the police officer's son) in the Men's Room of J. C. Penney's. The official account, printed in a local newspaper, attends solely to Dan's conduct: "According to authorities, he was apprehended while 'making sexual-type-suggestion-advances' to and 'having sustained manual contact with the privates of' a 15-year-old boy 'at the urinals of the new Penney's rest room facility, 2:32 P.M., Saturday" (48). Yet daily conversations about the event easily translated conduct into identity, in paranoid fashion: "Others claimed that this unlikely toilet had become a secret breeding place for capital-area inverts" (53). Inverts, a synonym for homosexuality at the time, marked those who partook in such activities as a specific kind of person; conduct became identity. Dan's homosexuality is further established as identity when his kids learn of their father's indiscretions: "[T]hey all knew first, knew first what their father really was" (54). Allan later reflects, "The rest of it interests me because I am one, too. Like Dan, who was locally noticeable and then became hyper-visible en route to being totally unseen, I am trying once again to make myself more opaquely and superstitiously visible an invert. I am trying, through this story" (54). Gurganus explains how this event, Dan's "getting caught," awakened his nine-year-old erotic fantasies about Dan and subsequently his own sexual identity. Young Allan catches himself out. Homosexuality, in this sense, functions as a secret content that passes between Dan, the community at large, and Allan. A thing about Dan is known. Allan knows a thing about his self. To catch a homosexual, as the police catch Dan, requires a formal distinction between "homosexual" and "heterosexual" persons. To catch a homosexual, as Allan catches himself, necessitates imitation or identification.

1957: A Matter of Hooking

"Hooking," in contrast to "getting caught," is a mode of becoming-homosexual, for it entails the sharing of something (no thing). Gurganus recalls, "*I once literally hooked literally all of him. It proved addicting. This was the year those others caught, then vanished him*" (64). Allan does not catch Dan; that is what the others do. Instead, Allan "hooks him," becoming-homosexual. It is not that Allan imitates Dan-as-homosexual. It is not that Allan identifies with Dan-as-homosexual. It is, rather, that Allan creates an alliance with Dan in the act of hooking him. Allan's becoming-homosexual is a happening or an event. It attracts, ensnares [takes in, not catches or traps], seizes, and connects. It creates a zone of indiscernibility, a zone between, in which the boundary between one body and another becomes a blur, for as Allan later asks, "Who'd *had* whom" (67)? Hooking, unlike catching, does not produce identities: one who hooks and one who is hooked. Both parties hook and are hooked simultaneously. Once hooked, this site of alliance compels the subject— "it proved addicting." Becoming-homosexual's influence, its appeal lies in an alliance, not in the coherence of a thing.

In his coming-out narrative, Allan revisits the event, the hooking. The event and the narrative are sites of becoming, sites of personal and social change. In April of Allan's ninth year, Dan offers to help him practice aiming the hook on his fly-casting rod. Standing sixty feet away from Dan, Allan casts his hook out toward the named target, a red plastic ring. What happens constitutes "pure relations of speed and slowness" (Deleuze and Guattari, *Thousand* 281).[6] The act of hooking momentarily dissolves the otherwise coherent boundary between self and other through anticipation and release. As the hook moves towards its target, it slows down and arches in the air. "I aimed. I recall the thumb release of line. 'Go!' The reel sang its precise ratcheting, pure play-out" (Gurganus 65). The narrative idles at this moment, experiencing an interruption (marked by parentheses). We must wait. We must slow down.

(Later, during sex, I'd recall this giddying suspension. A man feels his release 'go off,' you feel the aim-out pleasure upspiral into air, your reel line is moving, about to mainline joy throughout your groin, then flooding every cell of you. You know it's literally coming, you are. You know that nothing on the earth—not even a jealous macho God—can stop it now, your gusher, eureka! The Fellow Ship fullsteamahead!)

This depiction is not a metaphor, not the pure imitation of sexual orgasm. Rather, this parenthetical interruption becomes a mechanism for slowing down the creation of an alliance between Dan and Allan. It also constitutes an alliance between Allan and us—the text forces us to wait as the hook flies through the air: "My silver line lifts a C shape of rolling light, midair." We are, in the act of reading, becoming-homosexual. "Settling. Then I feel the snap of my hook find something hard/good— a surface firm yet yielding—springy, live, worthwhile." We wait in this moment between casting and reeling "it" in. The hook settles, finds "something" (no thing). The surface pulls and releases, resists and gives way. "There's much game 'play' in it." Finally, the event accelerates.

> And, even as I realize I've hit, not the red ring, but one pale human wrist (not the left, holding a target, but Dan's other one), some excitement, some malice unaccountable, makes me jerk it anyway. Gotcha, motherfucker! Snagging the arm of a man who's always been only kind to me, is a response so male, so savage, automatic— it scares me sick. The Sports Gene! 'Owwweesh!' Dan howls. (Might this not be Dan's exact sexual release cry?)

A distinction between the act of hooking Dan and the eroticism of that act becomes imperceptible due to the speed of the event. To "jerk it anyway" takes on speed ("automatic"). It occurs "even as I realize," at the same moment that Allan perceives what has been hooked. The hook is both perceived and imperceptible—the response to "jerk it" is blurred by the speed at which it happens. The possible reasons (excitement, malice?) for hooking and jerking Dan are "unaccountable," even upon later reflection. We cannot know or catch them with certainty, for the act is "automatic." In fact, the speed and consequent mysteriousness of such reasons "scares [Allan] sick." The imperceptibility of the event inhabits Dan's howl. This time, the parentheses mark out the speed of the cry, rather than its slowness. Due to speed, a distinction between a cry of pain and a cry of pleasure is imperceptible. "Might" it be one or the other? Is one "exactly" the same as the other? This is not a metaphor, a copy, a semblance. Mystery forever haunts the event. Hooking creates an alliance, a becoming, through its speeds and slownesses, rather than through its similarities with or mimicry of sexual activity.

As Allan runs to Dan ("I speed toward my prize"), to bear witness to the consequences of his hooking, we find ourselves waiting again. Allan's slowness contaminates us, in its relation to the hook and the "wound" it has caused. Although Allan's whole body accumulates a relative speed toward Dan, his eyes [and our eyes] experience a delay: "[Dan] shields me from seeing his bleeding arm" (65). The event then takes on a molecular quality. It "suddenly sweeps us up and makes us become—*a proximity, an indiscernibility* that extracts a shared element." These shared elements emerge from "an emission of particles" (Deleuze and Guattari, *Thousand* 279).[7] Allan's body, in becoming-homosexual, no longer experiences Dan as a whole subject (a form), but, rather, he encounters his part-icles. Finally, "His fibrous arm flips over, accidentally showing me white skin, powder-blue marbled veining, and one long spittle of opaque red leaving the silver beak of my own hook" (66). The arm's texture is tough, its contours outlining a shape. In its toughness, however, its fibers are separated from each other. Skin becomes transparent, displaying the faint "powder-blue" of a vein. Cells are extracted to create a marbled appearance. Eyes follow a line ("one long spittle") of blood, fluid, emitted from a puncture in the skin. The particles of Dan's body (its fibers, cells, fluids) constitute a zone of proximity between his body and Allan's. This is not a metaphor for homo-sexual acts, an exchange of seminal fluids. It permits, instead, a co-mingling of particles and an emission of particles.

Particles of flesh equally join within the zone of becoming-homosexual. "That surgical hook puckers a two-inch sample of someone's bacon-fat flesh" (Gurganus 66). Allan's later dream or fantasy about Dan's body produces a zone of indiscernibility, a site in which the hook and the flesh of the body enter into a relation of becoming.

> Lit by orange light in my tree, I understand how they have hurt you. Where I expected your manhood waiting, springy, perfectly cheerfully complete, they've slid a giant fishhook. It has been stuck all the way between your legs and I see its barbed tip gleaming in the flame. It's perfectly down-curved. I see how cleverly it's made, so it will go right through, but never get back out. (70)

Allan's tree house might be read conventionally as a metaphor for the homosexual closet. It both contains secrets (Allan's own homosexuality) and allows the secrets of others to permeate its boundaries ("I understand how they have hurt you"). It is equally an immanent space of becoming, for it is a site of alliance between Allan and Dan. The hook also serves an ambivalent function in the narrative, for it constitutes both how "they," the others, the police, have hurt Dan and how Allan has hurt him. In one instance, the hook catches Dan, and in the other, it hooks him into a zone of proximity. One might also read the presence of the hook as a metaphor for Dan's penis, for it replaced his "manhood" completely—"it will go right through, but never get back out." But this is not a metaphor. The hook is not a sexual object. It is not an organized form. Rather, its particles can be extracted and create a zone of proximity. Allan later writes, "*I place my mouth to it. I find the taste is ketchup, metal, Milk Duds, bitter money, milk, and salt and sugar mixed*" (70). The hook emits these particles of taste and texture; Allan's mouth shares these particles in his becoming-homosexual. This is not a sexual act between like-oriented individuals, but, rather, it is an erotic act that creates an alliance and proximity.

Allan's body also emits particles, which sweep Dan up into a becoming-child. Both bodies, subjects, become indiscernible: "I nuzzle, sobbing, 'Didn't mean to, to *you*, Dan . . . ' Dreading others' seeing us, hating how pain alone permits our union, I cry "Soory" into splayed legs. They remain wide open. I've run right into their V-shape shelter, a berth. I now wedge farther between. I am sobbing, he holds me fast" (66). A nine-year-old sobs, emits tears, fluids. These particles "permit" a "union," entry into "splayed legs." As a "shelter" or "berth," these legs function to create a space for rest, absolute slowness. One might perceive the tears as a lie, a falsity, which, by the nature of their façade, sanctions homosexual activity. We must resist this understanding of Allan's soft, wet particles. We must insist that such tears are a real and fundamental element in the act of becoming. Homosexuality, in its indiscernibility from hooking, requires the emission of fluids, tears, blood, semen. In its existence as an excessive surface, the gay male body becomes paradoxically a zone of safety, protection. Becoming-homosexual, in this way, does not imitate or identify with the "homosexual" subject, but, rather, troubles the very borders of the body.

Once sheltered, Allan returns to a "plane of organization," that belonging to sexuality. "So, sick with boldness, I tip against the inner fabric of his much-washed pants" (Gurganus 66). The relation between Allan and Dan, one of becoming-homosexual, one of alliance and contagion, one "sick with boldness," returns to a plane of sexual organization. "Mid-thigh, I read the Braille outline of sexual parts, his. They're presented plain, canine in guilelessness, grapelike in gentle plentiful cascade. The very symbol of abundance" (Gurganus 66). Dan, in this moment, is an individual subject, a sexual subject. His corporeal parts are identified by their sexual function, and they constitute Dan as a subject, for they are ", his." The comma renders this "his" as a possessive term— the parts belong to Dan. Dan's body, consequently, is a coherent substance with a gendered and sexualized identity, separated from Allan's body by a comma. "His" parts are containers, for they are full, "plentiful," or "abundant." Their contents determine or organize Dan as a sexual subject, as a subject with a capacity to reproduce. His parts, his body, his identity, linked through synecdoche, are full of seed. He is an organized subject, his body a code. Allan "reads" the outline of Dan's parts as a referential language ("Braille"), the parts become "*the* very symbol" that confirms and authenticates Dan's sexual organization, his boundaries, the constitution of his individual subjectivity. The code is transparent, unproblematic, for the parts are "presented plain," without mystery.

The comma separating Dan's body and Allan's body is repeated shortly thereafter, to different effect. "Using bloodshed as my excuse I find nerve to cup my open right hand lightly—light as light itself— against them, against all his. Just overtop, no pressure. I simply do it, crying as distraction" (66). We remain, with Dan and Allan, on the plane of sexual organization, for the comma traces a line of interpretation along the edge of Dan's parts—"against them, against all his." Corporeal particles, however, lead us to the threshold between this plane of organization and a plane of consistency or becoming. Bloodshed (Dan's particles) and tears (Allan's), we must remember, are not lies. Despite their status as "excuses" and "distractions," they are really and truly elements in this becoming-homosexual. We exist now between these two planes. "It is in jumping from one plane to the other, or from the relative thresholds to the absolute threshold that coexists with them, that the imperceptible becomes necessarily perceived" (Deleuze and Guattari, *Thousand* 282). If this is the case, then we might follow the path mapped out by the blood and the tears in order to return to a site of becoming-homosexual. The comma equally becomes a means of transportation across the lines of organized sexuality into a zone of proximity and alliance. Allan recalls, "Then my pleasure—stirred, overambitious— leads me to tighten my clamp on him, his. My reach exceeds my grasp" (66). We return to becoming-homosexual, "the moment when desire and perception meld" (Deleuze and Guattari, *Thousand* 283). The tactile alliance that is constituted by Allan's "clamp" exists between his desire (not necessarily "identifying with" Dan as a "homosexual subject") and his perception of Dan's body. It is neither organizing that desire nor that body, but, rather, it is caught up in a state of becoming-imperceptible. It is a relation of experimentation, rather than one of interpretation. "Everything is different on the plane of consistency or immanence, which is necessarily perceived in its own right in the course of its construction: experimentation replaces interpretation, now molecular, nonfigurative, and nonsymbolic" (284). We must observe becoming as a site where "everything is different." Becoming is *not* in opposition to interpretation. We are not destroying or escaping the sexual subject, but, rather, we are in the process of thinking "him" differently. Moreover, Allan is desiring/perceiving *no* thing, but, rather, "every"-thing, for "everything" is different. A thing is not eliminated; it is altered through elements of an other—particles, experimentation. His hand does not "grasp," but "reaches." Allan's touch exceeds organizational boundaries and reaches elsewhere—toward the unknown and unpredictable effects of experimentation. We move toward change, an alteration of bodies. Allan notes, "I see his face change, slow" (66). Dan enters into Allan's slowness. Change happens; it is an event in the course of becoming—the composition of an alliance, not the organization of Dan or Allan as sexual subjects. The change in Dan's face is neither a metaphor nor a code; it is "nonfigurative" and "nonsymbolic." It is an event itself. Change happens in the event of becoming. It does not represent, directly or indirectly, figuratively or symbolically, sexual pleasure. Instead, Dan's face becomes a site of mystery, the imperceptible perceived.

We are now in a space of becoming, a space between subjectivity and desire. "Dan himself glances down between Dan's own mighty legs. Definitely checking on a little scoop-shaped paw now curved against his right-dressed member" (Gurganus 66). Dan becomes split, subject and object at once. Dan, as a sexual subject, "himself glances down," and "checks on." His gaze travels to a site of becoming-homosexual— "between Dan's own mighty legs." We are guided down into a zone of proximity, alliance. Dan, as the object of his own gaze, disrupts his organization as a subject. "Nothing left but the word of speeds and slownesses without form, without subject, without a face" (Deleuze and Guattari, *Thousand* 283). We are in an event with a slowness all its own. There is "nothing," no thing, for it is Dan's gaze that perceives "his right-dressed member" rather than Allan's. There is no subject, for Dan's gaze disrupts the very corporeal borders that might produce such a coherent subject. There is no face, no appearance that contains a secure interior subject or identity. Dan's face is exhibited to Allan's gaze, which disrupts rather than maintains the surface of the face. The slowly changing face does not communicate an interior. It presents a mysterious exterior. It is simultaneously perceived and imperceptible.

In this alliance of becoming-homosexual, there is no face, no subject. There is no secret content or form. Dan's face, in its gaze, does not communicate an interior—the secret that he is a homosexual subject. Nor does it constitute Allan as a homosexual. Rather, Dan's face becomes a smooth surface of mystery. "Dan, metal-blue jaw, gives me one sleepy, dubious half smile. In it, amused recognition, some pity maybe, much fellow feeling, a father's patience for his own kid's guileless curiosity. Oh, the Fellow Ship. Dan says, 'Well, little buddy . . . '" (67). "In" the smile, "in" his face, lies a relation, a becoming, an alliance. What appears on the face, it is clear, is imperceptible, yet, at the same time, perceived. Is it the knowledge of Allan's homosexual desire? Is it sympathy for one so young? Is it a mutual understanding of a shared homosexual desire? Is it mere tolerance without pleasure? What does it mean to be a "fellow?" If we were on a plane of organization, "fellow" would be a space of identification, a site in which Dan and Allan discover, uncover their secret-content status as homosexual subjects. As "fellows," they are the same. As becoming-homosexual, "a fellow" is not a subject position, but rather, a site of affect between self and other. "A fellow" is an alliance, a relation of difference or otherness.

Allan returns to his tree house, which is not merely a closet or a container for his homosexual identity, but, rather, a site of transparency and desire. The walls of the tree house dissolve the content and form of the secret, and become a smooth space. Allan calls down to Dan, standing below, "I didn't know it hurt. To fish. Hurt the *fish,* Dan" (67). Here, hooking is transformed into "fishing." To fish relays us between a plane of organization or "catching" and a plane of consistency or "hooking." Let us remain becoming-homosexual, with the hook. The hook becomes a site of imperceptibility. Allan (the fisher) and Dan (the fish) are caught up in the affect of pain, of hurt, as well as an alliance of pleasure. Upon tasting the hook, Allan writes later, "*The taste is equal pleasure, equal pain*" (70). The affect, the taste is imperceptible, yet still perceived. We are in a zone of proximity between pleasure and pain—desire and perception. Dan replies: "Don't blame yourself. You've got the sporting touch . . . You'll land hundreds more ahead, and rainbows, too. Glad to be the first in line—a great long catch o' keepers, pal. Your only problem is, your aim's *too* good. Every man should have such trouble" (67). To jump to a plane of sexual organization would be simple. The "blame" [guilt, if private; shame, if public], "landing" future sexual partners, "rainbows" and coalitions, "catching" and "aiming" at secret identities and desires, all might work as code for homosexual subjectivity. But let us continue becoming-homosexual. These words are elements in the act of hooking, composing an alliance, not an identity. Allan later asks, "Had Dan talked to me in code?" The question, as a question, transports us to a zone of indiscernibility, rather than a plane of codes, subjects, and secret-contents. The borders of subjectivity, confirmed identity, remain open—never fully closed: "Who'd *had* whom?"

Dan's wrist is equally a site of becoming-homosexual; its scar becomes a signature, evidence of the hook. "Inside your right wrist, even with the lights out, can you not still touch a little scratchy signature of scarring?" (Gurganus 67). In a zone of perception and desire, we continue becoming. Something (not a thing) that might be seen can also be touched—a scar. Deleuze and Guattari remind us, "The signature, the proper name, is not the constituted mark of a subject, but the constituting mark of a domain, an abode" (*Thousand* 316). If the scar located on Dan's wrist is indeed a signature, then how might it disrupt or disconfirm Dan's identity as a "homosexual"? This is not to question Dan's sexual orientation, his status, but, rather, to interrogate the borders of his subjectivity—his constitution as a subject. The scar becomes permanent visual or tactile evidence of hooking, of becoming-homosexual. The scar, by its very nature, disturbs the borders of Dan's body. It cuts into his corporeal being, and leaves its mark, serving as a signature of becoming, of his alliance with Allan. The mark left by the scar is not a mark of identity. The mark-as-signature, thought differently, creates a "domain" or a zone of proximity between Allan and Dan. As a site of becoming, the scar constitutes a space of relation that continually changes. This is not to say the scar is without boundaries. It is, rather, to say that those boundaries are continually a site of experimentation and difference. If the abode of the scar is a home, those borders of subjectivity and alliance invite a guest to visit. An other always has the potential to alter the borders that constitute the relation or alliance. If the abode of the scar is a temporary locale of stability, change is inevitable. An abode is not merely a site of subjectivity and alliance. It is also a site of difference, for an other is frequently welcome to stay a while.

Coming Out as an Ethical Practice

Conceptualizing coming out's rhetorical force solely through the lens of identification significantly limits our understanding of its potential for queer resistance. This is not to say, however, that coming out does not operate as a mode of identification, for it surely does for both hetero-sexual and non-heterosexual audiences: it assimilates queer citizens into mainstream culture and forges an ethnic identity for political organiz-ing. Yet identification appears to restrict the conditions of speaking about homosexuality in American discourse at the dawn of the twenty-first century such that coming out is divorced from channels and net-works of desire. The knowledge of coming out as identification derives from the rhetorical secret and its performative contradictions: *Sexuality's disclosure performs the private in public; Sexuality's secrecy invents heteronor-mative claims of ignorance; Sexuality's enslavement to discourse is mistaken for mastery over that discourse; Sexuality's knowledge requires forgetting.* When mapped onto the rhetorical practice of coming out, these performative contradictions blind us to the ways in which coming out produces alli-ances through the enactment of desire.

Deleuze and Guattari's biophysical ethics, invoked through their con-cept of becoming, expands Foucault's genealogical project in substantive ways, enabling genealogy to function as critique. Becoming, in other words, enables the move from history to possibility. Both thinkers rec-ognize the modern shift in power from operations of repression to mechanisms of production and sites of knowledge, which privatized so-cial forces through subjection. Yet Foucault's genealogies specify mecha-nisms of power while Deleuze and Guattari emphasize forces of desire, which both produce normalization and create avenues of new connec-tions, new possibilities. Deleuze and Guattari, in their biophysical ethics, also give critical rhetoricians tools for judgment, a means of avoiding the trappings of historical determinism and historical relativism. The history of coming out thus becomes a history of desire as well as a his-tory of identification.

Coming out has proven to be a multifaceted rhetorical practice, one that addresses both heterosexual and non-heterosexual audiences, one that creates bonds of identification and desire. Across these diverse rhetorical operations, ethical concerns remain central to coming out's rhetorical role in queer resistance. Coming out is (in this instance) the ethical prac-tice of male homosexual identity. In contrast to its limited formulation as identification, coming out materializes desire, eroticism, and collectivity. Coming out, as the ethical practice of identity, is queer. Coming out mobilizes queer desire in and through the body rather than through words alone. Coming out mobilizes queer desire as an alliance grounded in difference rather than in sameness. Coming out mobilizes queer desire as a collective experience rather than a private one. In these ways, coming out is a rhetorical practice that challenges the rhetorical secret and its performative contradictions. In these ways, coming out is indeed a mode of queer resistance to heteronormative power relations.

Conclusion

The Conditions of Speaking About Homosexuality

On History and Rhetorical Criticism

The critical rhetoric project, taking material discourse as its object, reassesses the role of history within the critical act. Of course, any critical engagement with a rhetorical object is incomplete without some understanding of its historicity, for as Celeste Condit concludes, "The uniquely powerful province of rhetoric [is a] judgment of the collective human meaning-making process as it occurs in history through situated discourse-construction" ("Rhetorical" 342). Acknowledging rhetoric's historical situated-ness, however, produces different forms of critical practice, with no disciplinary consensus on history's referent.[1] For some, history refers to the extradiscursive context against which rhetorical objects appear and thus take on meaning. For others, history refers to the material, discursive context in which the rhetorical object circulates. The debates over history's double valence are not inconsequential to critical practice. It is not merely a matter of, as the classic song suggests: "I say 'discursive context,' you say 'extradiscursive context,' let's call the whole thing off." Our interpretations of "historical context" in critical practice, whether explicit or implicit, necessarily thematize the relationship between knowledge, power, and ethical practice. Rhetorical scholarship, in its treatment of the relationship between discourse and history, cannot avoid making larger claims about agency and social change. Foucault's genealogical method thus speaks directly to both rhetorical theory and rhetorical practice. These relationships are vital to the rhetorical study of social movements in particular.[2]

Two recent treatises on rhetorical scholarship demonstrate that such claims entail subtle differences rather than a forcible, "either/or" endgame. Arguing that texts and contexts are created (not discovered) by critics, Bonnie Dow writes: "Material constraints *do* exist, just as they do for the artist: paint and canvas can do thing that clay cannot, and vice versa. We always start with some kind of *thing,* and because of the vocabularies that critical communities agree upon, we are often constrained in what we can intelligibly make of it. Within those very basic parameters, however, there is enormous latitude for creativity" (340). The nature of material constraints, while recognized here, is significantly reduced by Dow's later claim that rhetorical agents have "enormous latitude" within those constraints. In contrast, Celeste Condit insists on a materialist account of language so as to avoid the charges of "objectivist" on the one hand and "relativist" on the other: "A materialist account of language does not deny that language shapes the particular meaningfulness of the material world in which we live, but it does not presume that the meaningfulness of language can be independent of material constraints" ("History in Rhetoric" 177). Unlike Dow's account, in which material constraints appear to be discursive ones (as paint, canvas, and clay are to the artist), material constraints seem to be extradiscursive in Condit's account. In the former, the force of discursive constraints appears negligible while in the latter, the force of extradiscursive constraints appears formidable. Theories of performative discourse enable critical rhetoricians to take discursive constraints as powerful ideological resources without collapsing them into extradiscursive determinants.

Ultimately, history's role in rhetorical theory and practice is a matter of discourse. In contrast to language, which produces "an infinite number of performances," discourse is "finite" (Foucault, *Archaeology* 27). As Foucault later concludes, "few things, in all, can be said" (119). Discourse not only limits *what* statements can be uttered within a field of knowledge, but also *who* can speak, for discourse "defines the possible position of speaking subjects" (122). Eschewing individual, collective, and transcendental notions of the speaking subject, Foucault creates a quandary for rhetorical scholars, especially those who study minority discourse and modes of social resistance. It is a quandary that has led Gayatri Chakravorty Spivak to ask: "Can the subaltern speak?" Rhetoricians have responded by attempting to recuperate the humanist subject within Foucault's philosophy (Blair and Cooper), and by carving out a space for "vernacular" or "out-law" discourses (Ono and Sloop, "Vernacular"; Sloop and Ono, "Outlaw"). In her reading of Foucault, Barbara Biesecker concludes, "[P]ower names not the imposition of a limit that constrains human thought and action but a being-able that is made possible by a grid of intelligibility" (356). As Butler's theory of performativity reminds us, however, being-able and constraint are concomitant, not oppositional states within relations of power and their particular field of discourse/knowledge.

The tension between rhetorical capacity and rhetorical limitation is never of the abstract, "glass-half-full" or "glass-half-empty" variety. The question of performative agency is always a specific one. Butler's analysis of universality, once again, deserves examination: "At stake here is the exclusionary function of certain norms of universality which, in a way, transcend the cultural locations from which they emerge. Although they often appear as transcultural or formal criteria by which existing cultural conventions are to be judged, they are precisely cultural conventions which have, through a process of abstraction, come to appear as post-conventional principles" ("Restaging" 39). How then do universal standards of judgment appear within a discursive field of knowledge? What is their particularity? What exclusions are performed in their cultural abstractions? What rhetorical processes mobilize this abstraction? Discourse, in its performative character, in its enabling and limiting functions, forces these questions upon the critical rhetoric project in such a way that they must be answered within each specific instance.

Upon entering public discourse, the queer subject is required to make an assertion of universality. For example, we deserve the protection of our rights because we constitute a recognizable minority group [like racial minorities] whose sexual identity is immutable [like heterosexuals] and who experience tangible forms of discrimination [like racial minorities]. On the surface, this logical argument should carry the day, so to speak. Yet the discourse of equal rights, as we now know, is never that simple, for as Butler observes, "The assertion of universality by those who have conventionally been excluded by the term often produces a performative contradiction of a certain sort" ("Restaging" 38). When queer citizens assert their own universality, they are quickly made aware that citizenship's universality is uniquely heterosexual. Yet this contradiction between that which can be uttered within a discourse and that which cannot has always been there. Contradiction, Foucault explains, "far from being an appearance or accident of discourse, far from being that from which it must be freed if truth is at last to be revealed, constitutes the very law of its existence" (*Archaeology* 151). Performative rhetoric, therefore, goes in search of the contradictions inherent to universalities that found dominating fields of knowledge within a historically situated society, within a specific time and place. It explores the relations of power and domination that derive from such fields of knowledge. Finally, performative rhetoric reworks knowledge to invent new possibilities of ethical practice.

Contingent Foundations for Queer Ethical Practice

If the rhetorical secret and its performative contradictions constitute heteronormative relations of knowledge-power within American society, as I have shown they do, then how might queer activists and citizens invent new modes of ethical engagement? Rather than outline a series of practical steps to change the place of non-heterosexual citizens through political means, I will argue that queer ethics begins with the concepts we use to understand our world and our relationships, both politically and personally. The rhetorical secret stands as the dominant concept of homosexuality in twenty-first-century America. Reworking the performative contradictions that inhabit it will enable queer citizens to reinvent the very conditions of speaking about their world and their experiences—it will enable new forms of social agency.

The rhetorical secret begins by performing the private in public, thus restricting queer citizen's rhetorical agency in public spaces, namely: law, medicine, culture, and community. Queer resistance, consequently, begins by announcing the publicness of sexuality rather than simply defending homosexuality in zones of privacy. Public policy issues such as repealing sodomy laws and legalizing same-sex marriage demonstrate the rhetorical potency of privatized sexual identity. Both issues are caught up in the performative contradiction that makes "privacy" a condition of speaking about homosexuality. There remains no doubt that sodomy laws invade non-heterosexual citizens' right to privacy. Yet when we limit homosexuality to zones of privacy, we forgo the right to be public. Debates over same-sex marriage also enact this performative contradiction, for marriage is both a private sexual relationship and a public institution. Performing the private in public also influences the practice of medicine and the use of medical information in queer communities. When HIV/AIDS discourse presumes that HIV transmission is a matter of individual decision making, we forget that HIV transmission is also a question of norm making within sexual cultures. Although queer communities are clearly sexual cultures, heterosexual relationship also exist within sexual cultures with rules and norms of behavior. Yet the conditions of speaking about heterosexuality readily enable those citizens to craft sexual norms publicly while eroticizing safe-sex in gay cultures remains a challenge. Homosexual and heterosexual cultures alike produce messages and circulate images that communicate sexuality and eroticism. Heterosexual culture, however, is less likely to perceive erotically charged public discourse and images as worthy of censure as they have become normalized through repetition. Queer culture's public discourse and images, in contrast, are more likely to be disciplined by both straight and gay audiences alike. Attempts to deeroticize gay culture in both mainstream media forms and within the LGBT movement itself demonstrates this double standard. Finally, LGBT visibility is often compromised in public spaces; from media to families, from the workplace to suburbia, queer citizens still lack the ability to occupy public spaces freely.

The right to be public is our most precious right as citizens.

The rhetorical secret also translates invention into ignorance. Heteronormative power must be understood as mobilized by knowledge, not by ignorance. American citizens learn heteronormative ideology through public discourse and discourse creates relations of power. Queer citizens often believe that coming out of the closet alone will change society by contributing knowledge and debunking ignorance. Yet challenging social knowledge involves more than simply countering ideological myths with the truth and social change entails more than simply making our voices heard. Once queer subjects begin to speak, their discourse is immediately conditioned by the rhetorical secret and its performative contradictions. Queer resistance must rework the discursive conditions from which we speak.

Invention is our most effective political and cultural resource.

The rhetorical secret, finally, positions speakers as masters of discourse, yet in this positioning, speakers become enslaved to discourse. To become a master of discourse requires one to become subservient to it. Mastering the legal discourse on homosexuality, for instance, enslaves interlocutors within essentialist and ethnic models of sexual identity. The right to privacy, while effectively overruling Texas's sodomy laws, also limits our understandings of sexuality to individual personhood and thus eclipses the presence of sexual collectives in American society. Arguing that same-sex marriage represents social and legal equality might eventually produce policy changes with real-world, material benefits and responsibilities for queer citizens; yet, the potential for same-sex marriage also carries normative implications for non-heterosexual citizens and their relationships. Mastering the medical discourse on homosexuality and HIV transmission, likewise, enslaves queer subjects within epidemiological, immunological, and viral narratives.

Through these discursive regimes, gay men become enemies rather than allies.

The mastery of heteronormative discourse is our most enduring oppressor.

Queer ethics begins with the body. The body is more than merely the residence of one's sexual identity; the body is also a collective entity, responsive and responsible to others. The queer body is a desiring body as well as a body that identifies. Desire, not identification, must become queer ethics' predominant form. Gazing upon the body of another, disclosing one's sexual identity to another—these are modes of creating alliances, not simply means of self-identification. Queer culture, queer ethics, queer resistance must reinvent "identity" and "secrecy" as desire.

Desire is our most powerful form of resistance.

Notes

Introduction

1. See Eric O. Clarke, *Virtuous Vice: Homoeroticism and the Public Sphere;* Shane Phelan, ed., *Playing with Fire: Queer Politics, Queer Theories;* Craig A. Rimmerman, *From Identity to Politics: The Lesbian and Gay Movements in the United States;* Steven Seidman, *Difference Troubles: Queering Social Theory and Sexual Politics;* Ralph R. Smith and Russel R. Windes, *Progay/Antigay: The Rhetorical War Over Sexuality;* Michael Warner, ed., *Fear of a Queer Planet: Queer Politics and Social Theory.*

2. Diana Helene Miller gestures toward this gap in rhetorical scholarship: "To date, however, no book has taken a rhetorical approach in examining lesbian and gay civil rights discourse. Nor has any book analyzed public speech by or about lesbians, separate from that by or about gay men or homosexuality in general" (162). Gail Mason advances a similar claim in her analysis of violent hate crimes committed against lesbian and bisexual women contending, "there are also signs that this 'typical' incident of homophobic violence may be a more accurate depiction of the violence that gay men report, than it is of the violence that lesbians report" (40).

3. Statistically speaking, studies of lesbian and gay public discourse are rarely found within the field of communication. The paucity of communication scholarship on lesbian, gay, bisexual, transgender issues is evidenced by an eight-page document distributed by the LGBT Division at the NCA convention in 2001. See Frederick C. Corey, Ralph R. Smith, and Thomas K. Nakayama, "A Bibliography of National Communication Association, Regional Communication Association, and International Communication Association Journal Articles addressing Lesbian, Gay, Bisexual, Transgender, and Queer Issues and Books addressing Lesbian, Gay, Bisexual, Transgender, and Queer Issues by members of NCA and ICA." This document cites a mere 66 journal articles and 24 books on LGBT issues that were published in the field of speech communication between 1973 and 2001. Existing books on communication and LGBT issues break down into four major categories: edited volumes, books whose primary focus is the HIV/AIDS crisis, media scholarship, and rhetorical studies of LGBT movements. Groundbreaking edited volumes on communication and LGBT issues include: *Gayspeak: Gay Male and Lesbian Communica-*

tion, ed. James Chesebro; *Queer Words, Queer Images: Communication and the Construction of Homosexuality,* ed. Jeffrey Ringer; and *Anti-Gay Rights: Assessing Voter Initiatives,* ed. Stephanie L. Witt and Suzanne McCorkle. Books on the HIV/AIDS crisis and communication include: *AIDS: A Communication Perspective,* ed. Timothy Edgar, Mary Anne Fitzpatrick, and Vicki S. Freimuth; and Roger Myrick, *AIDS, Communication, and Empowerment: Gay Male Identity and the Politics of Public Health Messages.* For studies on lesbian and gay representation in the mass media, see: Larry Gross, *Contested Closets: The Politics and Ethics of Outing;* Edward Alwood, *Straight News: Gays, Lesbians, and the News Media;* and Larry Gross, *Up From Invisibility: Lesbians, Gay Men, and the Media in America.*

4. "Queer Theory and Communication: From Disciplining Queers to Queering the Discipline(s)," a special issue of *Journal of Homosexuality* (2003), edited by Gust A. Yep, Karen E. Lovaas, and John P. Elia is a notable exception to this trend.

5. James Darsey's *The Prophetic Tradition and Radical Rhetoric in America,* for instance, adeptly critiques the recent shift from radical citizenship to consumer politics in the U.S. gay rights movement. Ralph R. Smith and Russel R. Windes present a neo-Burkean analysis of contemporary debates over public policy and the rights of sexual minorities in *Progay/Antigay.* This book brilliantly describes the formation of progay and antigay movements and how these collective actors organize around rhetorically charged symbols and meanings of sexuality.

6. Three exceptions to this general absence are noteworthy. In *Freedom to Differ: The Shaping of the Gay and Lesbian Struggle for Civil Rights,* Diane Helene Miller examines the discursive constitution of lesbian identity in two provocative case studies: a cabinet appointment and a military discharge. Adopting its critical edge from queer theory, Miller's study is similar to the project proposed here, except that it focuses on lesbian identity rather than gay male identity. Robert Brookey's recent publication, *Reinventing the Male Homosexual* challenges the gay and lesbian movement's reliance on gay gene studies to secure civil rights. Although Brookey frames his argument as a Foucauldian genealogy (in that it critiques scientific discourse), gay rights remain the measure of political success or failure. In other words, social power is embodied in social institutions and public policies rather than cultural norms. The rhetorical theory used to illuminate the problems with gay gene research and its claims about sexuality characterizes rhetorical action as rational argument rather than employing poststructuralist methods of criticism. While this methodological choice is not a weakness for the study, it does substantially distinguish Brookey's project from mine. Most recently, Julie M. Thompson's *Mommie Queerest* combines queer theory and the rhetorical tradition to explore public discourses on lesbian motherhood.

7. Although *Discipline and Punish* and *The History of Sexuality* witness disciplinary and productive operations of power during the 18th and 19th centuries in Europe, Foucault's analysis by no means eclipses repressive forms of power during those epochs. Rather, Foucault's analysis merely strips repression-based power of its "theoretical primacy" (McNay 91). Todd May concurs, "Disciplinary practices did

not replace but were integrated into—and in turn altered—more traditional (as well as other, capillary) discourses and practices of power" (46).

8. Although it is nearly impossible to identify the canon in queer theory or produce an exhaustive list of titles that might fall under that classification of scholarship, the following list evidences the claim that most seminal works in queer theory take place in English, Philosophy, and Sociology departments. In literary studies, for instance: Eve Kosofsky Sedgwick, *Epistemology of the Closet;* Eve Kosofsky Sedgwick, *Tendencies;* Lee Edelman, *Homographesis: Essays in Gay Literary and Cultural Theory;* David M. Halperin, *Saint Foucault: Towards a Gay Hagiography;* Michael Warner, *The Trouble with Normal: Sex, Politics, and the Ethics of Queer Life.* In philosophy: Judith Butler, *Gender Trouble: Feminism and the Subversion of Identity;* Judith Butler, *Bodies That Matter: On the Discursive Limits of 'Sex';* Shane Phelan, ed., *Playing with Fire: Queer Politics, Queer Theories.* In sociology: Cindy Patton, *Sex and Germs: The Politics of AIDS;* Cindy Patton, *Inventing AIDS;* Steven Seidman, ed. *Queer Theory/Sociology;* Steven Seidman, *Difference Troubles: Queering Social Theory and Sexual Politics.*

9. Many scholars view Foucault's move from genealogy to ethics as a corrective to imagining disciplinary modes of power as monolithic or totalizing. It is uncertain whether the notion of productive power as monolithic should be attributed to Foucault himself or those who read his genealogies in this fashion. Lois McNay, in her reading of Foucault's "bio-power," argues that conceptualizing power as merely domination in *Discipline and Punish* and *The History of Sexuality* becomes fatalistically "paradigmatic," "one-sided," "reductionist," "monolithic," "undifferentiated," and "totalizing" (100–106). In other words, positing power as a singularity leaves no room for resistive agency within a genealogical account. Foucault's move from bio-power to "governmentality," in McNay's estimation, provides a necessary corrective to this view of power. She clarifies, "The use of such concepts [free individual, autonomy, and will] signals an important shift in Foucault's work, but this should not be seen as a retraction of previous thought; rather it is a rethinking of the relation between his work and Enlightenment thought in general" (129). While the subject remains an effect of power for Foucault, there exists a certain amount of liberty or freedom within power relations that enables resistance (130–131). Thomas McCarthy, bridging Foucault and the Frankfurt School, echoes McNay's position. Mapping the shift from genealogy to ethics, McCarthy witnesses Foucault's incorporation of "strategic" power into his line of thought (445, 454), which leads to the following articulation of resistive agency: "Both the ethical subject and the strategic subject are now represented as acting intentionally and voluntarily—within, to be sure, cultural and institutional systems that organize their ways of doing things . . . This model now enables us to make sense of the possibilities of resistance and revolt which, Foucault always insisted, are inherent in systems of power" (459).

10. Discourse's materiality is equally problematic in Foucault's genealogies. Foucault writes: "[Genealogy's] task is to expose a body totally imprinted by history and the process of history's destruction of the body" (*Language* 148). Although there

is some dispute about Foucault's formulation of "bodily inscription" and its potential to privilege discourse over materiality (see, for example, Butler, "Foucault and Paradox"; Grosz), such arguments clarify rather than reject the relationship between discourse and the material body. In fact, examining this relationship within the broader context of Foucault's archaeological and genealogical work, the primacy of discourse over the body is (at least) attenuated in the genealogies. The inclusion of the corporeal body in historical analyses of knowledge-power, or the move from epistemology to emergence (May; Visker, *Genealogy*), is the very corrective to archaeology that Foucault seeks (Deleuze, *Foucault;* McNay). Deleuze, in his reading of Foucault, characterizes the relationship between discourse and materiality as a productive relation or "practical assemblage" (51) between "the articulable and the visible" (51), between "statements and visibilities" (60). Deleuze observes, "Even *The Archaeology of Knowledge,* which insists on the primacy [of the statement], will state that there is neither causality from the one to the other nor symbolization between the two, and that if the statement has an object, it is a discursive object which is unique to the statement and is not isomorphic with the visible object" (*Foucault* 61).

11. Understanding "identity" as an ideographic term is not altogether new to rhetorical studies. See, for example: Cloud, "Family Values"; Delgado; Lucaites and Condit, "Reconstructing Equality"; Smith and Windes, *Progay/Antigay;* Smith and Windes, "Identity."

12. The Stonewall Riots of 1969 in New York City are typically viewed as the "mythical origin of gay liberation" (Jagose 32). Yet this historical narrative suffers from a certain amount of amnesia, forgetting earlier forms of gay organizing (D'Emilio), the influence of student organizations and New Left politics (Adam), and lesbian and gay organizing in San Francisco (Armstrong).

13. This project, in many ways, parallels DeLuca's supplementation of ideographic analysis, which offers Laclau and Mouffe's concept of "articulation" as a means of analyzing synchronic structures (*Image* 34–44).

14. For a detailed critique of Butler's use of causality, see Kaufman-Osborn, "Fashionable Subjects."

15. The humanist subject appears to permeate contemporary rhetorical criticism. McKerrow notes, "Public address, as traditionally conceived, is *agent-centered.* Even the study of social movements has been dominated by this perspective" ("Theory and Praxis" 100). For further elaboration on the position of the humanist subject within rhetorical studies, see Thomas W. Benson (xix–xxi). Also, the exchange between Carole Blair and Martha Cooper's "The Humanist Turn in Foucault's Rhetoric of Inquiry" and Walter Fisher's "The Narrative Paradigm: An Elaboration" is instructive on this point. Maurice Charland's essay, "Constitutive Rhetoric" advances one of the most radical critiques of humanist subjectivity within the speech communication discipline.

16. Jacques Derrida's essay "Signature, Event, Context" presents a similar position on the category of intention and its relationship to performativity. J. L. Austin's

conceptualization of performativity, Derrida notes, hinges upon "what Austin calls the total context" (*Limited Inc* 14). One of the fundamental elements of this context "remains, classically, consciousness, the conscious presence of the intention of the speaking subject in the totality of his speech act. As a result, performative communication becomes once more the communication of intentional meaning" (14). Consequently, Austin's articulation of performativity maintains the intention of the speaking subject as its "organizing center" (15). Of course, we must recognize that Derrida is not eliminating the category of subjective intention, but, rather, its "place will no longer be able to govern the entire scene and system of utterance" (18).

17. For recent critiques of lesbian and gay politics of inclusion, see: Clarke, *Virtuous Vice;* Rimmerman, *From Identity to Politics;* and Lisa Bower, "Queer Problems/ Straight Solutions: The Limits of a Politics of 'Official Recognition.'"

Chapter 1

1. Chapter Two in William B. Turner's *A Genealogy of Queer Theory* provides an excellent survey of the scholarly controversies that accompany Foucault's claim regarding the so-called birth date of modern homosexuality and other histories of modern male homosexuality. Acknowledging these complexities, however, late-nineteenth-century Western discourse remains the discursive backdrop to which I refer.

2. The distinction between literary and rhetorical scholarship, historically speaking, has primarily concerned their objects of study—"literature" and "oratory" respectively. For a rhetorician to return to literary discourse may thus be the ultimate disciplinary betrayal. Bringing rhetorical studies [critical rhetoric] and literary studies [queer theory] together, however, provides necessary correctives to their individual blind spots (Leff, "Things" 223). In the first instance, this academic intersection better orients critical rhetoricians to the discourse on sexuality and its broader historical context. In the second, the persuasive dimensions of discourse become as significant as its formal devices when the study of public discourse becomes central, rather than peripheral to our understandings of how sexual identity is constructed. Both disciplines have also wrestled with the ideological turn in the humanities. The political and (as I am claiming here) rhetorical usages of literary theory and criticism have been articulated most recently in Butler, Guillary, and Thomas's compilation entitled *What's Left of Theory?* And, as literary critic Terry Eagleton argued earlier: "It is not that [literary theory] reads the texts 'disinterestedly' and then places what it has read in the service of its values: the values govern the actual reading process itself, inform what sense criticism makes of the works it studies" (209).

3. Contemporary discourse on male homosexuality also elides difference. Sedgwick marvels, "It is a rather amazing fact that, of the very many dimensions along which the genital activity of one person can be differentiated from that of another (dimensions that include preference for certain acts, certain zones or sensations, cer-

tain physical types, a certain frequency, certain symbolic investments, certain relations of age and power, a certain species, a certain number of participants, etc. etc.
etc.), precisely one, the gender of object choice, emerged from the turn of the century, and has remained, as *the* dimension denoted by the now ubiquitous category
of 'sexual orientation'" (*Epistemology* 8).

4. This approach to analyzing narrative as rhetorical form radically departs
from Walter Fisher's classic treatise on narrative and rhetorical invention, "The Narrative Paradigm." In Fisher's account, in contrast, narrative success requires narrative coherence, namely "narrative probability" and "narrative fidelity" ("Narration
as Paradigm" 8).

5. From here on, I will cite passages from Melville's *Billy Budd* as *BB*.

Chapter 2

1. For legal scholarship critiquing right to privacy and immutability of sexuality arguments, see: Halley, "Sexual Orientation and the Politics of Biology: A Critique of the Argument from Immutability"; Rubenfeld, "The Right of Privacy";
and Thomas, "Beyond the Privacy Principle."

2. Legally speaking, legislation displays "invidious intent" toward minority
groups in two ways: 1) legislation that disadvantages a minority from engaging in
the political process (Koppelman, "Invidious Intent" 91) and 2) legislation that "reflects prejudice" (Koppelman, "Why Discrimination" 280–82). Lesbian and gay citizens often claim the latter form of invidious intent through suspect classification
rather than choosing the former strategy of securing their political voice in the
democratic process. The distinction between these two legal strategies is illustrated
through *Romer v. Evans* (1996) and its overturning of Colorado's Amendment 2 (see
Duncan, "The Narrow and Shallow Bite of *Romer* and the Eminent Rationality of
Dual-Gender Marriage: A [Partial] Response to Professor Koppelman"; Koppelman,
"*Romer v Evans* and Invidious Intent"; and Gerstmann, *The Constitutional Underclass*).

3. In 1943, the Texas anti-sodomy statute prohibited anal and oral intercourse
for both same-sex and opposite-sex couples. The law was altered in 1973 to crimi-
nalize the conduct of same-sex couples only (Coyle, 2003).

4. For a concise history of sodomy laws, see Robbins, "Trendsetter or behind
the times?"

5. The oral arguments in *Lawrence v. Texas,* presented to the Supreme Court on
March 26, 2003, are available at http://www.supremecourtus.gov/oral_arguments/
argument_transcripts/02-102.pdf.

6. For accounts documenting the evolving concept of "the right to privacy" in
constitutional law, see: M. Farrell 598–601; Hafen 539–45; Wardle, "Critical Analysis" 40–45).

7. *Lawrence v. Texas,* 539 U.S. 558 (2003).

8. In his dissention, Justice Scalia countered this racial analogy. The Texas stat-

ute, Scalia reasoned, was less like anti-miscegenation laws [*Loving v. Virginia*] and more like "[a] law against public nudity [which] targets the conduct that is closely correlated with being a nudist." For further critiques of what has been termed "the *Loving* analogy" as it might apply to same-sex marriage, see: Coolidge, "Law and the Politics of Marriage: *Loving v. Virginia* After Thirty Years"; Destro, "Law and the Politics of Marriage: *Loving v. Virginia* After Thirty Years Introduction"; Wardle, "*Loving v. Virginia* and the Constitutional Right to Marry, 1790–1990."

9. In the 1998 elections, Hawaiian voters enabled the legislature to enact a constitutional amendment banning same-sex marriage (Gallagher 46).

10. Such benefits include: joint parental custody, insurance and health benefits, joint tax returns, alimony and child support, inheritance of property, hospital visitation rights, a spouse's Social Security and retirement benefits, family leave, confidentiality of conversations, and the right to decide what to do with a partner's body after death ("National Campaign"). For further discussion of the legal advantages that would derive from legalizing same-sex marriage, see Chambers, "What If? The Legal Consequences of Marriage and the Legal Needs of Lesbian and Gay Male Couples."

11. The legal climate for gay and lesbian couples, however, is not entirely hostile at the turn of the century. In 2000, Vermont recognized "civil unions" for same-sex couples, providing them with many of the benefits and privileges held by opposite-sex married couples ("Landmark legislation").

12. For an historical analysis of the diverse legal usages of the term "sodomy," see Halley, "Reasoning."

13. Legal scholarship echoes Eskridge's argument claiming sexual orientation as a suspect class. See, for example: Farrell, "*Baehr v. Lewin:* Questionable Reasoning; Sound Judgment"; Hodges, "*Dean v. The District of Columbia:* Goin' to the Chapel and We're Gonna Get Married"; Strasser, "Domestic Relations and the Great Slumbering Baehr: On Defending Preclusion, Equal Protection and Fundamental Interests"; and Sunstein, "Homosexuality and the Constitution." Although sexual orientation appears to meet the criteria for suspect class status, Gerstmann argues that this change is unlikely (see *The Constitutional Underclass*).

14. For further arguments on sexual orientation and natural law doctrine, see the exchange between John Finnis and Andrew Koppelman: Finnis, "Law, Morality, and 'Sexual Orientation'" and Koppelman, "Sexual Morality and the Possibility of Same-Sex Marriage: Is Marriage Inherently Heterosexual?"

15. Lee Chiaramonte observes: "In order to believe that lesbians are not at risk for AIDS . . . I would have to believe we are either sexless or olympically monogamous; that we are not intravenous drug users; that we do not sleep with men; that we do not engage in sexual activities that could prove as dangerous as they are titillating" (qtd. in Crimp, "Promiscuity" 251–52).

16. Although the Western depiction of the gay male body as an image of death and degeneration can be traced back to the late nineteenth century (Nunokawa), its scapegoating function has resulted in devastating consequences during the AIDS

crisis, ranging from refusals of medical care and medical insurance to a lack of medical research for AIDS to antigay violence (Altman, *AIDS in the Mind of America;* C. Patton, *Sex and Germs*).

Chapter 3

1. For scholarly treatments of these two practices, see Gauthier and Forsyth; and Yep, Lovaas, and Pagonis.

2. Identification with "risk" is equally (if not more) important for women because they have largely been excluded from "risk" categories within the national discourse on HIV transmission (Treichler, *Theory* Chapter 8).

3. Most sources date 1991 as the birth of "Queer Theory"; the term first appeared in Teresa DeLaurentis's essay, "Queer Theory: Lesbian and Gay Sexualities, An Introduction," in *Differences: A Journal of Feminist Cultural Studies.*

4. These institutional effects include: refusals of medical care; interference in the writing of wills and the making of medical decisions; refusals of medical insurance, employment, and housing; violating the confidentiality of medical records; objections to federal funding for AIDS research; and antigay violence (Altman, *AIDS;* C. Patton, *Sex and Germs*). AIDS activism responded to these injustices, affecting institutional change on many levels: expediting federal drug approvals, lowering medication costs, and increasing funding for AIDS research (Wachter). Activists also significantly altered medical practice itself, resulting in more humane research practices, for instance: providing equal access to experimental medications for women, children, and people of color and using surrogate markers (the rate of T-cell decline rather than death) to measure the success of a particular drug (Epstein, "Democratic Science"; Epstein, "Lay Expertise").

5. The rhetorical association between semen and masculine agency in HIV transmission narratives becomes even more potent when contrasted with the cultural perception of blood as an "involuntary" mode of HIV transmission (Clark).

6. For a more exhaustive review of the rhetoric of science literature, see Treichler (*Theory,* Chapter Five), which concludes: "[S]cientific discourse is a form of shorthand in which facts, once admitted, need no longer retain the history of their fabrication" (170).

7. Crimp marks AIDS epidemiology as a complex rhetorical invention: "But AIDS probably did *not* affect gay men first, even in the U.S. What is now called AIDS was first *seen* in middle-class gay men in America, in part because of our access to medical care. Retrospectively, however, it appears that IV drug users—whether gay or straight—were dying of AIDS in New York City throughout the '70s and early '80s, but a class-based and racist health care system failed to notice, and an epidemiology equally skewed by class and racial bias failed to begin to look *until* 1987" ("Promiscuity" 249).

8. Epidemiology had to ignore other infected populations in order to produce this chronology of cases (Oppenheimer; C. Patton, *Fatal Advice*).

9. The spatiality of AIDS epidemiology is local as well, identifying HIV infection with specific zip codes (C. Patton, "Performativity").

10. To offset the apparent idealism of this solution, Rotello later advocates "serial monogamy"—presumably the way of life for most lesbians (245–46)—which often relies upon the HIV antibody test to confirm the seronegative status of the partners. This method of safe-sex creates substantive problems when the partners fail to consider the three-month "window period" of the test during which individuals can transmit the virus before having produced HIV antibodies (J. Blake Scott 100–20).

11. Rotello's evidence for the failure of the condom code, however, is problematic on several levels (102–3). Based entirely upon survey research, condom "misuse" and "inconsistent" condom use are cited as the key reasons for condom failure. Additionally, two of the three studies cited rely solely upon data from *heterosexual* couples, which is entirely irrelevant to the discussion of gay male sexual practices and networks. The single study on gay men and condom use involves seven gay men who "reported" using condoms every time and were still infected with HIV. We might also logically expect that condoms do not work in HIV prevention when they are misused or used inconsistently. On this point, Rotello is discussing human failures, not condom failures.

12. See also: Atkins et al.; Birchard; Byrn et al.; Fackelmann; "HIV in Semen"; and Henry et al.

13. See also M. S. Cohen et al.

14. Infertility studies illustrate the synecdochic link between semen and the male body through the figure of sperm, for to diagnose the "infertile male" is to diagnose infertile semen or semen with "low sperm count" (Auger et al.; Bonde et al.; Irvine et al.; R. J. Levine et al.). This relationship is reproduced in the discourse on sperm donation (Daniels and Lewis; Daniels, Lewis, and Curson).

Chapter 4

1. For a detailed critique of this slippage between promiscuity and unsafe sex, see Crimp, "How to Have Promiscuity in an Epidemic."

2. For a critical discussion of the "pink dollar," see Bronski 138–57.

3. Allen Ellenzweig, in his chronology of homoerotic photography, warns: "[I]t would be a simplification of photographic history, and simple minded as well, to suppose that only homosexual photographers deal in homoerotic images" (3).

4. The Clone's "hypermasculine affect," we must remember, was "distinctly gay" rather than pure mimesis (M. Levine 56–58). Levine notes, "Clones rejected [heterosexual] nonchalance and stylized these looks. They kept their hair short, beards and mustaches clipped, and clothing tailored and matched. In a sense, the clone brought a gay sensibility to a gendered attire" (61).

5. The damaging social impacts of this phenomenon are said to range from an increase in steroid use among gay men (Freiss; Signorile, *Life* 133–75), to a decrease

in self-esteem generally (Mann 346), to "internalized homophobia" more narrowly (Feraios 427).

6. Next to knowledge and power, Foucault identifies the study of ethics as the third component of genealogy (*Ethics* 262) and in so doing provides the basis for queer ethics in several writings. In one sense, the discussion of queer ethics begins with gay culture. Foucault posits, for instance, "Rather than saying what we said at one time, 'Let's try to re-introduce homosexuality into the general norm of social relations,' let's say the reverse—'No! Let's escape as much as possible from the type of relations that society proposes for us and try to create in the empty space where we are new relational possibilities.' (*Ethics* 160). It is, therefore, logical to begin our discussion of queer ethics in cultural expressions of the erotic. In another sense, queer ethics is substantively linked to the body and pleasures. The move to the body does not supplant political uses of "identity" and "secrecy," but rather complicates what it means to enact queer ethics and queer resistance. In a different interview, Foucault explains, "Not only do we have to defend ourselves, not only affirm ourselves, as an identity but as a creative force" (*Ethics* 164). Gay culture's creative force, its capability to perform non-heteronormative practices, lies significantly within its ability to invent "new possibilities of pleasure" (165).

7. The basis of Mohr's critique becomes even clearer when we consider Leo Bersani's inverse treatment of gay anal sex and gay sadomasochism. Bersani argues, for instance, that gay anal sex enacts the death of phallic, masculinist, heteronormative agency ("Rectum" 222) while gay sadomasochism simply reinforces masculinist forms of domination and submission (*Homos* 87–107).

8. I borrow significantly here from Luce Irigaray's conception of phallic power as "the One" or Sameness (*The Sex Which Is Not One*).

9. Nick Crossley provides an adept critique of Foucault's critique of Merleau-Ponty. Specifically, he argues that Foucault's reading is often vague and lacking in direct evidence (137–45).

10. For a good summary of Merleau-Ponty's conceptualization of the body, see *Phenomenology of Perception,* pages 234–37.

11. To summarize this debate as it swirls around Foucault's genealogical work, I offer the following. Dick Pels argues that Foucault's knowledge-power relationship ought to be understood as "duality" rather than "dualism" (1022). Rather than opposing knowledge and power, thereby forcing a reductionist account in one direction or another, Pels's move toward knowledge-power as a "duality" privileges neither epistemology nor history; genealogy is neither transcendental nor deterministic. Yet both Todd May's *Between Genealogy and Epistemology* and Rudi Visker's *Genealogy as Critique* ask: how can genealogy justify its own invention of truth? May argues that genealogy lacks "epistemic justification" when it reduces knowledge to power and thus advances a wholesale relativist account of history, a reduction that Foucault inherits from Nietzsche's "perspectivism" (77). May creates an "epistemic space—a space without foundations to be sure, but epistemic nonetheless—that allows genealogy to be more than another expression of what it analyzes" (89). Genealogy as

political advocacy requires some kind of justification for its claims. But if this justification does not emerge in the form of universal or transcendental foundations, then what form must it take in order to avoid the pejorative charge of "relativist"? May succinctly articulates, "The answer to the question of power is not its rejection, however, nor the rejection of practices and discourses that participate in it . . . Rather, the answer is to study discourses and practices, to determine the nature and extent of the constraints they impose, and to evaluate whether those constraints are acceptable or not" (113). In other words, epistemic justifications for genealogical critique take the form of rhetoric, making its claims about power and resistance "acceptable." Rudi Visker's reading of Foucault's *Discipline and Punish* traces a similar problematic and comes to a similar conclusion regarding genealogical critique's potential. Visker locates the knowledge-power problematic in Foucault's discussion of the connection between the prison as a historical practice [emergence] and the human sciences that appeared simultaneously [possibility] (*Genealogy* 55–56). Once again, the potential for these two forces to be reduced to one another causes Visker to initially doubt genealogy's capacity as a mode of "critique" (58–71). And, like May, Visker views these reductionist accounts of knowledge-power as a path toward either fatalistic nihilism or idealistic relativism (100–102). In the end, the potential for genealogy to become "critique" exists in Foucault's later work on ethics, which enables agency through a concept of "liberty" or "freedom" (Visker, *Genealogy* 103).

Chapter 5

1. The Gay Liberation Front's explicitly cultural objectives are even more striking when compared to the Gay Activists Alliance (GAA), founded in March of 1970. The GAA, in contrast to GLF's vision of a cultural revolution, spoke in the language of "rights" and "personhood" (Teal 109–11). Creating an open, public gay identity was a significant part of GAA's political strategizing. Yet GAA saw itself as a purely political organization rather than a cultural and social form of activism.

2. This choice is informed by Jandt and Darsey's observation that next to friends, literature [novels, periodicals, poetry, etc.] is the most prevalent source of positive information about being gay and thus impacts non-heterosexual citizens' feelings about themselves (20).

3. Deleuze's claim in *Foucault* that resistance comes first is a matter of debate within the philosophical tradition. Françoise Proust, for instance, questions the primacy given to resistance, claiming that resistance is "a game of actions and reactions between being and its double. This is not 'extra-being' as Deleuze would have it. It is counter-being" (34). Proust later explicates, "Resistance . . . is the contemporary and double of the power it resists, neither primary nor secondary in relation to it. Resistance constantly accompanies power" (35). This reading of Deleuze stands in stark contrast to Rodowick's thematization of "the memory of resistance, which expresses the powers of the outside" (418). The Outside, in both Deleuze and Foucault, does not denote "exteriority" but rather a network of "forces" (Rodowick

419). As Rodowick concludes, "Resistance is the awakening of forces of life that are more active, more affirmative, richer in possibilities than the life we now live" (424).

4. See also Vivian, "Threshold of the Self"; Vivian, "Always a Third Party Who Says 'Me'"; and Lewin, "Dispersing the *Cogito*."

5. On the relationship between philosophy and literature, see also Colombat, "Deleuze and the Three Powers of Literature and Philosophy."

6. Deleuze and Guattari's becoming introduces movement and time into matters of subjectivity, giving voice to the molecular machines that serve as conditions of production for the subject. Doing so, they borrow from molecular biology to critique the psychoanalytic account of subjectivity, which eclipses the organism's dynamic relationship with the environment (see, for example, Pearson, *Germinal Life,* pages 179–85).

7. Taking their cue from bio-philosophy, Deleuze and Guattari argue that evolutionary change occurs in molecular compositions of particles-speeds rather than moral organizations of forms-functions (Pearson, *Germinal Life* 160). Pearson explains, "'Change,' therefore, cannot be conceived as the passage from one pre-established form to another but rather in terms of a process of decoding" (159). Although Deleuze and Guattari do not create a "dualist opposition between the molecular and the molar" (168), the aim of rhizomatics is to "give primacy to the molecular multiplicities" (183).

Conclusion

1. For diverse treatments of historical context in the rhetorical tradition, see: Browne; Condit, "Rhetorical Criticism"; Condit, "The Character of 'History'"; Dow; Leff and Sachs; Leff; Lucas; McGee, "Text"; Medhurst, "Public Address"; Soloman; Zarefsky.

2. James Darsey's work on lesbian and gay social movements presents two different accounts of the relationship between rhetoric and history and thus enables us to witness how these distinctive accounts impact rhetorical scholarship. Darsey's first account of LGBT activism locates the rhetorical object against the shifting backdrop of historical events, which then shaped the rhetorical choices of the movement. "Catalytic events," exigencies or dramatic changes in the rhetorical situation become "moments in the life of a movement that provide the appropriate conditions for discourse" ("Evolution" 46). The historical constraints on rhetorical discourse, in the catalytic event model, are extradiscursive, clearly marked off from rhetorical invention by space and time: "[Catalytic events] (1) are historical rather than rhetorical, (2) are nontactical (either extraneous to the movement in origin, spontaneous in origin, or both), (3) achieve tremendous significance for the movement, and (4) precede rhetorical responses that constitute demonstrably discrete internally homogeneous rhetorical eras" (46). Darsey's examples of catalytic events, in various social movements, further indicate this extradiscursivity: the Boston massacre influenced colonial rhetoric, the Kansas-Nebraska Act changed abolitionist rhetoric, both

world wars altered labor rhetoric, Rosa Parks's refusal in Montgomery mobilized the civil rights movement, Friedan's *The Feminine Mystique* galvanized feminism, the AIDS epidemic greatly impacted the LGBT movement (46). Darsey is correct on all counts. Extradiscursive events indeed catalyzed, influenced, or otherwise altered the course of these social movements. Turning to the final example, however, should remind us that the rhetorical choices available to social movements are also constrained by discursive conditions as well. The impact of HIV/AIDS on the LGBT movement and its rhetorical situation cannot be underestimated or overstated, yet the movement's rhetorical response to this catalytic event also took place within specific discursive fields, namely: epidemiology, virology, and immunology. The discursive conditions of scientific knowledge were thus equally restrictive on the LGBT movement's public discourse on HIV/AIDS, effectively governing its rhetorical choices. An analysis of catalytic events, however, cannot account for these forces of social power and ideological production because catalytic events (as exigencies only) exist outside of and prior to discourse.

Darsey's second account of LGBT activism, in contrast, recognizes the *discursive* constraints on a social movement's rhetorical tactics. Mapping the historical emergence of the Gay Liberation Movement in the 1950s, Darsey explains that public discourse on homosexuality had been effectively governed by specific social institutions: the law, the church, and medicine ("Die Non" 49). World War II was clearly an extradiscursive, "catalytic event" that enabled lesbian and gay populations to organize socially and politically in urban settings in an unprecedented manner. The war also substantively altered the discursive conditions in which public conversations on homosexuality occurred. These discursive conditions, "legal realism" specifically, produced the necessary ground from which a rhetoric of tolerance and rights emerged. This shift in the discursive conditions of American law, Darsey argues, produced a gay liberation rhetoric founded upon "legality" rather than "justice," characterized by the gay movement's "recognition of the law as the source of rights, and in its advocacy of a solution that is within the law" (55). Historical context, in this account, is discursive as well as extradiscursive. History places constraints on discourse, the very ground from which political activism speaks.

References

Abel, Marco. "*Fargo:* The Violent Production of the Masochistic Contract as a Cinematic Concept." *Critical Studies in Mass Communication* 16 (1999): 308–28.

Adam, Barry D. *The Rise of a Gay and Lesbian Movement,* rev. ed. New York: Twayne Publishers, 1995.

Altman, Dennis. *AIDS in the Mind of America: The Social, Political, and Psychological Impact of a New Epidemic.* Garden City, NY: Anchor Press, Doubleday, 1986.

———. *Power and Community: Organizational and Cultural Responses to AIDS.* London: Taylor & Francis, 1994.

Anderson, Deborah J., Thomas R. O'Brien, Joseph A. Politch, Adriana Martinez, George R. Seage III, Nancy Padian, Robert Horsburgh, Jr., and Kenneth H. Mayer. "Effects of Disease Stage and Zidovudine Therapy on the Detection of Human Immunodeficiency Virus Type 1 in Semen." *JAMA: The Journal of the American Medical Association* 267.20 (1992): 2769–74.

Arkes, Hadley. "Gay Marriage in 1996?" *American Enterprise* May 1995: 57–59.

———. "The Closet Straight." *Same-Sex Marriage: Pro and Con, A Reader.* Ed. Andrew Sullivan. New York: Vintage Books, 1997. 154–56.

Armstrong, Elizabeth A. *Forging Gay Identities: Organizing Sexuality in San Francisco, 1950–1994.* Chicago & London: The University of Chicago Press, 2002.

Arning, Bill. "'Achieving Failure': Gym Culture 2000." *Gay and Lesbian Review* 7 (2000): 39.

Atkins, M. C., E. M. Carlin, V. C. Emery, P. D. Griffiths, and F. Boag. "Fluctuations of HIV Load in Semen of HIV Positive Patients with Newly Acquired Sexually Transmitted Diseases." *British Medical Journal (International)* 313 n7053 (1996): 341–42.

Auger, Jacques, Jean Marie Kunstmann, Francoise Czyglik, and Pierre Jouannet. "Decline in Semen Quality among Fertile Men in Paris during the Past 20 Years." *New England Journal of Medicine* 332.5 (1995): 281–85.

Austin, J. L. *How to Do Things with Words.* 2nd ed. Ed. J. O. Urmson and Marina Sbisa. Cambridge, MA: Harvard University Press, 1962.

Babst, Gordon A. "Community, Rights Talk, and the Communitarian Dissent in

Bowers v. Hardwick." *Playing with Fire: Queer Politics, Queer Theories.* Ed. Shane Phelan. New York & London: Routledge, 1997. 139–72.

Barber, Stephen, and David Clark (eds.). *Regarding Sedgwick: Essays on Queer Culture and Critical Theory.* New York & London: Routledge, 2002.

Barthes, Roland. *The Pleasure of the Text.* Trans. Richard Miller. New York: Hill and Wang, 1975.

———. "Rhetoric of the Image." *Image-Music-Text.* Trans. Stephen Heath. New York: Hill and Wang, 1977. 32–51.

———. *A Lover's Discourse: Fragments.* Trans. Richard Howard. New York: Hill and Wang, 1978.

Bataille, Georges. *Erotism: Death and Sensuality.* Trans. Mary Dalwood. San Francisco: City Lights Books, 1986.

Beaver, Harold. "Homosexual Signs (In Memory of Roland Barthes)." *Critical Inquiry* 8 (1981): 99–119.

Bennett, Jeffrey A. "Citizenship in Vein: Queer Identity and the Stigma of Banned Blood." Diss. Indiana University, 2004.

Benson, Thomas W. "Beacons and Boundary-Markers: Landmarks in Rhetorical Criticism." *Landmark Essays on Rhetorical Criticism.* Ed. Thomas W. Benson. Davis, CA: Hermagoras Press, 1993. xi–xxii.

Bergman, David. "Books and Issues: *The Epistemology of the Closet.*" *Raritan* 11 (1991): 115–31.

Bergson, David. *Gaiety Transfigured: Gay Self-Representation in American Literature.* Madison: University of Wisconsin Press, 1991.

Berlant, Lauren, and Michael Warner. "Sex in Public." *Critical Inquiry* 24 (1998): 547–66.

Bernstein, Mary, and Renate Reimann. "Queer Families and the Politics of Visibility." *Queer Families, Queer Politics: Challenging Culture and the State.* Ed. Mary Bernstein and Renate Reimann. New York: Columbia University Press, 2001. 1–20.

Bersani, Leo. "Is the Rectum a Grave?" *AIDS: Cultural Analysis, Cultural Activism.* Ed. Douglas Crimp. Cambridge, MA: The MIT Press, 1988. 197–222.

———. *Homos.* Cambridge, MA: Harvard University Press, 1995.

"Bestsellers." *Lambda Book Review* June 1997: 5.

"Bestsellers." *Lambda Book Review* August 1997: 5.

Biesecker, Barbara. "Michel Foucault and the Question of Rhetoric." *Philosophy and Rhetoric* 25.4 (1992): 351–64.

Birchard, Karen. "Different HIV-1 Strains Found in Semen and Blood." *Lancet* 352.9137 (1998): 1363.

Blair, Carole. "The Statement: Foundation of Foucault's Historical Criticism." *Western Journal of Speech Communication* 51 (1987): 364–83.

Blair, Carole, and Martha Cooper. "The Humanist Turn in Foucault's Rhetoric of Inquiry." *Quarterly Journal of Speech* 73 (1987): 151–71.

Blasius, Mark. *Gay and Lesbian Politics: Sexuality and the Emergence of a New Ethic.* Philadelphia: Temple University Press, 1994.

Blasius, Mark, and Shane Phelan (eds.). *We Are Everywhere: A Historical Sourcebook of Gay and Lesbian Politics.* New York & London: Routledge, 1997.

Bonde, Jens Peter E., Erik Ernst, Tina Kold Jensen, Niels Henrik I. Hjollund, Henrik Kolstad, Tine Brink Henriksen, Thomas Scheike, Aleksander Giwercman, Jorn Olsen, and Niels Erik Skakkebaek. "Relation between Semen Quality and Fertility: A Population-Based Study of 430 First-Pregnancy Planners." *Lancet* 352.9135 (1998): 1172–77.

Bordo, Susan. *The Male Body: A New Look at Men in Public and Private.* New York: Farrar, Straus, and Giroux, 1999.

Bowers v. Hardwick, 478 U.S. 186 (1986).

Bower, Lisa. "Queer Problems/Straight Solutions: The Limits of a Politics of 'Official Recognition.'" *Playing with Fire: Queer Politics, Queer Theories.* Ed. Shane Phelan. New York & London: Routledge, 1997. 267–91.

Bronski, Michael. The Pleasure Principle: Sex, Backlash, and the Struggle for Gay Freedom. New York: St. Martin's Press, 1998.

Brookey, Robert Alan. "A Community Like Philadelphia." *Western Journal of Communication* 60.1 (1996): 40–56.

———. *Reinventing the Male Homosexual: The Rhetoric and Power of the Gay Gene.* Bloomington: Indiana University Press, 2002.

Browne, Stephen H. "Response: Context in Critical Theory and Practice." *Western Journal of Communication* 65.3 (2001): 330–35.

Browning, Frank. *The Culture of Desire: Paradox and Perversity in Gay Lives Today.* New York: Vintage Books, 1993.

Brownworth, Victoria. "Campus Queer Query." *OutWeek* 16 May 1990: 48–49.

Buchanan, Ian. *Deleuzism: A Metacommentary.* Durham, NC: Duke University Press, 2000.

Burke, Kenneth. *The Philosophy of Literary Form.* 3rd ed. Berkeley: University of California Press, 1973.

Butler, Judith. "Foucault and the Paradox of Bodily Inscriptions." *Journal of Philosophy* 11 (1989): 601–7.

———. "Contingent Foundations: Feminism and the Question of 'Postmodernism.'" *Feminists Theorize the Political.* Ed. Judith Butler and Joan W. Scott. New York: Routledge, 1992. 3–21.

———. *Bodies That Matter: On the Discursive Limits of "Sex."* New York: Routledge, 1993.

———. *Excitable Speech: A Politics of the Performative.* New York: Routledge, 1997.

———. "Restaging the Universal." *Contingency, Hegemony, Universality: Contemporary Dialogues on the Left.* Ed. Judith Butler, Ernesto Laclau, and Slavoj Zizek. London & New York: Verso, 2000. 11–43.

Butler, Judith, John Guillary, and Kendall Thomas. "Preface." *What's Left of Theory?:*

New Work on the Politics of Literary Theory. Ed. Judith Butler, John Guillary, and Kendall Thomas. London & New York: Routledge, 2000. viii–xii.

Byrn, Randal A., Dezhen Zhang, Robert Eyre, Katherine McGowan, and Ann A. Kiessling. "HIV-1 in Semen: An Isolated Virus Reservoir." *Lancet* 350.9085 (1997): 1141.

Cain, Patricia A. "Litigating for Lesbian and Gay Rights: A Legal History." *Virginia Law Review* 79 (1993): 1551–1642.

Casarino, Cesare. "Gomorrahs of the Deep or, Melville, Foucault, and the Question of Heterotopia." *Arizona Quarterly* 51 (1995): 1–25.

Chambers, David. "What If? The Legal Consequences of Marriage and the Legal Needs of Lesbian and Gay Male Couples." *Michigan Law Review* 95 (1996): 447–91.

Charland, Maurice. "Finding a Horizon and Telos: The Challenge to Critical Rhetoric." *Quarterly Journal of Speech* 77 (1991): 71–74.

———. "Constitutive Rhetoric: The Case of the *Peuple Quebecois.*" *Quarterly Journal of Speech* 73 (1987): 133–50.

Chauncey, George. *Gay New York: Gender, Urban Culture, and the Making of the Gay Male World, 1890–1940.* New York: Basic Books, 1994.

Clark, E. "Pink Water: The Archetype of Blood and the Pool of Infinite Contagion." *Power in the Blood: A Handbook on AIDS, Politics and Communication.* Ed. W. Elwood. Mahwah, NJ, & London: Lawrence Erlbaum Associates, Pub., 1999. 9–24.

Clarke, Eric O. *Virtuous Vice: Homoeroticism and the Public Sphere.* Durham and London: Duke University Press, 2000.

Cloud, Dana L. "The Rhetoric of Family Values: Scapegoating, Utopia, and the Privatization of Social Responsibility." *Western Journal of Communication* 62 (1998): 387–419.

———. "The Materiality of Discourse as Oxymoron: A Challenge to Critical Rhetoric." *Western Journal of Communication* 58 (1994): 141–63.

Cohen, Ed. *Talk on the Wilde Side: Toward a Genealogy of a Discourse on Male Sexualities.* London & New York: Routledge, 1993.

Cohen, Myron S., Irving F. Hoffman, Rachel A. Royce, Peter Kazembe, John R. Dyer, Celine Costello Daly, Dick Zimba, Pietro L. Vernazza, Martin Maida, Susan A. Fiscus, Joseph J. Eron, Jr., and the AIDSCAP Malawi Research Group. "Reduction of Concentration of HIV-1 in Semen after Treatment of Urethritis: Implications for Prevention of Sexual Transmission of HIV-1." *Lancet* 349.9069 (1997): 1868–73.

Cohen, Richard A. "Merleau-Ponty, the Flesh, and Foucault." *Philosophy Today* 28 (1984): 329–38.

Colombat, Andre Pierre. "Deleuze and the Three Power and Literature and Philosophy: To Demystify, to Experiment, to Create." *South Atlantic Quarterly* 96 (1997): 579–97.

Condit, Celeste. "The Character of 'History' in Rhetoric and Cultural Studies." *At the Intersection: Cultural Studies and Rhetorical Studies.* Ed. Thomas Rosteck. New York & London: The Guilford Press, 1999. 168–85.

———. "Rhetorical Criticism and Audiences: The Extremes of McGee and Leff." *Western Journal of Speech Communication* 54 (1990): 330–45.

Connolly, William E. "Beyond Good and Evil: The Ethical Sensibility of Michel Foucault." *Political Theory* 21 (1993): 365–89.

Conway, Daniel W. "Tumbling Dice: Gilles Deleuze and the Economy of *Répétition.*" *Deleuze and Philosophy: The Difference Engineer.* Ed. Keith Ansell Pearson. London & New York: Routledge, 1997. 73–90.

Coolidge, David Ogden. "Law and the Politics of Marriage: *Loving v. Virginia* After Thirty Years." *Brigham Young University Journal of Public Law* 12 (1998): 201–38.

Cooper, Martha. "Rhetorical Criticism and Foucault's Philosophy of Discursive Events." *Central States Speech Journal* 39.1 (1988): 1–17.

Corey, Frederick C., and Thomas K. Nakayama. "Sextext." *Text and Performance Quarterly* 17 (1997): 58–68.

Cosgrove, Peter. "Edmund Burke, Gilles Deleuze, and the Subversive Masochism of the Image." *ELH* 66 (1999): 405–37.

Coyle, Marcia. "In the Bedroom: Gay Rights Are at the Center of the Sodomy Case at the Supreme Court." *National Law Journal.* 2003, March 24, A1.

Crawford, Isiaah, Kevin Allison, Brian Zamboni, and Thomas Soto. "The Influence of Dual-identity Development on the Psychosocial Functioning of African-American Gay and Bisexual Men." *Journal of Sex Research* 39 (2002): 179–90.

Creech, James. *Closet Writing/Gay Reading: The Case of Melville's Pierre.* Chicago: University of Chicago Press, 1993.

Crimp, Douglas. "How to Have Promiscuity in an Epidemic." *AIDS: Cultural Analysis, Cultural Activism.* Ed. Douglas Crimp. Cambridge, MA: The MIT Press, 1988. 237–71.

Crossley, Nick. *The Politics of Subjectivity.* Brookfield, VT: Avebury, 1994.

Crowley, Sharon. "Reflections on an Argument That Won't Go Away: Or, A Turn of the Ideological Screw." *Quarterly Journal of Speech* 78 (1992): 450–65.

Daniels, Ken R., and Gillian M. Lewis. "Donor Insemination: The Gifting and Selling of Semen." *Social Science & Medicine* 42.11 (1996): 1521–36.

Daniels, Ken R., Gillian M. Lewis, and Ruth Curson. "Information Sharing in Semen Donation: The Views of Donors." *Social Science & Medicine* 44.5 (1997): 673–80.

Darsey, James. "Die Non: Gay Liberation and the Rhetoric of Pure Tolerance." *Queer Words, Queer Images: Communication and the Construction of Homosexuality.* Ed. Jeffrey Ringer. New York & London: New York University Press, 1994. 45–76.

———. "From 'Gay is Good' to the Scourge of AIDS: The Evolution of Gay Liberation Rhetoric, 1977–1990." *Communication Studies* 42 (1991): 43–66.

Dean, Craig R. "Gay Marriage: A Civil Right." *Journal of Homosexuality* 27.3–4 (1994): 111–15.

Deetz, Stanley. "Negation and the Political Function of Rhetoric." *Quarterly Journal of Speech* 69 (1983): 434–41.

DeLaurentis, Teresa. "Queer Theory: Lesbian and Gay Sexualities, An Introduction." *Differences* 3.2 (1991): iii–xviii.

Deleuze, Gilles. *Foucault.* Trans. Sean Hand. Minneapolis & London: University of Minnesota Press, 1988.

———. *Masochism: Coldness and Cruelty.* Trans. Jean McNeil. New York: Zone Books, 1989.

———. "Literature and Life." Trans. Daniel W. Smith and Michael A. Greco. *Critical Inquiry* 23 (1997): 225–30.

Deleuze, Gilles, and Felix Guattari. *Anti-Oedipus: Capitalism and Schizophrenia.* Trans. Robert Hurley, Mark Seem, and Helen R. Lane. Minneapolis: University of Minnesota Press, 1983.

———. *A Thousand Plateaus: Capitalism and Schizophrenia.* Trans. Brian Massumi. Minneapolis: University of Minnesota Press, 1987.

———. *What Is Philosophy?* Trans. Hugh Tomlinson and Graham Burchell. New York: Columbia University Press, 1994.

Delgado, Fernando Pedro. "Chicano Movement Rhetoric: An Ideographic Interpretation." *Communication Quarterly* 43 (1995): 446–54.

DeLuca, Kevin Michael. *Image Politics: The New Rhetoric of Environmental Activism.* New York & London: The Guilford Press, 1999.

D'Emilio, John. *Sexual Politics, Sexual Communities: The Making of a Homosexual Minority in the United States, 1940–1970,* 2nd ed. Chicago & London: The University of Chicago Press, 1983.

Derrida, Jacques. *Limited Inc.* Trans. Samuel Weber and Jeffrey Mehlman. Evanston, IL: Northwestern University Press, 1988.

Destro, Robert A. "Law and the Politics of Marriage: *Loving v. Virginia* After Thirty Years Introduction." *The Catholic University Law Review* 47 (1998): 1207–30.

Deverell, K., and A. Prout. "Sexuality, Identity, and Community: Reflections on the MESMAC Project." *AIDS: Safety, Sexuality, and Risk.* Ed. P. Applegate, P. Davies, and G. Hart. London: Taylor & Francis, 1995. 172–93.

Diaz, R. M. *Latino Gay Men and HIV: Culture, Sexuality, and Risk Behavior.* New York & London: Routledge, 1998.

Doel, Marcus A. "A Hundred Thousand Lines of Flight: A Machinic Introduction to the Nomad Thought and Scrumpled Geography of Gilles Deleuze and Felix Guattari." *Environment and Planning: Society and Space* 14 (1996): 421–39.

Dow, Bonnie J. "Response: Criticism and Authority in the Artistic Mode." *Western Journal of Communication* 65.3 (2001): 336–48.

Dowsett, Gary, Jonathan Bollen, David McInnes, Murray Couch, and Barry Edwards. "HIV/AIDS and Constructs of Gay Community: Researching Educational Practice within Community-based Health Promotion for Gay Men." *International Journal of Social Research Methodology* 4 (2001): 205–223.

Doyle, Richard. *On Beyond Living: Rhetorical Transformations of the Life Sciences.* Stanford, CA: Stanford University Press, 1997.

Duncan, Richard F. "Symposium: *Romer v. Evans:* The Narrow and Shallow Bite of Romer and the Eminent Rationality of Dual-Gender Marriage: A [Partial] Response to Professor Koppelman." *William and Mary Bill of Rights Journal* 6 (winter 1994): 147–66.

During, Simon. *Foucault and Literature: Toward a Genealogy of Writing.* London & New York: Routledge, 1992.

Dutton, Kenneth R. *The Perfectible Body: The Western Ideal of Male Physical Development.* New York: Continuum, 1995.

Dyer, Richard. *White.* London & New York: Routledge, 1997.

Eagleton, Terry. *Literary Theory: An Introduction.* Minneapolis: The University of Minnesota Press, 1983.

Edelman, Lee. *Homographesis: Essays in Gay Literary and Cultural Theory.* New York: Routledge, 1994.

Edwards, Tim. *Men in the Mirror: Men's Fashion, Masculinity, and Consumer Society.* London: Cassell, 1997.

Ellenzweig, Allen. *The Homoerotic Photograph: Male Images from Durieu/ Delacroix to Mapplethorpe.* New York: Columbia University Press, 1992.

Elliot, Patricia. "Politics, Identity, and Social Change: Contested Grounds in Psychoanalytic Feminism." *Hypatia* 10 (1995): 41–55.

Epstein, Steven. "Gay Politics, Ethnic Identity: The Limits of Constructionism." *Socialist Review* 93/94 (1987): 9–54.

———. "Democratic Science?: AIDS Activism and the Contested Construction of Knowledge." *Socialist Review* 21 (1991): 35–64.

———. "The Construction of Lay Expertise: AIDS Activism and the Forging of Credibility in the Reform of Clinical Trials." *Science, Technology, and Human Values* 20 (1995): 408–37.

Erni, John Nguyen. *Unstable Frontiers: Technomedicine and the Cultural Politics of 'Curing' AIDS.* Minneapolis & London: University of Minnesota Press, 1994.

Escoffier, Jeffrey. *American Homo: Community and Perversity.* Berkeley, Los Angeles, and London: University of California Press, 1998.

Eskridge Jr., William N. *The Case for Same-Sex Marriage: From Sexual Liberty to Civilized Commitment.* New York: The Free Press, 1996.

Fackelmann, Kathy A. "Seeking the AIDS Virus in Semen." *Science News* 138.18 (1990): 286.

Farrell, Megan E. "*Baehr v. Lewin:* Questionable Reasoning; Sound Judgment." *Journal of Contemporary Health and Law Policy* 11 (spring 1995): 589–616.

Farrell, Thomas B. "Knowledge, Consensus, and Rhetorical Theory." *Quarterly Journal of Speech* 62 (1976): 1–14.

Feraios, Andrew J. "If Only I Were Cute: Lookism and Internalized Homophobia in the Gay Male Community." *Looking Queer: Body Image and Identity in Lesbian,*

Bisexual, Gay, and Transgender Communities. Ed. Dawn Atkins. New York & London: Harrington Park Press, 1998. 415–29.

Finnis, John M. "Law, Morality, and 'Sexual Orientation.'" *Notre Dame Law Review* 69 (1994): 1049–76.

Fisher, Walter. "The Narrative Paradigm: An Elaboration." *Communication Monographs* 52 (1985): 347–67.

———. "Narration as a Human Communications Paradigm: The Case of Public Moral Argument." *Communication Monographs* 51 (1984): 1–22.

Foss, Sonja K., and Ann Gill. "Michel Foucault's Theory of Rhetoric as Epistemic." *Western Journal of Speech Communication* 51 (1987): 384–401.

Foucault, Michel. *The Order of Things: An Archaeology of the Human Sciences.* New York: Vintage Books, 1970.

———. *The Archaeology of Knowledge.* Trans. A. M. Sheridan Smith. New York: Pantheon Books, 1972.

———. *Discipline and Punish: The Birth of the Prison.* Trans. Alan Sheridan. New York: Vintage Books, 1977.

———. *Language, Counter-Memory, Practice: Selected Essays and Interviews.* Ed. Donald F. Bouchard. Trans. Donald F. Bouchard and Sherry Simon. Ithica, NY: Cornell University Press, 1977.

———. *The History of Sexuality Volume 1: An Introduction.* Trans. Robert Hurley. New York: Vintage Books, 1978.

———. *Power/Knowledge: Selected Interviews and Other Writings, 1972–1977.* Ed. Colin Gordon. Trans. Colin Gordon, Leo Marshall, John Mepham, Kate Soper. New York: Pantheon Books, 1980.

———. *The Use of Pleasure: Volume 2 of The History of Sexuality.* Trans. Robert Hurley. New York: Vintage Books, 1985.

———. *The Care of the Self: Volume 3 of The History of Sexuality.* Trans. Robert Hurley. New York: Vintage Books, 1986.

———. *Politics, Philosophy, Culture: Interviews and Other Writings 1977–1984.* Ed. Lawrence D. Kritzman. Trans. Alan Sheridan and others. New York: Routledge, 1988.

———. *Ethics: Subjectivity and Truth.* Ed. Paul Rabinow. New York: The New Press, 1997.

Freeman, Gregory A. "In Search of Death." *Rolling Stone* (6 February 2003). 45–48.

Friess, Steve. "At What Price Beautiful?" *The Advocate* 22 Dec. 1998: 26–29, 31.

Fuss, Diana. *Essentially Speaking: Feminism, Nature, and Difference.* New York: Routledge, 1989.

Gallagher, John. "Marriage-Go-Round." *The Advocate* 19 Jan. 1999: 46–47.

Gamson, Josh. "Must Identity Movements Self-Destruct?: A Queer Dilemma." *Queer Theory/Sociology.* Ed. Steven Seidman. Cambridge, MA: Blackwell Publishers, Ltd., 1996. 395–420.

Gatter, P. "One of Us, One of Them, or One of Those?: The Construction of Identity and Sexuality in Relation to HIV/AIDS." *AIDS: Safety, Sexuality, and Risk.* Ed. P. Applegate, P. Davies, and G. Hart. London: Taylor & Francis, 1995. 159–71.

Gauthier, Deann, & Craig Forsyth. "Bareback Sex, Bug Chasers, and the Gift of Death." *Deviant Behavior* 20.1 (1999): 85–100.

Gearhart, Suzanne. "Foucault's Response to Freud: Sado-masochism and the Aestheticization of Power." *Style* 29 (1995): 389–404.

Gerstmann, Evan. *The Constitutional Underclass: Gays, Lesbians, and the Failure of Class-based Equal Protection.* Chicago: University of Chicago Press, 1999.

Gilliam, Bruce L., John R. Dyer, Susan A. Fiscus, Cheryl Marcus, Susan Zhou, Lynne Wathen, William W. Freimuth, Myron S. Cohen, and Joseph J. Eron, Jr. "Effects of Reverse Transcriptase Inhibitor Therapy on the HIV-1 Viral Burden in Semen." *Journal of Acquired Immune Deficiency Syndromes & Human Retrovirology* 15.1 (1997): 54–60.

Goldstein, Anne B. "History, Homosexuality, and Political Values: Searching for the Hidden Determinants of *Bowers v. Hardwick.*" *The Yale Law Journal* 97 (1988): 1073–1103.

Gould, Timothy. "The Unhappy Performative." *Performativity and Performance.* Ed. Andrew Parker and Eve Kosofsky Sedgwick. New York & London: Routledge, 1995. 19–44.

Graff, E. J. "Wedding March." *The American Prospect* 28 Feb. 2000: 32–34.

Greaves, William. "The Boys in the Band." *Lambda Book Review* June 1997: 19–20.

Grindstaff, Davin Allen. "Sodomy Laws and Rhetorical Secrets: The Social Construction of Privacy in *Lawrence v. Texas.*" *Critical Problems in Argumentation: Selected Papers from the 13th Biennial Conference on Argumentation.* Ed. Charles Arthur Willard. Washington, DC: National Communication Association, 2003. 187–93.

———. "Queering Marriage: An Ideographic Interrogation of Heteronormative Subjectivity." *Journal of Homosexuality,* 45, nos. 2–4 (2003): 257–76.

Gross, Larry. *Contested Closets: The Politics and Ethics of Outing.* Minneapolis: The University of Minnesota Press, 1993.

———. *Up From Invisibility: Lesbians, Gay Men, and the Media.* New York: Columbia University Press, 2001.

Grosz, Elizabeth. *Volatile Bodies: Toward a Corporeal Feminism.* Bloomington and Indianapolis: Indiana University Press, 1994.

Grover, Jan Zita. "AIDS: Keywords." *AIDS: Cultural Analysis, Cultural Activism.* Ed. Douglas Crimp. Cambridge, MA: The MIT Press, 1988. 17–30.

Gunn, Joshua, and David Beard. "On the Apocalyptic Sublime." *Southern Communication Journal* 65.4 (2000): 269–86.

Gurganus, Allan. "He's One, Too." *Boys Like Us: Gay Writers Tell Their Coming Out Stories.* Ed. Patrick Merla. New York: Avon Books, 1996. 40–72.

Hackett, Thomas. "The Execution of Pvt. Barry Winchell: The Real Story Behind the 'Don't Ask, Don't Tell' Murder." *Rolling Stone* 2 March 2000: 81–88, 108.

Hafen, Bruce C. "The Constitutional Status of Marriage, Kinship and Sexual Privacy: Balancing the Individual and Social Interests." *Michigan Law Review* 81 (January 1983): 463–509.

Halley, Janet. "Misreading Sodomy: A Critique of the Classification of 'Homosexuals' in Federal Equal Protection Law." *Body Guards: The Politics of Gender Ambiguity.* Ed. Julia Epstein and Kristina Straub. New York: Routledge, 1991. 351–77.

———. "Reasoning About Sodomy: Act and Identity in and after *Bowers v. Hardwick.*" *Virginia Law Review* 79 (1993): 1721–80.

———. "The Politics of the Closet: Towards Equal Protection for Gay, Lesbian, and Bisexual Identity." *Reclaiming Sodom.* Ed. Jonathan Goldberg. New York & London: Routledge, 1994. 145–204.

———. "Sexual Orientation and the Politics of Biology: A Critique of the Argument from Immutability." *Stanford Law Review* 46 (1994): 503–69.

———. "'Like Race' Arguments." *What's Left of Theory?: New Work on the Politics of Literary Theory.* Ed. Judith Butler, John Guillary, and Kendall Thomas. London & New York: Routledge, 2002.

Hallward, Peter. "The Limits of Individuation: Or How to Distinguish Deleuze and Foucault." *Angelaki* 5 (2000): 93–111.

Halperin, David M. *One Hundred Years of Homosexuality: And Other Essays on Greek Love.* New York: Routledge, 1990.

———. *Saint Foucault: Towards a Gay Hagiography.* New York: Oxford University Press, 1995.

———. "Forgetting Foucault: Acts, Identities, and the History of Sexuality." *Representations* 63 (1998): 93–120.

———. "How to Do the History of Male Homosexuality." *GLQ: A Journal of Lesbian and Gay Studies.* 6 (2000): 87–123.

Hanson, Ellis. "Undead." *Inside/Out: Lesbian Theories, Gay Theories.* Ed. Diana Fuss. New York: Routledge, 1991. 324–40.

Hariman, Robert. "Critical Rhetoric and Postmodern Theory." *Quarterly Journal of Speech* 77 (1991): 67–70.

———. "Status, Marginality, and Rhetorical Theory." *Quarterly Journal of Speech* 72 (1986): 38–54.

Harris, Daniel. *The Rise and Fall of Gay Culture.* New York: Hyperion, 1997.

Hayden, Patrick. *Multiplicity and Becoming: The Pluralist Empiricism of Gilles Deleuze.* New York: Peter Lang, 1998.

Healey, Murray. "The Mark of a Man: Masculine Identities and the Art of Macho Drag." *Critical Quarterly* 35 (1994): 86–93.

Hendershot, Cyndy. "Revolution, Femininity, and Sentimentality in *Billy Budd, Sailor,*" *The Iowa Review* 63 (1996): 99–113.

Henry, Keith, Barbara J. Chinnock, Richard P. Quinn, Courtney V. Fletcher, Paulo de Miranda, and Henry H. Balfour. "Concurrent Zidovudine Levels in Semen and Serum Determined by Radioimmunoassay in Patients with AIDS or AIDS-Related Complex." *JAMA: The Journal of the American Medical Association* 259.20 (1988): 3023–26.

"HIV in Semen: Considering the Source." *American Journal of Nursing* 97.12 (1997): 25.

Hocks, Richard A. "Melville and 'The Rise of Realism'" The Dilemma of History in *Billy Budd.*" *American Literary Realism* 26 (1994): 60–81.

Hodges, Heather. "*Dean v. The District of Columbia:* Goin' to the Chapel and We're Gonna Get Married." *American Journal of Gender and the Law* 5 (1996): 93–146.

Holland, Eugene W. "Infinite Subjective Representation and the Perversion of Death." *Angelaki* 5 (2000): 85–91.

Howard, Ken, and Gavin Yamey. "Magazine's HIV Claim Rekindles 'Gay Plague' Row." *British Medical Journal* 326 (2003): 326, 454.

Humphries, Martin. "Gay Machismo." *The Sexuality of Men.* Ed. Andy Metcalf and Martin Humphries. London & Sydney: Pluto Press, 1985. 70–85.

Humphrey, Laud. *Out of the Closets: The Sociology of Homosexual Liberation.* Englewood Cliffs, NJ: Prentice-Hall, 1972.

Hunter, Nan. "Life After Hardwick." *Sex Wars: Sexual Dissent and Political Culture.* Ed. Lisa Duggan and Nan Hunter. New York & London: Routledge, 1995. 85–100.

Hutchinson, George B. "The Conflict of Patriarchy and Balanced Sexual Principles in *Billy Budd.*" *Studies in the Novel* 13 (1981): 388–97.

Idelson, Holly. "Panel Give Swift Approval to Gay Marriage Bill." *Congressional Quarterly Weekly Report* 1 June 1996: 1539.

Irigaray, Luce. *This Sex Which Is Not One.* Trans. Catherine Porter. Ithaca, NY: Cornell University Press, 1985.

Irvine, Stewart, Elizabeth Cawood, David Richardson, Eileen MacDonald, and John Aitken. "Evidence of Deteriorating Semen Quality in the United Kingdom: Birth Cohort Study in 577 Men in Scotland over 11 Years." *British Medical Journal (International)* 312 (1996): 467–71.

Jagose, Annamarie. *Queer Theory: An Introduction.* Washington Square, NY: New York University Press, 1996.

Jandt, Fred E., and James Darsey. "Coming Out as a Communicative Process." *Gay Speak: Gay Male and Lesbian Communication.* Ed. James Cheseboro. New York: Pilgrim Press, 1981. 12–27.

Jay, Karla, and Allen Young (eds.). *Out of the Closets: Voices of Gay Liberation.* New York: New York University Press, 1972.

Johnson, Barbara. "Melville's Fist: The Execution of Billy Budd." *Herman Melville: A Collection of Critical Essays.* Ed. Myra Jehlen. Englewood Cliffs, NJ: Prentice-Hall Inc., 1994. 235–48.

Kaufman-Osborn, Timothy V. "Fashionable Subjects: On Judith Butler and the Causal Idioms of Postmodern Feminist Theory." *Political Research Quarterly* 50 (1997): 649–74.

Kevles, Daniel J. "A Culture of Risk." *New York Times Book Review* 25 May 1997: 8.

Knoebel, John. "Somewhere in the Right Direction: Testimony of My Experience in a Gay Male Living Collective." *Out of the Closets: Voices of Gay Liberation.* Ed. Karla Jay and Allen Young. New York: New York University Press, 1972. 301–14.

Koffler, Judith S. "The Feminine Presence in Billy Budd." *Cardoza Studies in Law and Literature* 1 (1989): 1–14.

Koppelman, Andrew. "Why Discrimination Against Lesbians and Gay Men Is Sex Discrimination." *New York University Law Review* 69 (1994): 197–287.

——. "*Romer v Evans* and Invidious Intent." *William and Mary Bill of Rights Journal* 6 (1997): 89–146.

——. "Forum: Sexual Morality and the Possibility of Same-Sex Marriage: Is Marriage Inherently Heterosexual?" *American Journal of Jurisprudence* 42 (1997): 51–95.

Krafft-Ebing, R. Von. *Psychopathia Sexualis, Contrary Sexual Instinct: A Medico-Legal Study.* Philadelphia & London: F. A. Davis Co., Publishers, 1893.

Kuypers, Jim A. "*Doxa* and a Critical Rhetoric: Accounting for the Rhetorical Agent Through Prudence." *Communication Quarterly* 44.4 (1996): 452–62.

"Landmark for gay rights." *The Oregonian* 2003, March 25: C6.

"Landmark legislation in Vermont raises questions for other states." *State Legislatures* July/August 2000: 11.

Lawrence v. Texas. 539 U.S. 558 (2003).

Leff, Michael. "Things Made by Words: Reflections on Textual Criticism." *Quarterly Journal of Speech* 78 (1992): 223–31.

Leff, Michael, and Andrew Sachs. "Words the Most Like Things: Iconicity and the Rhetorical Text." *Western Journal of Speech Communication* 54 (1990): 252–73.

Levine, George. *The Realistic Imagination: English Fiction from Frankenstein to Lady Chatterley.* Chicago: University of Chicago Press, 1981.

Levine, Martin P. *Gay Macho: The Life and Death of the Homosexual Clone.* New York & London: New York University Press, 1998.

Levine, Richard J., Ravi M. Mathew, C. Brandon Chenault, Michelle H. Brown, Mark E. Hurtt, Karin S. Bentley, Kathleen L. Mohr, and Peter K. Working. "Differences in the Quality of Semen in Outdoor Workers during Summer and Winter." *New England Journal of Medicine* 323.1 (1990): 12–16.

Lewin, Philip. 2001. "Dispersing the *Cogito:* A Response to Vivian's Rhetorical Self." *Philosophy and Rhetoric* 34: 335–342.

Lingis, Alphonso. *Foreign Bodies.* New York & London: Routledge, 1994.

——. *The Imperative.* Bloomington: Indiana University Press, 1998.

Long, Ron. "The Fitness of the Gym." *The Harvard Gay and Lesbian Review* 4 (1997): 20–22.

Lucaites, John L., and Celeste M. Condit. "Reconstructing Equality: Culturetypal and Counter-Cultural Rhetorics in the Martyred Black Vision." *Communication Monographs* 57 (1990): 5–24.

Lucas, Stephen E. "The Renaissance of American Public Address: Text and Context in Rhetorical Criticism." *Quarterly Journal of Speech* 74 (1988): 241–60.

Maguire, Daniel. "The Morality of Homosexual Marriage." *Same-Sex Marriage: The Moral and Legal Debate.* Ed. Robert M. Baird and Stuart E. Rosenbaum. Amherst, NY: Prometheus Books, 1997. 57–71.

Mann, William J. "Laws of Desire: Has Our Imagery Become Overidealized?" *Look-*

ing Queer: Body Image and Identity in Lesbian, Bisexual, Gay, and Transgender Communities. Ed. Dawn Atkins. New York & London: Harrington Park Press, 1998. 345–53.

Martin, Robert K. *Hero, Captain, and Stranger: Male Friendship, Social Critique, and Literary Form in the Sea Novels of Herman Melville.* Chapel Hill: The University of North Carolina Press, 1986.

Mason, Dyana. "Supreme Court can end sodomy laws in VA, elsewhere." *The Virginian-Pilot* (9 June 2003): B11.

Mason, Gail. *The Spectacle of Violence: Homophobia, Gender, and Knowledge.* London & New York: Routledge, 2000.

Matthiessen, F. O. *American Renaissance: Art and Expression in the Age of Emerson and Whitman.* New York: Oxford University Press, 1941.

May, Todd. *Between Genealogy and Epistemology: Psychology, Politics, and Knowledge in the Thought of Michel Foucault.* University Park, PA: Pennsylvania State University Press, 1993.

McCabe, Neil C. "Review of Sodomy Case Validates Justices' Opinion." *Texas Lawyer* 19 (14 April 2003): 49.

McCarthy, Thomas. "The Critique of Pure Reason: Foucault and the Frankfurt School." *Political Theory* 18 (1990): 437–69.

McElroy, John Harmon. "The Uncompromising Truth of Billy Budd: Its Miraculous Climax." *Christianity and Literature* 38 (1998): 47–62.

McGee, Michael Calvin. "The 'Ideograph:' A Link between Rhetoric and Ideology." *Quarterly Journal of Speech* 66 (1980): 1–16.

———. "Text, Context, and the Fragmentation of Contemporary Culture." *Western Journal of Speech Communication* 54 (1990): 274–89.

McGowan, Gerard. "Christian Masochism and Melville." *Northeast Regional Meeting of the Conference on Christianity and Literature.* Ed. Joan F. Hallisey. Weston, MA: Regis College, 1996. 91–96.

McIntosh, James. "Billy Budd, Sailor: Melville's Last Romance." *Critical Essays on Melville's Billy Budd, Sailor.* Ed. Robert Midler. Boston: Hall, 1989. 223–37.

McIntosh, Mary. "Queer Theory and the War of the Sexes." *Activating Theory: Lesbian, Gay, Bisexual Politics.* Ed. Joseph Bristow and Angelia R. Wilson. London: Lawrence & Wishart, 1993. 30–52.

McKerrow, Raymie E. "Critical Rhetoric and Propaganda Studies." *Communication Yearbook* 14 (1991): 249–55.

———. "Critical Rhetoric in a Postmodern World." *Quarterly Journal of Speech* 77 (1991): 75–78.

———. "Critical Rhetoric: Theory and Praxis." *Communication Monographs* 56 (1989): 91–111.

McNay, Lois. *Foucault: A Critical Introduction.* New York: Continuum, 1994.

Medhurst, Martin J. "Public Address and Significant Scholarship: Four Challenges to the Rhetorical Renaissance." *Texts in Context.* Ed. Michael C. Leff and Fred Kauffeld. Davis, CA: Hermagoras Press, 1989. 29–42.

Melville, Herman. *Billy Budd and Other Stories.* New York: Penguin Books, 1986.

Merleau-Ponty, M. *Phenomenology of Perception.* Trans. Colin Smith. London & New York: Routledge, 1962.

———. *The Visible and the Invisible.* Ed. Claude Lefort. Trans. Alphonso Lingis. Evanston, IL: Northwestern University Press, 1968.

Miller, D. A. *Bringing Out Roland Barthes.* Berkeley, CA: University of California Press, 1992.

———. *The Novel and the Police.* Berkeley, Los Angeles, & London: University of California Press, 1988.

Miller, Diane, H. *Freedom to Differ: The Shaping of the Gay and Lesbian Struggle for Civil Rights.* New York & London: New York University Press, 1998.

Mills, Thomas, Ron Stall, Lance Pollack, Jay Paul, Diane Binson, Jesse Canchola, and Joseph Catania. "Health-related Characteristics of Men Who Have Sex With Men: A Comparison of Those Living in 'Gay Ghettos' with Those Living Elsewhere." *American Journal of Public Health* 91 (2001): 980–83.

Mizruchi, Susan. "Cataloguing the Creatures of the Deep: 'Billy Budd, Sailor' and the Rise of Sociology." *Boundary 2* 17 (1990): 272–304.

Mohr, Richard. *Gay Ideas: Outing and Other Controversies.* Boston: Beacon Press, 1992.

Morris III, Charles E. "'The Responsibilities of the Critic': F. O. Matthiessen's Homosexual Palimpsest." *Quarterly Journal of Speech* 84 (1998): 261–82.

Morris, Martin. "On the Logic of the Performative Contradiction: Habermas and the Radical Critique of Reason." *The Review of Politics* 58.4 (1996): 735–60.

Mosse, George L. *Nationalism and Sexuality: Respectability and Abnormal Sexuality in Modern Europe.* New York: Howard Fertig, 1985.

Murphy, John M. "Critical Rhetoric as Political Discourse." *Argumentation and Advocacy* 32 (1995): 1–15.

"National Campaign for Same-Sex Marriage Draws Political and Religious Opposition." *CQ Researcher* 10 May 1996: 420–23.

Nealon, Jeffrey T. *Alterity Politics: Ethics and Performative Subjectivity.* Durham, NC: Duke University Press, 1998.

Noyes, John K. *The Mastery of Submission: Inventions of Masochism.* Ithaca & London: Cornell University Press, 1997.

Nunokawa, Jeff. "'All the Sad Young Men': AIDS and the Work of Mourning." *Inside/Out: Lesbian Theories, Gay Theories.* Ed. Diana Fuss. New York: Routledge, 1991. 311–23.

Ono, Kent A., and John M. Sloop. "The Critique of Vernacular Discourse." *Communication Monographs* 62 (1995): 19–46.

———. "Commitment to Telos: A Sustained Critical Rhetoric." *Communication Monographs* 59 (1992): 48–60.

Oppenheimer, Gerald M. "Causes, Cases, and Cohorts: The Role of Epidemiology in the Historical Construction of AIDS. *AIDS: The Making of a Chronic Disease.*

Ed. E. Fox and D. M. Fee. Berkeley, Los Angeles & Oxford: University of California Press, 1992. 49–83.

Oral argument. *Lawrence v. Texas.* http://www.supremecourtus.gov/oral_arguments/argument_transcripts/02-102.pdf.

Padgug, Robert A., and Gerald M. Oppenheimer. "Riding the Tiger: AIDS and the Gay Community." *AIDS: The Making of a Chronic Disease.* Ed. E. Fox and D. M. Fee. Berkeley, Los Angeles & Oxford: University of California Press, 1992. 245–78.

Parsi, Novid. "Don't Worry, Sam, You're not Alone: Bodybuilding Is So Queer." *Building Bodies.* Ed. Pamela Moore. New Brunswick, NJ: Rutgers University Press, 1997. 103–34.

Patton, Cindy. *Sex and Germs: The Politics of AIDS.* Montreal & New York: Black Rose Books, 1986.

———. *Inventing AIDS.* New York and London: Routledge, 1990.

———. "Visualizing Safe Sex: When Pedagogy and Pornography Collide." *Inside/Out: Lesbian Theories, Gay Theories.* Ed. Diana Fuss. New York: Routledge, 1991. 373–86.

———. "Tremble, Hetero Swine!" *Fear of a Queer Planet: Queer Politics and Social Theory.* Ed. Michael Warner. Minneapolis, MN: University of Minnesota, 1993. 143–77.

———. "Performativity and Spatial Distinction: The End of AIDS Epidemiology." *Performativity and Performance.* Ed. Andrew Parker and Eve Kosofsky Sedgwick. New York & London: Routledge, 1995. 173–96.

———. *Fatal Advice: How Safe-Sex Education Went Wrong.* Durham & London: Duke University Press, 1996.

Patton, Paul. *Deleuze and the Political.* London & New York: Routledge, 2000.

Pearson, Keith Ansell. *Germinal Life: The Difference and Repetition of Deleuze.* London & New York: Routledge, 1999.

Pease, Donald E. "Melville and Cultural Persuasion." *Ideology and Classic American Literature.* Ed. Sacvan Bercovitch and Myra Jehlen. Cambridge: Cambridge University Press, 1987: 384–417.

Pela, R. L. "Beyond the Cult." *The Advocate* 27 May 1997: 86.

Pels, Dick. "The Politics of Critical Description: Recovering the Normative Complexity of Foucault's *pouvoir/savoir.*" *American Behavioral Scientist.* 38 (1995): 1018–41.

Phelan, Shane. *Getting Specific: Postmodern Lesbian Politics.* Minneapolis & London: University of Minnesota Press, 1994.

Phillips, Kathy J. "Billy Budd as Anti-Homophobic Text." *College English* 56.8 (1994): 896–910.

Prager, Dennis. "Homosexuality, the Bible, and Us: A Jewish Perspective." *Same-Sex Marriage: Pro and Con, A Reader.* Ed. Andrew Sullivan. New York: Vintage Books, 1997. 61–67.

Proust, Françoise. "The Line of Resistance." *Hypatia* 15 (2000): 23–37.

"Quick Hits: Sex in the News." *Contemporary Sexuality* 37 (2003): 7–9.

Rajchman, John. *Michel Foucault: The Freedom of Philosophy.* New York: Columbia University Press, 1985.

Rauch, Jonathan. "For Better or Worse?" *Same-Sex Marriage: Pro and Con, A Reader.* Ed. Andrew Sullivan. New York: Vintage Books, 1997. 169–81.

Reske, Henry J. "Gay Marriage Ban Unconstitutional." *ABA Journal* July 1993: 28.

Ricco, John Paul. "Queering Boundaries: Semen and Visual Representations from the Middle Ages and in the Era of the AIDS Crisis." *Journal of Homosexuality* 27.1–2 (1994): 57–80.

Rimmerman, Craig A. *From Identity to Politics: The Lesbian and Gay Movements in the United States.* Philadelphia: Temple University, 2002.

Robbins, Mary Alice. "Gay rights showdown at High Court." *Legal Times* (24 March 2003): 7.

———. "Trendsetter or behind the times?" *Texas Lawyer* 19 (24 March 2003): 16.

Rodowick, D. N. "The Memory of Resistance." *South Atlantic Quarterly* 96 (1997): 417–37.

Ross, Michael, and Mark Williams. "Effective Targeting and Community HIV/STD Prevention Programs." *Journal of Sex Research* 39 (2002): 58–62.

Rotello, Gabriel. *Sexual Ecology: AIDS and the Destiny of Gay Men.* New York: Plume Books, 1998.

Rubenfeld, Jed. "The Right of Privacy." *Harvard Law Review* 102 (1989): 737–808.

Ruttenburg, Nancy. "Melville's Handsome Sailor: The Anxiety of Innocence." *American Literature* 66 (1994): 83–103.

Sarotte, Georges-Michel. *Like a Brother, Like a Lover: Male Homosexuality in the American Novel and Theater from Herman Melville to James Baldwin.* Garden City, NY: Anchor, 1978.

Schwartz, Michael. "Repetition and Ethics in Late Foucault." *Telos* 117 (1999): 113–33.

Scott, J. Blake. *Risky Rhetoric: AIDS and the Cultural Practices of HIV Testing.* Carbondale & Edwardsville: Southern Illinois University Press, 2003.

Scott, Robert L. "On Viewing Rhetoric as Epistemic." *Central States Speech Journal* 18 (1967): 9–17.

Sealts, Merton M, Jr. "Innocence and Infamy: Billy Budd, Sailor." *A Companion to Melville Studies.* Ed. John Bryant. Westport, CT: Greenwood, 1986. 407–30.

Sedgwick, Eve Kosofsky. *The Epistemology of the Closet.* Berkeley: University of California Press, 1990.

———. *Tendencies.* Durham, NC: Duke University Press, 1993.

Seidman, Steven. "Identity and Politics in a 'Postmodern' Gay Culture: Some Historical and Conceptual Notes." *Fear of a Queer Planet: Queer Politics and Social Theory.* Ed. Michael Warner. Minneapolis, MN: University of Minnesota, 1993. 105–42.

———. *Difference Troubles: Queering Social Theory and Sexual Politics.* Cambridge, MA: Cambridge University Press, 1997.

Seppa, Nathan. "Blood, Semen Harbor Distinct HIV Mutations." *Science News* 154.18 (1998): 279.

Shilts, Randy. *And The Band Played On: Politics, People, and the AIDS Epidemic.* New York: Penguin Books, 1988.

Signorile, Michelangelo. *Queer in America: Sex, the Media, and the Closets of Power.* New York: Anchor Books Doubleday, 1993.

———. *Life Outside.* New York: Harper Collins Publishers, 1997.

Silverman, Kaja. "Masochism and Male Subjectivity." *Male Trouble.* Ed. Constance Penley and Sharon Willis. Minneapolis & London: University of Minnesota Press, 1993. 33–66.

Silvestre, Anthony, Scott Arrowood, Jan Ivery, and Sylvia Barksdale. "HIV-prevention Capacity in Building Gay, Racial, and Ethnic Minority Communities in Small Cities and Towns." *Health and Social Work* 27 (2002): 61–67.

Simmons, Todd. "Falwell, Gingrich . . . Signorile?" *The Advocate* 16 Sept. 1997: 43–45.

Simpson, Mark. *Male Impersonators: Men Performing Masculinity.* New York: Rutledge, 1994.

Slagle, R. Anthony. "In Defense of Queer Nation: From Identity Politics to a Politics of Difference." *Western Journal of Communication* 59 (1995): 85–102.

Sloop, John M., and Kent A. Ono. "Out-law Discourse: The Critical Politics of Material Judgment." *Philosophy and Rhetoric* 30.1 (1997): 50–69.

Smart, C. "Collusion, Collaboration, and Confession: On Moving Beyond the Heterosexuality Debate." *Theorizing Heterosexuality: Telling it Straight.* Ed. D. Richardson. Buckingham & Philadelphia: Open University Press, 1996: 161–77.

Smith, Ralph R. "Queer Theory, Gay Movements, and Political Communication." *Journal of Homosexuality* 45.2/3/4 (2003): 345–48.

Smith, Ralph R., and Russel R. Windes. *Progay/Antigay: The Rhetorical War Over Sexuality.* Thousand Oaks, London, & New Delhi: Sage Publications, 2000.

———. "Identity in Political Context: Lesbian/Gay Representation in the Public Sphere." *Journal of Homosexuality* 37.2 (1999): 25–45.

Soloman, Martha. "The Things We Study: Texts and Their Interactions." *Communication Monographs* 60 (1993): 62–68.

Sontag, Susan. *AIDS and Its Metaphors.* New York: Farrar, Straus, and Giroux, 1989.

Spivak, Gayatri C. "Can the Subaltern Speak?" *Marxism and the Interpretation of Culture.* Ed. Cary Nelson and Lawrence Grossberg. Urbana & Chicago: University of Illinois Press, 1988. 271–316.

Stanton, Michael N. "Blake, 'B.V.,' and Billy Budd." *Melville Society Extracts* 71 (1987): 12–16.

Strasser, Mark. "Domestic Relations and the Great Slumbering Baehr: On Defending Preclusion, Equal Protection and Fundamental Interests." *Fordham Law Review* 64 (December 1995): 921–86.

Sullivan, Andrew. "The Conservative Case." *Same-Sex Marriage: Pro and Con, A Reader.* Ed. Andrew Sullivan. New York: Vintage Books, 1997. 146–54.

Sunstein, Cass. "Homosexuality and the Constitution." *Indiana Law Journal* 70 (1994): 1–28.

Teal, Donn. *The Gay Militants.* New York: St. Martin's Press, 1995.

Thomas, Kendall. "Beyond the Privacy Principle." *Columbia Law Review* 92 (1992): 1431–1517.

Thompson, Julie M. *Mommie Queerest: Contemporary Rhetorics of Lesbian Maternal Identity.* Amherst & Boston: University of Massachusettes Press, 2002.

Treichler, Paula A. *How to Have Theory in an Epidemic: Cultural Chronicles of AIDS.* Durham & London: Duke University Press, 1999.

Turner, William B. *A Genealogy of Queer Theory.* Philadelphia: Temple University Press, 2000.

Tyler, Carole-Anne. "Boys Will Be Girls: The Politics of Gay Drag." *Inside/Out: Lesbian Theories, Gay Theories.* Ed. Diana Fuss. New York: Routledge, 1991. 32–70.

U.S. Senate, "Employment of Homosexuals and Other Sex Perverts in the U.S. Government." *We Are Everywhere: A Historical Sourcebook of Gay and Lesbian Politics.* Ed. Mark Blasius and Shane Phelan. New York & London: Routledge, 1997. 241–50.

Vaid, Urvashi. "After Identity." *The New Republic* 10 May 1993: 28.

———. *Virtual Equality: The Mainstreaming of Gay and Lesbian Liberation.* New York: Doubleday, 1995.

Visker, Rudi. "Raw Being and Violent Discourse: Foucault, Merleau-Ponty, and the (Dis-)Order of Things." *Merleau-Ponty in Contemporary Perspectives.* Ed. Patrick Burke and Jan Van Der Veken. Dordrecht, Boston, & London: Kluwer Academic Publishers, 1993. 109–29.

———. *Michel Foucault: Genealogy as Critique.* Trans. Chris Turner. New York: Verso, 1995.

Vivian, Bradford. "The Threshold of the Self." *Philosophy and Rhetoric* 33 (2000): 303–18.

———. "Always a Third Party Who Says 'Me': Rhetoric and Alterity." *Philosophy and Rhetoric* 34 (2001): 343–54.

Wachter, Robert M. "AIDS, Activism, and the Politics of Health." *New England Journal of Medicine* 326 (1992): 128–33.

Waldby, Catherine. *AIDS and the Body Politic: Biomedicine and Sexual Difference.* London & New York: Routledge, 1996.

Wander, Philip. "The Third Persona: An Ideological Turn in Rhetorical Theory." *Central States Speech Journal* 35 (1984): 197–216.

———. "The Ideological Turn in Modern Criticism." *Central States Speech Journal* 34 (1983): 1–18.

Wardle, Lynn D. "A Critical Analysis of Constitutional Claims for Same-Sex Marriage." *Bringham Young University Law Review* (1996): 1–102.

———. "*Loving v. Virginia* and the Constitutional Right to Marry, 1790–1990." *Howard Law Journal* 41 (1998): 289–347.

Warner, Michael. Introduction. *Fear of a Queer Planet: Queer Politics and Social Theory.* Ed. Michael Warner. Minneapolis: University of Minnesota, 1993. vii–xxxi.

———. "Normal and Normaller: Beyond Gay Marriage." *GLQ: A Journal of Lesbian and Gay Studies* 5 (1999): 119–71.

———. *The Trouble with Normal: Sex, Politics, and the Ethics of Queer Life.* New York: The Free Press, 1999.

Watney, Simon. "The Spectacle of AIDS." *AIDS: Cultural Analysis, Cultural Activism.* Ed. Douglas Crimp. Cambridge, MA: The MIT Press, 1988. 71–86.

Wendt, Ronald F. "Answers to the Gaze: A Genealogical Poaching of Resistances." *Quarterly Journal of Speech* 82 (1996): 251–73.

West, Robin. "The Feminine Silence: A Response to Professor Koffler." *Cardozo Studies in Law and Literature* 1 (1989): 15–20.

Weston, Kath. *Gender in Real Time: Power and Transience in a Visual Age.* New York & London: Routledge, 2002.

Whang, Selena. "The White, Heterosexual Couple: On Masculinity, Sadism, and Radicalized Lesbian Desire." *College Literature* 24 (1997): 116–33.

White, Edmund. *The Burning Library: Essays.* Ed. David Bergman. New York: Vintage Books, 1994.

Wieder, Judy. "The End of the Gay 90's." *The Advocate* 19 Jan. 1997: 9.

Wilson, James Q. "Against Homosexual Marriage." *Same-Sex Marriage: Pro and Con, A Reader.* Ed. Andrew Sullivan. New York: Vintage Books, 1997. 159–68.

Wittman, Carl. "A Gay Manifesto." Ed. Mark Blasius and Shane Phelan. *We Are Everywhere: A Historical Sourcebook of Gay and Lesbian Politics.* New York & London: Routledge, 1997. 380–88.

Yingling, Thomas. "AIDS in America: Postmodern Governance, Identity, and Experience." *Inside/Out: Lesbian Theories, Gay Theories.* Ed. Diana Fuss. New York: Routledge, 1991. 291–310.

Yep, Gust A., Karen E. Lovaas, and Alex Pagonis. "The Case of 'Riding Bareback': Sexual Practices and the Paradoxes of Identity in the Era of AIDS." *Journal of Homosexuality* 42.4 (2002): 1–14.

Yoder, Jonathan A. "The Protagonists' Rainbow in *Billy Budd:* Critical Trimming of Truth's Ragged Edges." *ATQ: The American Transcendental Quarterly* 7 (1993): 97–113.

Zarefsky, David. "The State of the Art in Public Address Scholarship." *Texts in Context.* Ed. Michael C. Leff and Fred Kauffeld. Davis, CA: Hermagoras Press, 1989. 13–28.

Index